WINDSOR LIBRARY

KT-380-405

743940

Collins

easy
French

RBWM
LIBRARY
SERVICES

0007 208 405 0 535 3C

HarperCollins Publishers
Westerhill Rd, Bishopbriggs, Glasgow, G64 2QT

www.harpercollins.co.uk

First published 2001
This edition published 2006

© HarperCollins Publishers 2006

Reprint 10 9 8 7 6 5 4 3 2 1 0

ISBN 0 00 720840 5

A catalogue reference for this book is available from
The British Library

All rights reserved

Consultants: Christian Salzedo

Photography: Gonzalo Corvalan and Gaëlle Amiot-Cadey
With additional photography/material from:
Keith Gibson, Hôtel XII Apôtres, Contrexeville,
Christopher Riches, Fiona Steel, The Printer's Devil,
Artville (pp 95, 99, 100, 101, 103, 105, 106),
Anthony Blake Photo Library (pp 96, 97, 98[tl], 99[tr], 100[t],
101[tr], 102, 104, 107, 108, 109, 110, 111)
Wine guide: Andrea Gillies
Food Map: Heather Moore
Layout & Origination: The Printer's Devil and
Davidson Pre-Press Graphics Ltd, Glasgow

Other titles in the Collins Easy Photo Phrase Book series:
German (0 00 720839 1)
Greek (0 00 720837 5)
Italian (0 00 720836 7)
Portuguese (0 00 720835 9)
Spanish (0 00 720833 2)
These titles are also published in a CD pack containing
a 60-minute CD and Easy Photo Phrase book.

Printed in China by Imago

Contents

Useful Websites

Currency converters
www.xe.com
www.oanda.com

UK Passport Office
www.passport.gov.uk

Foreign Office travel advice
www.fco.gov.uk

Health advice
www.traveldoctor.co.uk
www.dh.gov.uk

Pet advice
www.defra.gov.uk/animalh/
  quarantine/index.htm

Facts and figures
www.cia.gov/cia/publications/
  factbook
www.//cybevasion.com/france

Weather
www.bbc.co.uk/weather

Driving
www.drivingabroad.co.uk
www.autoroutes.fr

Internet cafés
www.cybercafes.com

Hostels
www.hostels.com
www.europeanhostels.com

Hotels
www.hrs.com
www.francehotelreservation.com
www.hotels-france.com

Rail Travel
www.raileurope.co.uk
www.eurostar.com
www.sncf.com

Planning your trip
www.willgoto.com

Skiing
www.goski.com
www.ski-nordic-france.com
  (*in French*)

Canal holidays
www.barginginfrance.com

Châteaux
www.chateaux-france.com

Tourism
www.paris.org
www.paris-tours-guides.com
www.parisinfo.com/en
www.louvre.fr
www.la-cote-dazur.com
www.normandy-tourism.org
www.visit-alsace.com

Introduction

In the age of the euro, the internet and cash machines that offer a choice of languages, foreign travel might seem less of an adventure than it once was. But English is not the universal language yet, and there is much more to communication than knowing the right words for things. Once out of the airport you will not get far without some idea of the language, and also the way things are done in an unfamiliar culture. Things you might assume are the same everywhere, such as road signs and colour-coding, can turn out not to be. Red for trunk roads and skimmed milk, blue for motorways and full cream? Not everywhere! You may know the word for 'coffee' but what sort of coffee will you get? Will they understand what you mean when you say you're a vegetarian? What times do the shops open, and which ticket gives you the best deal? *Collins Easy Photo Phrase Books* keep you up to speed with handy tips for each topic, and a wealth of pictures of signs and everyday objects to help you understand what you see around you. Even if your knowledge of the language is excellent, you may still find yourself on the back foot when trying to understand what's on offer in a restaurant, so the food and drink section features a comprehensive menu reader to make sure eating out is a pleasure.

The unique combination of practical information, photos and phrases found in this book provides the key to hassle-free travel. The colour-coding below shows how information is presented and how to access it as quickly as possible.

i   General, practical information which will provide useful tips on getting the best out of your trip.

keywords

keywords
droite
drwat
right
gauche
gohsh
left

< keywords

these are words that are useful to know both when you see them written down or when you hear them spoken

key talk >

short, simple phrases that you can change and adapt to suit your own situation

talking	
excuse me!	**where is...?**
s'il vous plaît!	où est...?
seel voo play	*oo ay...*
how do I get to...?	
pour aller à...?	
poor a-lay a...	

The **Food Section** allows you to choose more easily from what is on offer both for snacks and at restaurants.

The practical **Dictionary** means that you will never be stuck for words.

Speaking French

We've tried to make the pronunciation under the phrases as clear as possible by breaking the words up with hyphens, but don't pause between syllables.

The consonants are not difficult, and are mostly pronounced as in English: **b, d, f, k, l, m, n, p, s, t, v, x** and **z**. The letter **h** is always silent, and **r** should be pronounced at the back of the throat in the well-known French way, although an English 'r' will be understood. When **c** comes before the vowels **e** or **i** it is pronounced like 's'; otherwise it is a hard 'k'. Likewise, **g** before **e** or **i** is 'zh' like 's' in 'pleasure', not hard 'g'. The letter **ç** is pronounced the same as **s**; **q** is always like **k** in 'kick' (not the 'kw' sound in 'quick'); **ch** is 'sh'; **gn** is 'ny', something like the sound in 'onion'; and **w** is either 'v' or 'w'.

Final consonants, especially **s** and **n**, are often silent, but sometimes not, for example when the following word begins with a vowel – just follow the pronunciation guide.

The sound spelt **ou** in French is something like 'oo' in English, while the sound represented by **u**, which many English speakers have difficulty with, is not really so hard: simply round your lips as if about to say 'ee' but pronounce 'oo'. We use the symbol '**<u>oo</u>**' in the pronunciation guide.

There are two **o** sounds in French; one is something like the 'o' in English 'hope' and one something like 'hop'. We've represented the first by 'oh' and the second by 'o' in the transcriptions. Meanwhile 'uh' represents both the rounded sounds of **peu** *puh* and **peur** *puhr* and also the sound (like 'a' in English 'ago' or 'sofa') found in **je** *zhuh* and **se** *suh* and the first syllables of **retard** *ruh-tar* and **demain** *duh-mañ*. Look out for the following letter combinations: **au** and **eau** are 'oh'; **oi** is 'wa'; and **ui** is something like 'wee'.

There are various 'nasalised' vowels in French. When you see a 'ñ' you should nasalise the vowel before it rather than pronouncing an n. For example 'mañ' in the pronunciation guide represents 'm' plus the vowel in the well-known French words **fin** *fañ* or **rien** *ryañ*, rather than the sounds in English 'man'. The others are 'uñ' (as in **brun** *bruñ*) and 'oñ', which we use to cover the similar vowel sounds in **dans** *doñ* or **en** *oñ* or **blanc** *bloñ* and **mon** *moñ* or **blond** *bloñ*.

Everyday Talk

*There are two forms of address in French, formal (**vous**) and informal (**tu**). You should always stick with the formal until you are on a first-name basis. For this book, we will use the formal.*

yes
oui
wee

no
non
noñ

ok/that's fine
très bien
tray byañ

please
s'il vous plaît
seel voo play

thank you
merci
mehr-see

thanks very much
merci beaucoup
mehr-see boh-koo

don't mention it
de rien
duh ryañ

that's very kind
c'est très gentil
say tray zhoñ-tee

hello
bonjour/salut
boñ-zhoor/sa-loo

goodbye
au revoir
oh ruh-vwar

good evening
bonsoir
boñ-swar

good night
bonne nuit
bon nwee

see you later
à plus tard
a ploo tar

excuse me!
excusez-moi
eks-koo-zay mwa

sorry!
pardon
par-doñ

I am sorry
je suis désolé
zhuh swee day-zo-lay

I don't understand
je ne comprends pas
zhuh nuh koñ-proñ pa

I don't know
je ne sais pas
zhuh nuh say pa

Addressing people

The French might seem rather formal with their frequent use of *Monsieur* and *Madame*, but it is simply a form of politeness. So although the phrases above do not indicate it, remember to add *Monsieur* or *Madame* when talking to someone. It doesn't matter that you don't know their name. It is what you will hear being used to you and will guarantee you a much smoother passage through France. The greeting *salut* is used more among young people and means both hello and goodbye.

excuse me!
pardon, Monsieur/Madame!
par-don muhs-yuh/ma-dam

that is very kind of you
vous êtes très gentil
vooz et tray zhoñ-tee

hi, Christian
salut, Christian
sa-loo Christian

bye, Claudine
salut, Claudine
sa-loo Claudine

see you tomorrow
à demain
a duh-mañ

i The simplest way to ask for something in a shop or bar is by
naming what you want and adding **s'il vous plaît**.

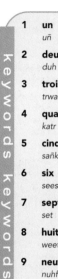

keywords keywords keywords

1	**un** *uñ*
2	**deux** *duh*
3	**trois** *trwah*
4	**quatre** *katr*
5	**cinq** *sañk*
6	**six** *seess*
7	**sept** *set*
8	**huit** *weet*
9	**neuf** *nuhf*
10	**dix** *deess*

a ... please
un/une ... s'il vous plaît
uñ/oon ... seel voo play

a white coffee please
un crème s'il vous plaît
uñ krem seel voo play

a tea please
un thé s'il vous plaît
uñ tay seel voo play

the...
le/la/les...
luh/la/lay...

the menu please
la carte s'il vous plaît
la kart seel voo play

my...
mon/ma/mes...
moñ/ma/may...

another beer
encore une bière
oñkor oon byehr

more bread
encore du pain
oñkor doo pañ

3 tickets
trois billets
trwah bee-yay

a beer please
une bière s'il vous plaît
oon byehr seel voo play

a phonecard please
une télécarte s'il vous plaît
oon te-le-kart seel voo play

some...
du/de la/des...
doo/duh la/day...

the bill please
l'addition s'il vous plaît
la-dee-syoñ seel voo play

another/more...
encore (du/de la/des)...
oñ-kor (doo/duh la/day)...

2 more beers
encore deux bières
oñkor duh byehr

2 more coffees
encore deux cafés
oñ-kor duh ka-fay

4 ice creams
quatre glaces
katr glass

To catch someone's attention

To catch the attention of a passerby, you should begin your request with
Pardon, Monsieur/Madame or *S'il vous plaît, Monsieur/Madame*. This
will induce the right kind of mood. You should not take it for granted that
they speak English and address them in English.

excuse me!
s'il vous plaît!
seel voo play

do you know where...?
est-ce que vous savez où...?
ess-kuh voo savay oo...

can you help me?
est-ce que vous pouvez m'aider?
ess kuh voo poo-vay may-day

how do I get to...?
pour aller à...?
poor a-lay a...

> *In French you can turn a statement into a question simply by changing the intonation and putting a question mark in your voice:* **vous avez une chambre?**

est-ce que
vous avez...?
do you have...?

do you have a room?
est-ce que vous avez une chambre?
ess kuh vooz a-vay <u>oo</u>n shombr

c'est combien?
how much?

how much is the ticket?
c'est combien le billet?
say koñ-byañ luh bee-yay

how much is the wine?
c'est combien le vin?
say koñ-byañ luh vañ

je voudrais...
I'd like...

I'd like a red wine
je voudrais un vin rouge
zhuh voo-dray uñ vañ roozh

I'd like an ice cream
je voudrais une glace
zhuh voo-dray <u>oo</u>n glass

j'ai besoin de...
I need...

I need a taxi
j'ai besoin d'un taxi
zhay buhz-wañ duñ taxi

I need to phone
j'ai besoin de téléphoner
zhay buhz-wañ duh te-le-fo-nay

à quelle heure?/
quand?
when?

when does it open?
ça ouvre à quelle heure?
sa oovr a kel uhr

when does it close?
ça ferme à quelle heure?
sa fehrm a kel uhr

when does it leave?
quand est-ce qu'il part?
koñt ess-keel par

when does it arrive?
quand est-ce qu'il arrive?
koñt ess-keel a-reev

où?
where?

where is the bank?
où est la banque?
oo ay la boñk

where is the hotel?
où est l'hôtel?
oo ay loh-tel

est-ce
qu'il y a...?
is there...?

is there a market?
est-ce qu'il y a un marché?
ess keel ee a uñ mar-shay

where is there a market?
où est-ce qu'il y a un marché?
oo ess keel ee a uñ mar-shay

il n'y a pas de...
there is no...

there is no bread
il n'y a pas de pain
eel nee a pa duh pañ

there is no soap
il n'y a pas de savon
eel nee a pa duh sa-voñ

est-ce que je
peux...?
can I...?

can I smoke?
est-ce que je peux fumer?
ess kuh zhuh puh <u>foo</u>-may

can I phone?
je peux téléphoner?
zhuh puh te-le-fo-nay

where can I buy milk?
où est-ce que je peux acheter du lait?
oo ess kuh zhuh puh ash-tay d<u>oo</u> lay

c'est...?
is it...?

is it expensive?
c'est cher?
say shehr

is it far?
c'est loin?
say lwañ

j'aime...
I like...

I like red wine
j'aime le vin rouge
zhem luh vañ roozh

I don't like cheese
je n'aime pas le fromage
zhuh nem pa luh froh-mazh

These are a selection of small but very useful words.

keywords keywords keywords keywords keywords

grand
groñ
large

petit
puh-tee
small

un peu
uñ puh
a little

ça suffit
sa soo-fee
that's enough

le/la plus proche
luh/la ploo prosh
the nearest

loin
lwañ
far

trop cher
troh shehr
too expensive

et
ay
and

avec/sans
a-vek/soñ
with/without

pour
poor
for

mon/ma/mes
moñ/ma/may
my

celui-ci/-là
suhl-wee-see/-la
this one/that one

tout de suite
toot sweet
straight away

plus tard
ploo tar
later

a large white coffee
un grand crème
uñ groñ krem

a little please
un peu s'il vous plaît
uñ puh seel voo play

where is the nearest chemist?
où est la pharmacie la plus proche?
oo ay la far-ma-see la ploo prosh

is it far?
c'est loin?
say lwañ

it is too expensive
c'est trop cher
say troh shehr

is it engaged?
c'est occupé?
sayt o-koo-pay

a tea and a coffee
un thé et un café
uñ tay ay uñ ka-fay

with sugar
avec sucre
a-vek sookr

without sugar
sans sucre
soñ sookr

for me
pour moi
poor mwah

my passport
mon passeport
moñ pass-por

I'd like this one
je voudrais celui-ci
zhuh voo-dray suhl-wee-see

a small car
une petite voiture
oon puh-teet vwa-toor

that's enough thanks
ça suffit merci
sa soo-fee mehr-see

it is too small
c'est trop petit
say troh puh-tee

is it free?
c'est libre?
say leebr

a beer and a red wine
une bière et un vin rouge
oon byehr ay uñ vañ roozh

with cream
avec crème
a-vek krem

without cream
sans crème
soñ krem

for her/him
pour elle/lui
poor el/lwee

my keys
mes clés
may klay

I'd like that one
je voudrais celui-là
zhuh voo-dray suhl-wee-la

I need a taxi straight away
j'ai besoin d'un taxi tout de suite
zhay buhz-wañ duñ tak-see toot sweet

I'll call you later
je vais vous appeler plus tard
zhuh vay vooz ap-lay ploo tar

It is always good to be able to say a few words about yourself to break the ice, even if you won't be able to tell your life history. Remember there are different endings for male and female.

my name is...
je m'appelle...
zhuh ma-pel...

I am from...
je suis de...
zhuh swee duh...

I am on holiday
je suis en vacances
zhuh sweez oñ va-koñss

I am on business
je suis en voyage d'affaires
zhuh sweez oñ vwa-yazh da-fehr

I am single
je suis célibataire
zhuh swee say-lee-ba-tehr

I am married
je suis marié(e)
zhuh swee mar-yay

I have a boyfriend/a girlfriend
j'ai un ami/une amie
zhay un am-ee/oon am-ee

I have a partner *(male/female)*
j'ai un compagnon/une compagne
zhay uñ kom-pan-yoñ/oon kom-pañ-yuh

I am a widow
je suis veuve
zhuh swee vuhv

I am a widower
je suis veuf
zhuh swee vuhf

I am divorced
je suis divorcé(e)
zhuh swee dee-vor-say

I am separated
je suis séparé(e)
zhuh swee sep-a-ray

I have a child
j'ai un enfant
zhay un oñ-foñ

I have ... children
j'ai ... enfants
zhay ... oñ-foñ

I work
je travaille
zhuh tra-vah-yuh

I am retired
je suis à la retraite
zhuh swee a la ruh-tret

I am a student
je suis étudiant(e)
zhuh swee ay-tood-yoñ(t)

this is a beautiful country
c'est un très beau pays
sayt uñ tray boh pay-ee

people are very kind
les gens sont très gentils
lay zhoñ soñ tray zhoñ-tee

see you next year!
à l'année prochaine!
a la-nay pro-shen

thank you very much for your kindness
merci beaucoup pour votre gentillesse
mehr-see boh-koo poor votr zhoñ-tee-ess

I have enjoyed myself very much
je me suis très bien amusé(e)
zhuh muh swee tray byañ a-moo-zay

we'd like to come back
nous voudrions revenir
noo voo-dree-oñ ruh-vuh-neer

I'll write to you
je vais vous écrire
zhuh vay vooz ay-kreer

here is my address
voici mon adresse
vwa-see mon ad-ress

i People are generally helpful and, if in the right mood, will do all they can to help you. You should always try to use your French, however bad!

excuse me!
s'il vous plaît!
seel voo play

can you help me?
pouvez-vous m'aider?
poo-vay voo may-day

I don't speak French
je ne parle pas français
zhuh nuh parl pa froñ-say

I am sorry, I did not know
pardon, je ne savais pas
par-doñ zhuh nuh sa-vay pa

I am lost
je me suis perdu(e)
zhuh muh swee pehr-doo

we are lost
nous nous sommes perdus
noo noo som pehr-doo

I have lost...	**my money**	**my tickets**	**my passport**
j'ai perdu...	mon argent	mes billets	mon passeport
zhay pehr-doo...	*moñ ar-zhoñ*	*may bee-yay*	*moñ pass-por*

I have left...	**in the restaurant**		**on the train**
j'ai laissé...	dans le restaurant		dans le train
zhay less-ay...	*doñ luh res-toh-roñ*		*doñ luh trañ*

I have missed...	**my flight**	**the train**	**my connection**
j'ai manqué...	mon avion	le train	ma correspondance
zhay moñ-kay...	*mon av-yoñ*	*luh trañ*	*ma ko-res-poñ-doñss*

someone has stolen...	**my purse**		**my wallet**
on m'a volé...	mon porte-monnaie		mon portefeuille
on ma vo-lay...	*moñ port-mo-nay*		*moñ por-tuh-fuh-yuh*

	my handbag	**my traveller's cheques**
	mon sac à main	mes travellers
	moñ sak a mañ	*may tra-vuh-luhrs*

I need to get to...
je dois aller à/au...
zhuh dwa a-lay a/oh...

how can I get there?
comment je peux y aller?
ko-mañ zhuh puh ee a-lay

my luggage hasn't arrived
mes bagages ne sont pas arrivés
may ba-gazh nuh soñ pa a-ree-vay

my case has been damaged
ma valise a été abîmée
ma va-leez a ay-tay a-bee-may

I need to go to hospital
je dois aller à l'hôpital
zhuh dwa a-lay a lo-pee-tal

I have no money
je n'ai pas d'argent
zhuh nay pa dar-zhoñ

my child is missing
mon enfant s'est perdu
moñ oñ-foñ say pehr-doo

he/she is ... old
il/elle a ... ans
eel/el a ... oñ

go away!
allez-vous-en!
a-lay vooz oñ

that man is following me
cet homme me suit
set om muh swee

Although no-one wants to consider the possibility, you may come across the odd problem and it is best to be armed with a few phrases to help you cope with the situation.

there is no...
il n'y a pas de...
eel nee a pa duh...

there is no soap
il n'y a pas de savon
eel nee a pa duh sa-voñ

it is dirty
c'est sale
say sal

they are dirty
ils sont sales
eel soñ sal

it is broken
c'est cassé
say kass-ay

they are broken
ils sont cassés
eel soñ kass-ay

the ... does not work
le/la ... ne marche pas
luh/la ... nuh marsh pa

the ... do not work
les ... ne marchent pas
lay ... nuh marsh pa

the window doesn't open
la fenêtre n'ouvre pas
la fuh-netr noovr pa

the door doesn't close
la porte ne ferme pas
la port nuh fehrm pa

it is too noisy
il y a trop de bruit
eel ee a troh duh brwee

the room is too small
la chambre est trop petite
la shoñbr ay trop puh-teet

it is too hot
il fait trop chaud
eel feh troh shoh

it is too cold
il fait trop froid
eel feh troh frwa

it is too expensive
c'est trop cher
say troh shehr

I'd like another room
je voudrais une autre chambre
zhuh voo-dray oon otr shoñbr

I want to complain
je veux faire une réclamation
zhuh vuh fehr oon rek-la-mass-yoñ

where is the manager?
où est le directeur?
oo ay luh dee-rek-tuhr

we want to order
nous voudrions commander
noo vood-ree-yoñ ko-moñ-day

the service is very bad
le service est très mauvais
luh sehr-vees ay tray moh-vay

this dish is cold
ce plat est froid
suh pla ay frwa

this coffee is cold
ce café est froid
suh ka-fay ay frwa

there is a mistake
il y a une erreur
eel ee a oon e-ruhr

please check the bill
pouvez-vous vérifier l'addition?
poo-vay voo ve-ree-fyay la-dee-syoñ

this isn't what I ordered
ce n'est pas ce que j'ai commandé
suh nay pa suh kuh zhay ko-moñ-day

I want a refund
je veux être remboursé(e)
zhuh vuh etr roñ-boor-say

Everyday France

i *The following four pages should give you an idea of the type of things you will come across in France.*

OUVERT 24H / 24H
open 24 hours

FERME
closed

Horaires d'ouverture

MARDI	9ʰ - 12ʰ
MERCREDI	
JEUDI	14ʰ30 - 19ʰ

opening hours

Shops in France generally shut in the afternoon from about 12 noon to 2pm. Food shops close at around 7.30pm. Shops are usually closed on Sunday and Monday mornings. There are no markets on Monday.

the red lozenge: sign of the tabac

travel cards in Paris

lottery tickets

The **tabac** is an extremely useful place. Often it has a bar attached (**bar-tabac**) and is open all day until about 8pm. It sells cigarettes, envelopes, stamps, transport tickets and lottery tickets.

Accueil
information/reception

There are lottery draws on Wednesdays and Saturdays.

---

talking

do you sell...?	**stamps**	**phonecards**
est-ce que vous vendez...?	des timbres	des télécartes
ess-kuh voo voñ-day...	*day tañbr*	*day te-le-kart*
where can I get...?	**plasters**	**a map**
où est-ce que je peux acheter...?	du sparadrap	un plan
oo ess kuh zhuh puh ash-tay...	*doo spa-ra-dra*	*uñ ploñ*

entrance
The words *entrée libre*
mean free entry
(for museums, etc.)

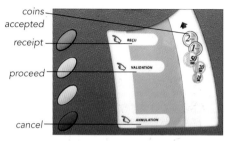

coins accepted
receipt
proceed
cancel

The use of bank cards in paying machines is more widespread in France. In car parks, you often have the option of either getting a ticket and paying at the machine, or just inserting your bank card on the way in and out of the car park without having to queue at the paying machine. British bank cards don't always work in French paying machines, but you'll always have the option of paying with cash.

exit
Sortie is also used for
exit on motorways.

push   **pull**

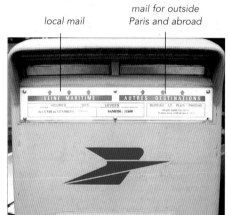

local mail

mail for outside
Paris and abroad

pay here
The word *caisse* actually
means *till* or *cash box*.

Postboxes are usually split into two: local mail (for the *département* – here *Seine Maritime*), and any other mail – national and international (*autres destinations* – other destinations).

excuse me...
pardon, Monsieur/Madame...
par-doñ muhs-yuh/ma-dam...

what do I have to do?
qu'est-ce qu'il faut faire?
kess keel foh fehr

how does this work?
comment ça marche?
ko-moñ sa marsh

what does that mean?
qu'est-ce que ça veut dire?
kess kuh sa vuh deer

talking

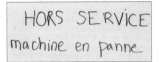

out of service
If something is working,
you will see the words **en service**.
The words **en panne** mean
broken down.

Service Non Compris

service not included
Tipping in France is not compulsory and
should be simply an appreciation of good
service. In a restaurant, you might consider
tipping the waiter 5–10% of the bill.

When friends
or family meet
up, they kiss
each other on
the cheeks
between two
and four times,
depending on
the tradition in
the area.

Sortie de secours
Défense
d'encombrer

emergency exit
défense de... means
no... ; *forbidden...*

Smoking is still popular in France
and although all bars and
restaurants have no-smoking
areas, you may find that the
whole bar is filled with smoke.

no smoking

Bars and cafés are open throughout the day and
close around 8pm. Bars that open later tend to
be shut during the day. Unlike in pubs, you sit at
your table and a waiter will come and take your
order. You generally pay when you leave. It is
cheaper to have a drink at the bar, *au comptoir*.

talking

can I smoke here?
est-ce que je peux fumer ici?
ess kuh zhuh puh foo-may ee-see

I don't smoke
je ne fume pas
zhuh nuh foo-may pa

an ashtray, please
un cendrier s'il vous plaît
uñ soñd-ree-ay seel voo play

do you mind if I smoke?
ça vous dérange si je fume?
sa voo day-roñzh see zhuh foom

please don't smoke
s'il vous plaît ne fumez pas
seel voo play nuh foo-may pa

a non-smoking table, please
une table non-fumeur s'il vous plaît
oon tabl noñ-foo-muhr seel voo play

In Paris the scarcity of coin-operated toilets means you have to rely on cafés, which are numerous, but where you almost always have to pay, and where standards vary greatly. In big cafés you can go straight to the toilets, generally downstairs. The toilet door is coin-operated. In standard cafés the toilets are for patrons only and you will be expected to buy a drink. Department stores (**les grandes magasins**) will usually have toilets. You'll often find that shopping centres charge for toilet facilities (about 30 euro cents). It's best to have small change on you just in case!

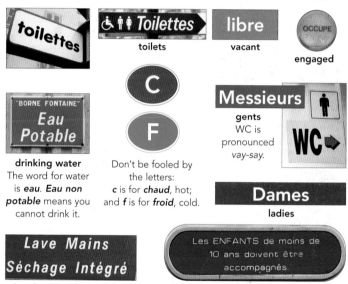

toilettes

Toilettes
toilets

libre
vacant

OCCUPE
engaged

"BORNE FONTAINE"
Eau Potable
drinking water
The word for water is *eau*. *Eau non potable* means you cannot drink it.

C
F
Don't be fooled by the letters: *c* is for *chaud*, hot; and *f* is for *froid*, cold.

Messieurs
gents
WC is pronounced *vay-say*.
WC ➜

Dames
ladies

Lave Mains Séchage Intégré
handwash and dryer in one

Les ENFANTS de moins de 10 ans doivent être accompagnés.
children under 10 must be accompanied

excuse me! where is the toilet?
s'il vous plaît où sont les toilettes?
seel voo play oo soñ lay twa-le

do you have the key for the toilet?
est-ce que vous avez la clé pour les toilettes?
ess kuh vooz a-vay la klay poor lay twa-le

are there toilets for the disabled?
est-ce qu'il y a des toilettes pour handicapés?
ess keel ee a day twa-let poor oñ-dee-ka-pay

where can I change my baby?
où est-ce que je peux changer mon bébé?
oo ess kuh zhuh puh shoñ-zhay moñ bay-bay

talking

Asking the Way

i **Tabacs** and newsagents sell very handy street directories (**répertoire des rues de Paris**) and you can ask for a free map with metro lines and bus routes when you buy your metro/bus tickets from the metro booth.

Maps of the area at Metro and RER stations are generally located near exits.

The dispenser on the side of the area map sells a portable copy of the map (*un plan*).

bikes
pedestrians   roller-skates

Sundays and public holidays from 9-5 all year round

talking talking talking

excuse me!
s'il vous plaît, Monsieur/Madame
seel voo play muhs-yuh/ma-dam

do you know where...?
est-ce que vous savez où...?
ess kuh voo sa-vay oo...

how do I get to...?
pour aller à/au...?
poor a-lay a/oh...

is this the right way to...?
c'est la bonne direction pour...?
say la bon dee-reks-yoñ poor...

do you have a map of the town?
est-ce que vous avez un plan de la ville?
ess kuh vooz a-vay uñ ploñ duh la veel

can you show me on the map?
pouvez-vous me montrer sur la carte?
poo-vay voo muh moñ-tray soor la kart

we're looking for...
nous cherchons...
noo shehr-shoñ...

where is...?
où est...?
oo ay...

is it far?
c'est loin?
say lwañ

a street directory
un répertoire des rues
uñ rep-er-twar day roo

pedestrians caution
cross in two stages

ZONE

15

PRIORITE AUX PIETONS

pedestrians have priority

9e Arrt

BOULEVARD
DES
CAPUCINES

In cities, street plates
display the **arrondissement**
(district) number at the top.

L.B.L
Syndicat Initiative ℹ
✉ ✕ Hôtel de LA PAIX

Syndicat d'Initiative
is another word for
tourist office. Hotels are
signposted. The knife
and fork means it has
a restaurant (open to
non-residents).

SORTIE ↓
RUE NÉLATON

exit

Hôtel de Ville

town hall
Don't be fooled by the
word **hôtel**.

town centre

Pedestrian routes
with symbol.
Places of interest
are signposted in
brown and public
services are in blue.

à droite
a drwat
to the right

à gauche
à gohsh
to the left

tout droit
too drwa
straight ahead

allez
a-lay
go

tournez
toor-nay
turn

rue
roo
street

place
plass
square

feux
fuh
traffic lights

église
eg-leez
church

première
pruhm-yehr
first

deuxième
duhz-yehm
second

loin
lwañ
far

près de
pray duh
near to

à côté de
a ko-tay duh
next to

en face de
oñ fass duh
opposite

jusqu'à
zhoos-ka
until

keywords keywords keywords keywords keywords keywords keywords

Banks & Money

French bank cards are the 'chip and pin' sort. Your British card may or may not be accepted by cash machines, but it's worth a try. Many banks are not freely accessible and you have to go through a locked door. Once you have rung the bell, you will see either a red light indicating to wait, or a green light indicating that you should enter.

REÇU

receipt

BILLETS

banknotes

PIÈCES ACCEPTEES :

(0,10€) (0,20€) (0,50€) (1€)

Ne rend pas la monnaie

pièces acceptées = coins accepted
ne rend pas la monnaie = no change given.

Cash machines operate as at home.

annulation = cancel

correction = error

validation = proceed

ANNULATION

CORRECTION

VALIDATION

wait (red light) — Attendez

come in (green light) — Passez

ring here — Sonnez Ici

You will have to ring a bell and wait to be let into most banks.

carte de crédit

credit card

carte bleue

debit card

Cash machines are known as *distributeurs de billets* and are widely available. You can carry out the transaction in English and it saves time queuing in banks to change money.

SOCIÉTÉ GÉNÉRALE

RETRAIT

CL CREDIT LYONNAIS

Banque is the word for bank, but you will also see words such as *crédit* (*Crédit Agricole*) and *société* (*Société Générale*).

Du Lundi au Jeudi
de 8h50 à 17h15

Vendredi
de 8h50 à 16h45

Opening times may
vary from bank to bank.

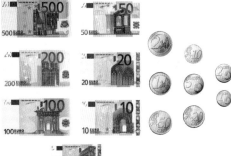

500 EURO · 50 EURO
200 EURO · 20 EURO
100 EURO · 10 EURO
5 EURO

The euro is the currency of France. It breaks down
into 100 euro cent.
Notes: 5, 10, 20, 50, 100, 200, 500
Coins: 2 euro, 1 euro, 50 cent, 20 cent, 10 cent,
5 cent, 2 cent, 1 cent.
Although coins are officially *cent*, you will find that
French people prefer to call them *centimes*, a more
familiar term for them. Euro notes are the same
throughout Europe. The backs of coins carry different
designs from each of the member European countries.

keywords keywords keywords

carte de crédit
kart duh kray-dee
credit card

distributeur
dees-tree-boo-tuhr
cash dispenser

code secret
kod suh-kray
PIN number

monnaie
mo-nay
change

insérez
añ-seh-ray
insert

tapez le
montant
ta-pay luh moñ-toñ
press amount

billets
bee-yay
notes

espèces
ess-pess
cash

puce
poos
chip

where is there...?
où est-ce qu'il y a...?
oo ess keel ee a...

a bank
une banque
oon boñk

a bureau de change
un bureau de change
uñ boo-roh duh shoñzh

where can I change money?
où est-ce que je peux changer de l'argent?
oo ess kuh zhuh puh shoñ-zhay duh lar-zhoñ

I would like small notes
je voudrais des petites coupures
zhuh voo-dray day puh-teet koo-poor

where is the nearest cash dispenser?
où est le distributeur le plus proche?
oo ay luh dees-tree-boo-tuhr luh ploo prosh

I want to change these traveller's cheques
je voudrais changer ces travellers
zhuh voo-dray shoñ-zhay say tra-vuh-luhrs

the cash dispenser has swallowed my card
le distributeur a mangé ma carte
luh dees-tree-boo-tuhr a moñ-zhay ma kart

talking talking talking

When is...?

*The 24-hour clock is used in timetables. With the 24-hour clock, the words half (**demie**) and quarter (**quart**) are not used.*

keywords		
matin *ma-tañ* morning		

at...

matin *ma-tañ* morning	13:00	**à treize heures** *a trez uhr*
après-midi *a-pray mee-dee* afternoon	14:00	**à quatorze heures** *a ka-torz uhr*
ce soir *suh swar* this evening	15:00	**à quinze heures** *a kañz uhr*
aujourd'hui *oh-zhoor-dwee* today	16:00	**à seize heures** *a sez uhr*
demain *duh-mañ* tomorrow	17:00	**à dix-sept heures** *a dees-set uhr*
hier *ee-yehr* yesterday	18:00	**à dix-huit heures** *a deez-weet uhr*
plus tard *ploo tar* later	19:00	**à dix-neuf heures** *a deez-nuhf uhr*
tout de suite *toot sweet* straight away	20:00	**à vingt heures** *a vañt uhr*
maintenant *mañ-tuh-noñ* now	21:00	**à vingt et une heures** *a vañt ay oon uhr*
	22:00	**à vingt-deux heures** *a vañt-duhz uhr*
	23:00	**à vingt-trois heures** *a vañt-trwaz uhr*
	24:00	**à vingt-quatre heures** *a vañt-katr uhr*

---

when is the next...? quand part le prochain...? *koñ par luh pro-shañ...*	**train** train *trañ*	**bus** bus *boos*	**boat** bateau *ba-toh*
at what time is...? à quelle heure est...? *a kel uhr ay...*	**breakfast** le petit déjeuner *luh puh-tee day-zhuh-nay*		**dinner** le dîner *luh dee-nay*

when does the ... leave?
quand est-ce que le/la ... part?
koñt ess kuh luh/la ... par

when does the ... arrive?
quand est-ce que le/la ... arrive?
koñt ess kuh luh/la ... a-reev

when does the ... open?
le/la ... ouvre à quelle heure?
luh/la ... oovr a kel uhr

when does the ... close?
le/la ... ferme à quelle heure?
luh/la ... fehrm a kel uhr

at…

à douze heures
a dooz uhr

à onze heures
a oñz uhr

à une heure
a <u>oon</u> uhr

à dix heures
a dees uhr

à deux heures
a duhz uhr

à neuf heures
a nuhf uhr

à trois heures
a trwaz uhr

à huit heures
a weet uhr

à quatre heures
a katr uhr

à sept heures
a set uhr

à cinq heures
a sañk uhr

à six heures
a seez uhr

à dix-huit heures quarante-cinq
a deez-weet uhr ka-roñt-sañk
at 18.45

à … moins le quart
a … mwañ luh kar
at quarter to…

à minuit
a meen-wee
at midnight

à … et quart
a … ay kar
at quarter past…

à … moins vingt
a … mwañ vañ
at twenty to…

à midi
a mee-dee
at midday

à … et demie
a … ay duh-mee
at half past…

what time is it please?
quelle heure est-il s'il vous plaît?
kel uhr et-eel seel voo play

what is the date?
quelle est la date d'aujourd'hui?
kel ay la dat doh-zhoor-dwee

it is the 8th May
nous sommes le huit mai
noo som luh wee may

16 September 2006
le seize septembre deux mille six
luh sez sept-toñbr duh meel seess

which day?
quel jour?
kel zhoor

which month?
quel mois?
kel mwa

talking

Timetables

Timetables use the 24-hour clock. Bus and train timetables usually change once a year. French Summer Time starts on the last Sunday in March and ends on the last Sunday in October. France is always 1 hour ahead of the UK.

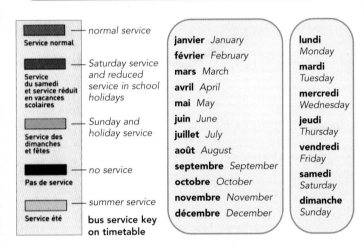

Service normal — normal service

Service du samedi et service réduit en vacances scolaires — Saturday service and reduced service in school holidays

Service des dimanches et fêtes — Sunday and holiday service

Pas de service — no service

Service été — summer service

bus service key on timetable

janvier January	
février February	
mars March	
avril April	
mai May	
juin June	
juillet July	
août August	
septembre September	
octobre October	
novembre November	
décembre December	

lundi Monday

mardi Tuesday

mercredi Wednesday

jeudi Thursday

vendredi Friday

samedi Saturday

dimanche Sunday

lignes de correspondance
connecting buses

bus timetable
(on bus stop)

vous êtes ici
you are here

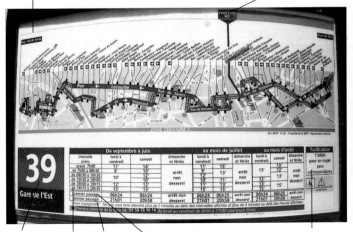

bus/route no.   times   last bus   first bus
location

journey limit
with 1 ticket

train timetable

numéro de train *notes à consulter*		50431 *1*	50433 *1*	3131 *2*	50007 *1*	3133 *2*
		🚲	🚲	🍴♿		🍴♿
Paris-St-Lazare	Dép.			06.39	06.45	07.32
Mantes-la-Jolie	Dép.				07.18	
Vernon (Eure)	Dép.			07.19	07.39	
Gaillon-Aubevoye	Dép.				07.48	
Val-de-Reuil	Dép.				08.03	
Oissel	Dép.				08.17	
Rouen-Rive-Droite	Arr.			07.49	08.33	08.38
Rouen-Rive-Droite	Dép.	06.35	06.49	07.51		08.40
Yvetot	Arr.	07.01	07.21	08.10		09.00
Bréauté-Beuzeville	Arr.	07.18	07.41	08.24		
Le Havre	Arr.	07.35	08.07	08.40		09.26

du 12 décembre 2004 au 02 juillet 2005

Paris ↑
Rouen
Le Havre ↓

HORAIRES

Paris ●
Mantes ●
Vernon ●
Gaillon-Aubevoye ●
Val-de-Reuil ●
Oissel ●
Rouen ■
Yvetot ■
Bréauté-Beuzeville ■
Le Havre ■

www.voyages-sncf.com

SNCF

This Paris-Rouen-Le Harve rail timetable runs from end of May to start of December.

horaire
o-rehr
timetable

tous les jours
too lay zhoor
everyday

sauf
sohf
except for

jusqu'au
zhoos-koh
until

à partir de
a par-teer duh
from

fêtes
fet
holidays

été
ay-tay
summer

hiver
ee-vehr
winter

keywords keywords keywords

trains run daily (dark background)

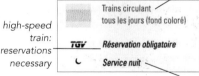

	Trains circulant tous les jours (fond coloré)
TGV	**Réservation obligatoire**
🌙	**Service nuit**

high-speed train: reservations necessary

night service

key to services

JOURS DE CIRCULATION ET SERVICES DISPONIBLES

1. les sam.
2. jusqu'au 25 juin : les ven, sam, dim et fêtes sauf le 1er juin ; circule du 26 juin au 3 sept : tous les jours;du 8 sept au 3 nov : les ven, sam et dim;les 10, 17, 24 nov et 1er déc.
3. tous les jours sauf les 23 juil et 24 sept 🍴assuré certains jours-♿ certains jours.

Days of operation and services available
1. *Saturdays*
2. *Until 25 Jun: Fri, Sat, Sun & hols exc. 1 Jun; 26 Jun-3 Sep: daily; 8 Sep-3 Nov: Fri, Sat, Sun; 10, 17, 24 Nov & 1 Dec.*
3. *Daily except 23 Jul & 24 Sep; refreshment trolley some days; reclining seats some days.*

Tickets

i Remember to try and begin your request with **Bonjour Monsieur** or **Bonjour Madame**. You should attempt to ask in French, even if you have to resort to English pretty quickly. Even though you might expect people working in such places to speak English, they will regard it as arrogant if you assume they do.

Carte Orange
is a Parisian travel pass (weekly, monthly or yearly)

Cut your photo to fit and fix it onto the white square.

Logo of RATP, Parisian transport authority (travel tickets and cards are sold wherever you see this logo).

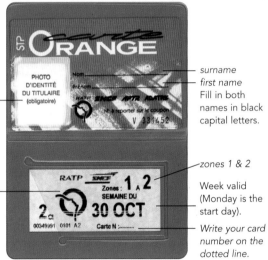

surname
first name
Fill in both names in black capital letters.

zones 1 & 2

Week valid (Monday is the start day).

Write your card number on the dotted line.

Train tickets carry various information.

période de pointe
peak period

à composter avant l'accès au train
validate ticket before boarding train

conservez tous vos billets
retain all your tickets

2 adults

voit coach
place no
seat nos
non fum
no smoking

fenêtre
window
couloir
aisle

découverte à deux
type of ticket

A/R à 2 obligatoire this type of ticket is for 2 people. Both people must travel there and back. **A/R = aller-retour**

prix price

A RATP transport ticket allowing travel in the Paris area.

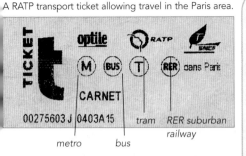

metro   bus   tram   RER suburban railway

A ticket like this bought in a book of 10 (*un carnet*), saves time and money: single tickets work out around 40% more expensive than when bought in a *carnet*.

Bus ticket for Boulogne-sur-Mer bought in a *carnet*.

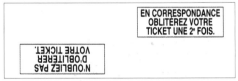

The ticket has been validated in the machine at the front of the bus (see page 29). This stamps it and slices the corner off.

Reverse of the ticket.

If you are catching a connection, remember to validate the ticket a second time (it will slice off the opposite corner).

carnet
kar-nay
book of 10 tickets

ticket
tee-kay
bus/metro ticket

billet
bee-yay
ticket

aller simple
a-lay sañpl
single

aller-retour
a-lay ruh-toor
return

adulte
a-doolt
adult

enfant
oñ-foñ
child

étudiant
ay-tood-yoñ
student

senior
sen-yor
over 60

handicapé
oñ-dee-ka-pay
disabled

famille
fa-meey
family

carte
kart
travel card/pass

Public Transport

i There is no zone system on Parisian buses. One ticket will get you to the end of the line or just one stop away. If you are using both metro and bus for one journey you cannot use the same ticket. You need to use two separate tickets. The bus timetable is posted in bus shelters (see pages 24-25). You have to stick your hand out if it is a request stop (**faire signe au machiniste**). If you haven't bought your ticket in advance, you can buy a single ticket from the driver (about 40% more expensive than when bought by the book, or **carnet**). There are 18 night-bus lines in Paris, indicated by letters. Night buses (**Noctambus** – a pun on **noctambule** meaning night-owl) operate 7 days a week from 1am to 5.30am. They serve Paris and its suburbs, up to 30kms away from the city centre. On night buses you pay a fixed fare.

The destination and route number appear on the front of the bus.

night buses

As well as in the **tabac** and at metro booths, you can buy bus tickets from the newsagent's.

newsagent's sign

Bus stop for route numbers 24, 27, 69 and 72. Lines are colour-coded.

sign for the night bus
Night bus services that stop here.

You must validate
your ticket when you
get on the bus.

night bus B timetable

validate tickets for each trip

talking talking talking

is there a bus to...?
il y a un bus pour...?
eel ee a uñ boos poor...

where can I catch a bus to...?
où est-ce que je peux prendre le bus pour...?
oo ess kuh zhuh puh proñdr luh boos poor...

which number goes to...?
quel numéro va à/au...?
kel noo-may-roh va a/oh...

does this bus go to...?
est-ce que ce bus va à/au...?
ess kuh suh boos va a/oh...

excuse me, is this a request stop?
s'il vous plaît, c'est un arrêt facultatif?
seel voo play say un a-ray fa-kool-ta-teef

which bus goes to the centre?
quel bus va au centre-ville?
kel boos va oh soñ-truh-veel

please tell me when to get off
pourriez-vous me dire quand descendre?
poo-ree-ay voo muh deer koñ day-soñdr

excuse me, I'm getting off!
pardon! je descends
par-doñ zhuh day-soñ

where can I catch the bus to the airport?
où est-ce que je peux prendre le bus pour l'aéroport?
oo ess kuh zhuh puh proñdr luh boos poor la-ehr-o-por

has the number 5 bus been already?
est-ce que le bus nº 5 est déjà passé?
ess kuh luh boos noo-may-roh sañk ay day-zha pas-say

i The Paris metro operates daily from 5.30am to 12.30 at night and the city's 6 main train stations connect to the metro system. There is a zone system (the centre of Paris is zone 1-3). The **Paris Visite** card allows you to travel around for 1, 2, 3 or 5 days (with a reduced price for children between 4 and 11). It is a safe and fast way to travel, even late at night.

ticket barriers

Metro signs

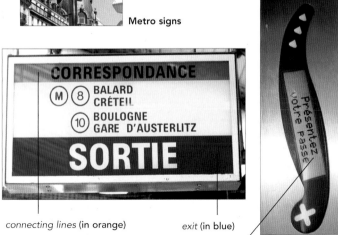

connecting lines **(in orange)**   exit **(in blue)**

insert ticket

en cas d'affluence
ne pas utiliser
les strapontins

when crowded, do not use the foldable seats

When catching a metro, let people get out first, then go in and stand clear of the door. If travelling with a rucksack, take if off and move towards the back of the carriage where you won't be in the way of people getting on and off.

RER is Paris' suburban train network, which is linked to the metro network (for instance, you'd take line A of the RER to go to Disneyland Paris, or line C or D to go to the *Stade de France*). You can take the RER with a standard metro/bus ticket as long as you don't leave zone 2, i.e. Paris *intramuros*. Some stations have disabled and pram access.

first train   *last train*

PREMIER TRAIN	**DIRECTION**	DERNIER TRAIN
5H41	(M) (6)	1H03

CHARLES DE GAULLE-ÉTOILE

Paris' 14 metro lines are called by their numbers as well as by their terminuses at each end.

where is the nearest metro station?
où est la station de métro la plus proche?
oo ay la stass-yoñ duh met-roh la ploo prosh

a carnet (book of 10 tickets) please
un carnet s'il vous plaît
uñ kar-nay seel voo play

a weekly card please
une carte hebdomadaire s'il vous plaît
oon kart eb-do-ma-dehr seel voo play

have you a pocket map of the underground?
est-ce que vous avez un plan de poche du métro?
ess kuh vooz av-ay uñ ploñ duh posh doo met-roh

which station is it for...?
c'est quelle station pour...?
say kel stass-yoñ poor...

I want to go to...
je voudrais aller à/au...
zhuh vood-ray a-lay a/oh...

do I have to change?
est-ce qu'il faut changer?
ess keel foh shoñ-zhay

where do I change?
où est-ce qu'il faut changer?
oo ess keel foh shoñ-zhay

which line do I take?
je dois prendre quelle ligne?
zhuh dwah proñdr kel leen-yuh

in which direction?
dans quelle direction?
doñ kel dee-reks-yoñ

which stop is it for...?
c'est quel arrêt pour...?
say kel a-reh poor...

excuse me! this is my stop
s'il vous plaît! c'est mon arrêt
seel voo play say moñ a-reh

talking talking talking talking

i The train is not an especially cheap way to travel in France, but it's often the only one since coach companies cannot serve domestic destinations, only international ones (the SNCF has the monopoly on domestic transport). Several types of reduction are available under a scheme called **Découverte** (Discovery). You can get 25% off just by being over 60, being under 26, by travelling with at least one other person and at most eight others, accompanying (up to four people) a child under 12 years of age. To take advantage of these discounts, you must be travelling during off-peak times (**pèriode bleue**) and not peak times (**pèriode blanche** or **de pointe**). Check the **Calendrier voyageurs** (Travellers' Calendar) in train stations.

The logo for French railways. The word for station is **gare**.

TGV Départ immédiat — leaving straight away

Billets — tickets

Abonnements — season tickets

Billets Grandes Lignes

Tickets for main lines.

talking talking talking talking

a single to...	**2 singles to...**	**first class**
un aller simple pour...	deux allers simples pour...	première classe
un a-lay sañple poor...	*duhz a-lay sañpl pour...*	*pruhm-yehr klass*

a return to...	**2 returns to...**	**second class**
un aller-retour pour...	deux allers-retours pour...	seconde classe
un a-lay ruh-toor poor...	*duhz a-lay ruh-toor poor...*	*suh-goñd klass*

a child's ticket to...	**2 senior tickets**	
un billet enfant pour...	deux billets senior pour...	
uñ bee-yay oñ-foñ poor...	*duh bee-yay seen-yor poor...*	

do I have to pay a supplement?
je dois payer un supplément?
zhuh dwa pay-ay uñ soop-lay-moñ

do I need a reservation?
est-ce qu'il faut une réservation?
ess keel foh <u>oon</u> ray-zehr-va-syoñ

do I have to change?
est-ce qu'il faut changer?
ess keel foh shoñ-zhay

I want to book...	**2 seats**	**a couchette**
je voudrais réserver...	deux places	une couchette
zhuh voo-dray ray-zehr-vay...	*duh plass*	*<u>oon</u> koo-shet*

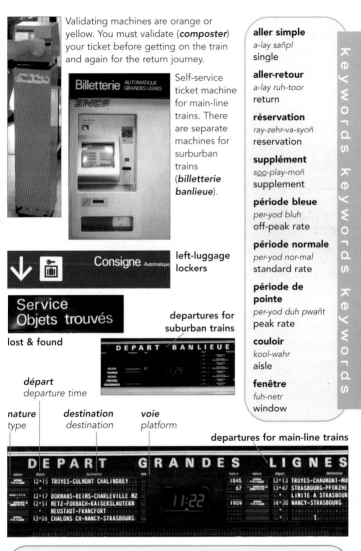

Validating machines are orange or yellow. You must validate (*composter*) your ticket before getting on the train and again for the return journey.

Self-service ticket machine for main-line trains. There are separate machines for surburban trains (*billetterie banlieue*).

Consigne Automatique — left-luggage lockers

Service Objets trouvés — lost & found

departures for suburban trains

départ
departure time

nature
type

destination
destination

voie
platform

keywords

aller simple
a-lay sañpl
single

aller-retour
a-lay ruh-toor
return

réservation
ray-zehr-va-syoñ
reservation

supplément
soo-play-moñ
supplement

période bleue
per-yod bluh
off-peak rate

période normale
per-yod nor-mal
standard rate

période de pointe
per-yod duh pwañt
peak rate

couloir
kool-wahr
aisle

fenêtre
fuh-netr
window

departures for main-line trains

DEPART GRANDES LIGNES

nature	départ	destination	voie	train n°	nature	départ	destination
	12¤15	TROYES-CULMONT CHALINDREY		1845		13¤13	TROYES-CHAUMONT-HUI
	12¤17	DORMANS-REIMS-CHARLEVILLE MZ		67		13¤47	STRASBOURG-PFORZHE
	12¤51	METZ-FORBACH-KAISERSLAUTERN					LIMITE A STRASBOUR
		NEUSTADT-FRANCFORT		1909		14¤30	NANCY-STRASBOURG
	13¤06	CHALONS CH-NANCY-STRASBOURG					

11:22

the train to...
le train pour...
luh trañ poor...

is this the train for...?
c'est le train pour...?
say luh trañ poor...

which platform does it leave from?
il part de quel quai?
eel par duh kel kay

this is my seat
c'est ma place
say ma plass

talking

Taxi

> *You cannot hail taxis in the street – you will have to catch them at a stand. In Paris these are usually located near train stations and metro stations. Otherwise you will have to phone for a taxi. You can ask for a special price (**un forfait**) if you are going on a long journey (perhaps to the airport).*

Paris taxi sign
A (white), B (orange) and C (green) lights correspond to the 3 different tariffs (see below). The taxi is free (**libre**) when the 'taxi' sign is lit and the A, B, C lights are off.

taxi meter
(**le compteur**)

taxi stand

map showing different taxi tariff zones around Paris
Taxi tariff A corresponds to the white central zone (Paris *intramuros*); tariff B to the orange zone (the nearest suburbs) and tariff C to the green zone (the departments of Seine et Marne, Yvelines and Val d'Oise.)

where is the nearest taxi stand?
où est la station de taxi la plus proche?
oo ay la stass-yoñ duh tak-see la ploo prosh

to ... please
à ... s'il vous plaît
a ... seel voo play

how much is it to...?
c'est combien pour aller à...?
say koñ-byañ poor a-lay a...

please order me a taxi
pouvez-vous m'appeler un taxi?
poo-vay voo map-lay uñ tak-see

for now
pour maintenant
poor mañ-tuh-noñ

for ... o'clock
pour ... heures
poor ... uhr

can I have a receipt?
est-ce que je peux avoir un reçu?
ess kuh zhuh puh av-war uñ ruh-soo

keep the change
gardez la monnaie
gar-day la mo-nay

is there a special rate for the airport?
est-ce qu'il y a un forfait pour l'aéroport?
ess keel ee a uñ for-fay poor la-ehr-o-por

Car Hire

> To hire a car in France you have to be at least 21 and have held a driving licence for a year. If you are under 25 you might have to pay a young driver's supplement, depending on the type of car. Mileage (or **kilométrage**) is usually unlimited (**forfait kilométrage illimité**).

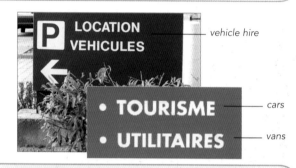

LOCATION VEHICULES — vehicle hire

• TOURISME — cars
• UTILITAIRES — vans

I want to hire a car
je voudrais louer une voiture
zhuh voo-dray loo-ay <u>oon</u> vwa-t<u>oo</u>r

for one day
pour un jour
poor uñ zhoor

for ... days
pour ... jours
poor ... zhoor

I want...
je voudrais...
zhuh voo-dray...

a small car
une petite voiture
<u>oon</u> puh-teet vwa-t<u>oo</u>r

a large car
une grosse voiture
<u>oon</u> gross vwa-t<u>oo</u>r

a people carrier
un monospace
uñ mo-no-spass

an automatic
une automatique
<u>oon</u> oh-toh-ma-teek

how much is it?
c'est combien?
say koñ-byañ

is mileage included?
est-ce que le kilométrage est compris?
ess kuh luh kee-lo-me-trazh ay koñ-pree

I am ... old
j'ai ... ans
zhay ... oñ

here is my driving licence
voici mon permis de conduire
vwa-see moñ per-mee duh koñ-dweer

what is included in the price?
qu'est-ce qui est compris dans le prix?
kess kee ay koñ-pree doñ luh pree

where are the documents?
où sont les papiers?
oo soñ lay pap-yay

can you show me the controls?
vous pouvez me montrer les commandes?
voo poo-vay muh moñ-tray lay ko-moñd

what do we do if we break down?
qu'est-ce qu'il faut faire si la voiture tombe en panne?
kess keel foh fehr see la vwa-t<u>oo</u>r toñb oñ pan

we need a baby seat
nous avons besoin d'un siège pour bébés
nooz a-voñ buh-zwañ duñ syehzh poor bay-bay

talking talking talking talking talking talking

Driving

French drivers tend to be quite aggressive and the high incidence of road deaths has become a cause for national concern. There are speed restrictions for drivers who have held their licence for less than 2 years (110km/h on motorways and 100km/h on dual carriageways and 80km/h on ordinary roads). Seatbelts are compulsory for both front and rear. Children under 10 should travel in the back, if possible. Babies and young children should be restrained appropriately, with a booster seat (**siège réhausseur**) or babyseat (**siège pour bébés**).

Speed restrictions

built up area	50 km/h
ordinary roads	90 km/h
dual carriageway	110 km/h
motorway	130 km/h

F

French car nationality badge

French road signs are colour-coded.

motorways

primary routes

local routes

temporary routes

places of interest

north **Nord**

Ouest west

east **Est**

Sud south

TOUTES DIRECTIONS

Centre Ville

town centre

all routes

AUTRES DIRECTIONS 7.5t

other routes

Itinéraire Poids Lourds

route for heavy vehicles

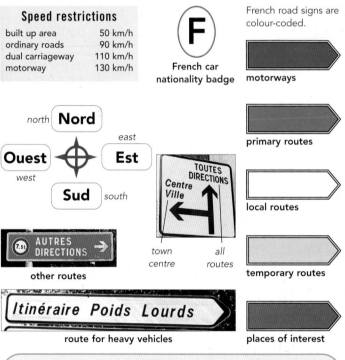

we are going to...
nous allons à...
nooz a-loñ a...

is the road good?
est-ce que la route est bonne?
ess kuh la root ay bon

is the pass open?
est-ce que le col est ouvert?
ess kuh luh kol ayt oo-vehr

which is the best route?
quel est le meilleur itinéraire?
kel ay luh may-yuhr ee-tee-nay-rehr

can you show me on the map?
pouvez-vous me montrer sur la carte?
poo-vay voo muh moñ-tray soor la kart

do we need snow chains?
est-ce qu'il faut des chaînes?
ess keel foh day shen

talking

If main roads are busy, look out for the *Bis* signs – these indicate alternative (and less busy) routes to main towns.

road closed detour
Follow the yellow detour signs to rejoin your route.

slow down

Indicates a roundabout and reminds drivers approaching to give way.

leaving **Petit-Quevilly** entering **Grand-Quevilly**

learner driver (*apprenti*)

give way

frequent speed checks

vers means *towards*
A6 means *Autoroute 6*

reminder that restriction is still in force

is this the road to...?
c'est bien la route de...?
say byañ la root duh...

how do I get to...?
pour aller à...?
poor a-lay a...

I am sorry, I did not know
je suis désolé, je ne savais pas
zhuh swee day-zo-lay zhuh nuh sa-vay pa

do I have to pay the fine straight away?
est-ce qu'il faut payer l'amende tout de suite?
ess keel foh pay-ay la-moñd toot sweet

talking

Although some portions of motorways are free around cities, you have to pay a toll if travelling over long distances. You get a ticket when you join the motorway. On leaving it you hand the ticket in at the **station péage** and the amount to pay is flashed up on an illuminated sign. Remember it is the front passenger who pays if you have a right-hand-drive car. Take care over speeding: limits are lowered in wet weather – by 20km/h on motorways and 10km/h on other roads.

Motorway signs are blue; local signs are white.

inner ring-road

motorway junction/exit

motorway emergency phone

The motorway routes signposted here are toll-paying (**péage**).

aire de...
Don't be fooled by the word *aire*, it means area not air.

Motorway services are located every 30-40km.

stop toll station

You pay a toll on most French motorways. Don't use the orange 't' lane. These are for drivers with a special device in their car, i.e. pre-paid. They can just drive through.

If you break down on the motorway

If you break down on the motorway, first you should put on your hazard lights and place the warning triangle about 30m behind the car. You should alert the police on emergency number 17 stating your exact location. If you are using an emergency SOS phone (located every 2km along the motorway) they will know your location. The police will arrange for a recovery vehicle to come to you.

my car has broken down
ma voiture est en panne
ma vwa-toor ay oñ pan

what do I do?
qu'est-ce que je dois faire?
kess kuh zhuh dwa fehr

I am on my own *(female)*
je suis seule
zhuh swee suhl

my children are in the car
mes enfants sont dans la voiture
mayz oñ-foñ soñ doñ la vwa-toor

the car is near junction number...
la voiture est près de la sortie numéro...
la vwa-toor ay pray duh la sor-tee noo-may-roh...

it's a blue Fiat Uno
c'est une Fiat Uno bleue
say ooñ fyat oo-noh bluh

registration number...
numéro d'immatriculation...
noo-may-roh dee-mat-ree-koo-las-yoñ...

In Paris, you generally pay to park. Outside Paris, in some parts of many towns, parking is only allowed on one side of the road. The system is that for the first 15 days of the month, parking is on the side of the road with odd house numbers. During the second half of the month, parking is on the even-numbered-house side.

Wherever you see this sign there will be some kind of parking restriction.

no parking anywhere along street

parking – pay at meter

no parking on the pavement

parking meter

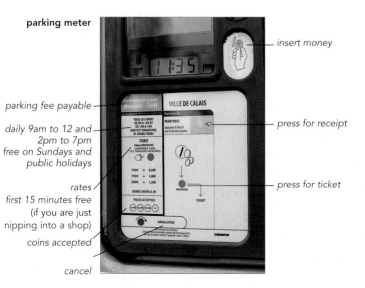

insert money

parking fee payable

daily 9am to 12 and 2pm to 7pm free on Sundays and public holidays

press for receipt

rates

press for ticket

first 15 minutes free (if you are just nipping into a shop)

coins accepted

cancel

no stopping for more
than 15mins

Don't be fooled: *libre* means there are spaces, not that parking is free. Full is **complet**.

no parking Tuesday
Friday from midnight
to 3pm

no HGVs

you will be towed away

no parking except taxis

on both sides

no parking

vehicle exit

dropping-off point

I am looking for a car park
je cherche un parking
zhuh shehrsh uñ par-keeng

can I park here?
est-ce que je peux me garer ici?
ess kuh zhuh puh muh ga-ray ee-see

the ticket machine doesn't work
l'horodateur ne marche pas
lo-ro-da-tuhr nuh marsh pa

do I need to pay?
il faut payer?
eel foh pay-ay

how long for?
pour combien de temps?
poor koñ-byañ duh toñ

talking

Petrol stations in small towns are generally manned and closed Sundays and in the evenings. The big towns have 24-hour petrol stations and you can buy petrol at most large supermarkets.

Colour-coding matches the pump handle: green is usually for unleaded (**sans plomb**), blue or red for super and yellow or black for diesel. The figure to the right (98, 95, 97) refers to the octane rating. Most cars run on the lower rating. The higher one is for powerful cars or towing cars.

Diesel is spelt a number of ways, **gazole**, **gaz oil** and **gazoil**. It is usually the black pump.

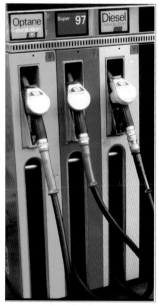

Petrol pumps are colour-coded. You will find the pump number at the side.

is there a petrol station near here?
est-ce qu'il y a une station-service près d'ici?
ess keel ee a oon stass-yoñ sehr-vees pray dee-see

fill it up please
le plein s'il vous plaît
luh plañ see voo play

40 euro worth of unleaded petrol
quarante euros d'essence sans plomb
ka-roñt uh-roh dess-oñss soñ ploñ

pump number...
pompe numéro...
poñp noo-may-roh...

I'd like to wash the car
je voudrais laver la voiture
zhuh voo-dray la-vay la vwa-toor

how much is that?
c'est combien?
say koñ-byañ

talking

i You should carry a red warning triangle in case of breakdown. It is also compulsory to carry a first-aid kit in the car. Neither of these is compulsory. It is advisable to have a box of spare bulbs as you could get fined on the spot by the police (unless you're able to change the bulb straightaway). You will have no trouble in France finding a **garage** to do repairs.

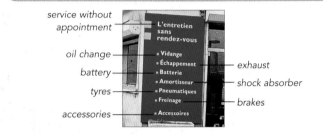

service without appointment — L'entretien sans rendez-vous

oil change — Vidange

battery — Batterie

tyres — Pneumatiques

accessories — Accessoires

exhaust — Échappement

shock absorber — Amortisseur

brakes — Freinage

I have broken down
je suis en panne
zhuh swee oñ pan

the car won't start
la voiture ne démarre pas
la vwa-toor nuh day-mar pa

I have a flat tyre
j'ai un pneu crevé
zhay uñ pnuh kruh-vay

the battery is flat
la batterie est à plat
la ba-tree ayt a pla

I need tyres
j'ai besoin de pneus
zhay buh-zwañ duh pnuh

I have run out of petrol
je suis en panne d'essence
zhuh swee oñ pan dess-oñss

where is the nearest garage?
où est le garage le plus proche?
oo ay luh ga-razh luh ploo prosh

something is wrong with...
il y a un problème avec...
eel ee a uñ pro-blehm a-vek...

the ... is not working
le/la ... ne marche pas
luh/la ... nuh marsh pa

the ... are not working
les ... ne marchent pas
lay ... nuh marsh pa

can you repair it?
vous pouvez le réparer?
voo poo-vay luh ray-pa-ray

how long will it take?
ça va prendre combien de temps?
sa va proñdr koñ-byañ duh toñ

when will it be ready?
ça sera prêt quand?
sa suh-ra pray koñ

how much will it cost?
combien ça va coûter?
koñ-byañ sa va koo-tay

can you replace the windscreen?
pouvez-vous changer le pare-brise?
poo-vay voo shoñ-zhay luh par-breez

please check...	**the oil**	**the water**	**the tyres**
vous pouvez vérifier...	l'huile	l'eau	les pneus
voo poo-vay vay-ree-fyay...	*lweel*	*loh*	*lay pnuh*

talking talking talking talking talking

Paris District

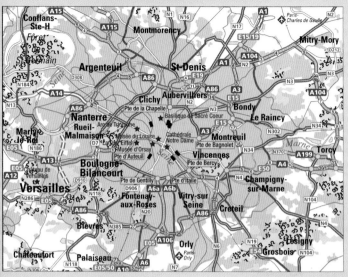

french speed limits

in built-up areas
on open roads
on motorways
Remember speeds are in kilometres per hour. When it rains, the speed limit is reduced by 20kph on the motorway and 10kph on all other roads.

VITESSE LIMITEE EN FRANCE

SAUF SIGNALISATION CONTRAIRE

50 en agglomération

90 sur route ordinaire

130 sur autoroute

priority to right

PRIORITE A DROITE

This means *priorité a droite* (*priority to vehicles on your right*) is suspended and that you have priority.

70

Green roads are major French routes (E = European, N = National). Motorways are signposted blue with *A* for *Autoroute*. The yellow D-roads (*départementale*) are what we would term b- or secondary roads. However, these can be good roads with little traffic. Many French roads have a solid white central line. You should not overtake or cross this line.

Paris City

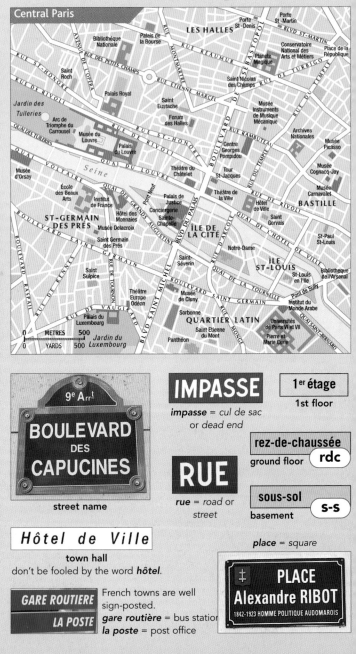

Central Paris

(Map of Central Paris showing labelled landmarks including:)

LES HALLES, Porte St-Denis, Porte St-Martin, BLVD ST-MARTIN, Place de la République, Conservatoire National des Arts et Métiers, Bibliothèque Nationale, Palais de la Bourse, RUE REAUMUR, Planète Magique, Saint Roch, AVENUE DE L'OPERA, RUE DES PETITS CHAMPS, RUE ETIENNE MARCEL, RUE DE TURBIGO, Saint Nicolas des Champs, RUE ST-HONORE, Palais Royal, Saint Eustache, Musée Instruments de Musique Mécanique, Jardin des Tuileries, Arc de Triomphe du Carrousel, Forum des Halles, RUE DE RIVOLI, RUE RAMBUTEAU, Archives Nationales, Musée Picasso, Musée du Louvre, RUE DE RIVOLI, RUE ST-HONORE, Centre Georges Pompidou, Palais du Louvre, QUAI DU LOUVRE, Seine, Théâtre du Châtelet, Tour St-Jacques, Musée Cognacq-Jay, QUAI DES TUILERIES, QUAI VOLTAIRE, Musée d'Orsay, Pont Neuf, Théâtre de la Ville, Musée Carnavalet, BASTILLE, École des Beaux Arts, Institut de France, QUAI DES GRANDS AUGUSTINS, Palais de Justice, Conciergerie, Sainte-Chapelle, Hôtel de Ville, Saint Gervais, St-Paul St-Louis, Hôtel des Monnaies, Musée Delacroix, ÎLE DE LA CITÉ, BLVD DU PALAIS, QUAI DE L'HOTEL DE VILLE, ST-GERMAIN DES PRÉS, Saint Germain des Prés, BOULEVARD SAINT GERMAIN, Notre-Dame, ÎLE ST-LOUIS, St-Louis en l'Île, Bibliothèque de l'Arsenal, Saint Sulpice, RUE DE TOURNON, Saint-Séverin, QUAI DE LA TOURNELLE, Pont de Sully, BOULEVARD RASPAIL, BOULEVARD DE RENNES, Théâtre Europe Odéon, Musée de Cluny, BOULEVARD SAINT GERMAIN, Institut du Monde Arabe, QUAI SAINT-BERNARD, RUE DE VAUGIRARD, Palais du Luxembourg, Sorbonne, QUARTIER LATIN, Universités de Paris VI et VII, Pierre et Marie Curie, BLVD SAINT MICHEL, RUE MONGE, Saint Etienne du Mont, Panthéon, Jardin du Luxembourg

METRES 500
YARDS 500

IMPASSE

impasse = cul de sac or *dead end*

RUE

rue = road or street

1er étage
1st floor

rez-de-chaussée rdc
ground floor

sous-sol s-s
basement

9e Arrt

BOULEVARD DES CAPUCINES

street name

Hôtel de Ville

town hall
don't be fooled by the word *hôtel*.

place = square

GARE ROUTIERE

LA POSTE

French towns are well sign-posted.
gare routière = bus station
la poste = post office

---

‡ **PLACE Alexandre RIBOT**
1842-1923 HOMME POLITIQUE AUDOMAROIS

Calais District

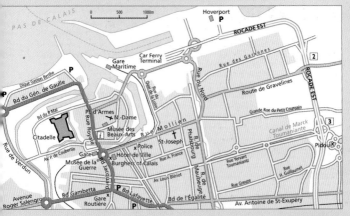

If you don't see your destination signposted, follow the *autres directions* (other routes) or *toutes directions* (all routes). To get to the town centre, follow *centre ville*.

15kph speed limit

In towns, local destinations are signposted in white. Motorways are signposted in blue.

heavy vehicles

slow down

RALENTIR

detour

give way
Indicates a roundabout and reminds drivers to give way.

Brussels City

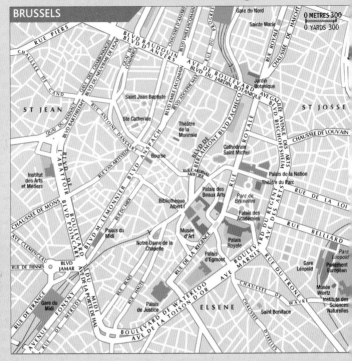

talking talking talking

have you a map of Brussels?
vous avez un plan de Brussels?
vooz av-ay uñ ploñ du broo-say

have you a map of the region
vous avez une carte de la région
vooz av-ay oon kart duh la ray-zhyoñ

can you show me where ... is on the map?
pouvez-vous me montrer où est ... sur la carte?
poo vay voo muh moñ-tray oo eh ... soor la kart

do you have a detailed map of the area?
vous avez une carte détaillée de la région?
vooz av-ay oon kart day-ta-yay duh la ray-zhyoñ

can you draw me a map with directions?
vous pouvez me dessiner un plan avec les directions?
voo poo-vay muh deh-see-nay uñ ploñ a-vek lay dee-rek-syoñ

Shopping

> Many shops are closed on Sundays and Monday morning. There are no markets on Mondays. Shops generally open at 9am and close for lunch around 12pm. Business resumes at 2pm and the shops stay open until around 7pm.

Alimentation générale is the classic corner shop. It stays open late and on Sunday and is generally open when everything else is closed. It sells drinks (including alcohol), fruit and veg, bread and all kind of things. These shops are handy but their prices are about 20–30% dearer than supermarkets.

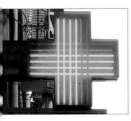

pharmacy symbol
You can buy nappies and baby food here but it tends to be more expensive than at the supermarket.

keywords keywords keywords

boulangerie
boo-loñzh-ree
baker's

boucherie
boosh-ree
butcher's

charcuterie
shar-koot-ree
delicatessen

alimentation générale
a-lee-moñ-tass-yoñ zhay-nay-ral
grocer's

pâtisserie
pa-teess-ree
cake shop

supermarché
soo-pehr-marsh-ay
supermarket

diététique
dee-ay-tay-teek
health food

pharmacie
far-ma-see
pharmacy

The red lozenge sign of the **tabac**. An extremely useful place, often it sells cigarettes, envelopes, stamps, transport tickets and lottery tickets. You can also have a flutter on the horses. If it is just a shop it is open till 7pm. If a bar is attached, it is open till late.

Boucherie

Butcher's

Pâtés, sausages, ham and other pork products.

Charcuterie

i Supermarkets are generally open from 8.30am to 8.30pm
Monday to Friday and 8.30am to 8pm on Saturday. Quite a few are
also open between 10am and 1pm on Sundays. Among the big chains
are **Auchan**, **Intermarché**, **Champion** and **Carrefour**. Most products are
cheaper than in smaller shops. Postcards are also much cheaper than in
tourist shops. You can also get petrol at many of the larger ones. At an
hypermarchè (superstore) you can also find non-food items such as
electrical goods, car parts, bicycles and so on.

supermarket
Welcomes you
Monday to
Saturday from
8.30am to
9pm. Late
night shopping
on Friday till 10pm. Sunday opening is
not very common in France.

Fruit and veg
must be weighed
and stickered
before you go
to the checkout.

You need a
1 euro coin
to release
the trolley.

— special offer

talking talking

where can I buy...?
où est-ce que je peux acheter...?
oo ess kuh zhuh puh ash-tay...

do you have...?
est-ce que vous avez...?
ess kuh vooz a-vay...

I am looking for...
je cherche...
zhuh shehrsh...

is there a market?
est-ce qu'il y a un marché?
ess keel ee a uñ mar-shay

can I pay with this card?
je peux payer avec cette carte?
zhuh puh pay-ay a-vek set kart

batteries
des piles
day peel

how much is it?
c'est combien?
say koñ-byañ

a present
un cadeau
uñ ka-doh

which day?
quel jour?
kel zhoor

a tin-opener
un ouvre-boîtes
un oovr-bwat

a good wine
un bon vin
uñ boñ vañ

*Quantities are expressed in kilos and grams. However, in everyday language, **une livre**, and **une demi-livre** (roughly equivalent to 1lb and ½lb) are often preferred to 500g (**cinq cents grammes**) and 250g (**deux cent cinquante grammes**). And they are easier to say! Remember to begin any shopping requests with **Bonjour Monsieur** or **Bonjour Madame**, as the French do.*

Bakers

Bread is bought freshly baked, whether from the local food shop, the baker's or the supermarket. Bakers bake at least twice a day, sometimes on Sunday mornings too, and they also sell snacks.

Milk comes in three varieties: wholemilk **entier**, semi-skimmed **demi-écrémé**, and skimmed **écrémé**.

The standard French stick is a **baguette**. The thinner version is **une ficelle**, the fatter version **un pain**. Some bakers specialise in different types of bread: **seigle** (rye), **complet** (wholemeal), **châtaignes** (chestnut) and **olives** (olive).

There are over 350 varieties of French cheeses (one for every day of the year). If you want to buy cheese at the **fromager**, you could ask, pointing to the one you want, **un morceau de ce fromage, s'il vous plaît**.

made with unpasteurised milk

keywords keywords keywords keywords keywords keywords

a piece of that cheese
un morceau de ce fromage
uñ mor-soh duh suh froh-mazh

a little more
un peu plus
uñ puh plooss

a little less
un peu moins
uñ puh mwañ

that's fine thanks
ça suffit merci
sa soo-fee mehr-see

10 slices of ham
dix tranches de jambon
dee troñsh duh zhoñ-boñ

thick slices
des tranches épaisses
day troñsh ay-pess

thin slices
des tranches fines
day troñsh feen

a bottle of mineral water
une bouteille d'eau minérale
oon boo-tay doh mee-nay-ral

still	**sparkling**
plate	gazeuse
plat	*gaz-uhz*

a tin of…
une boîte de…
oon bwat duh…

a jar of…
un pot de…
uñ poh duh…

a packet of…
un paquet de…
uñ pa-kay duh…

a bottle of…
une bouteille de…
oon boo-tay duh…

a plastic bag please
un sac en plastique s'il vous plaît
uñ sak oñ plas-teek seel voo play

that is everything thanks
c'est tout merci
say too mehr-see

Ham is sold by the slice, *à la tranche*, (*+ 1 tranche gratuite* = plus one free slice)

Eggs are sometimes sold individually, *à la pièce*.

organic eggs

Sign for organic produce.

take-away

Average nutritional value per 100g.

	Valeur	
energy (calories)	Valeur énergétique	64 kcal (271 kJ)
protein	Protéines	3,15g
carbohydrates	Glucides	4,9g
fat	Lipides	3,6g

Everyday Foods

> If you want some of something, change **le** to **du**, **la** to **de la**, **l'** to **de l'** and **les** to **des**. For low fat foods, look out for the words **allégé**, **light** and **minceur**. The word for frozen is **surgelé**.

6 sausages, pure pork, no colouring

Everyday foods

bread le pain *pañ*
  bread stick la baguette *ba-get*
  bread roll le petit pain *puh-tee pañ*
  sliced bread le pain de mie *pañ duh mee*
butter le beurre *buhr*
cereal les céréales *say-ray-al*
cheese le fromage *fro-mazh*
chicken le poulet *poo-leh*
coffee le café *ka-fay*
cream la crème *krem*
crisps les chips *sheeps*
eggs les œufs *uh*
fish le poisson *pwas-soñ*
flour la farine *fareen*
ham *(cooked)* le jambon cuit *zhoñ-boñ kwee*
ham *(cured)* le jambon cru *zhoñ-boñ kroo*
herbal tea la tisane *tee-zan*
honey le miel *myel*
jam la confiture *koñ-fee-toor*
juice le jus de fruits *zhoo duh frwee*

margarine la margarine *mar-ga-reen*
marmalade la confiture d'orange *koñ-fee-toor do-roñzh*
meat la viande *vyoñd*
milk le lait *lay*
mustard la moutarde *moo-tard*
oil l'huile *weel*
orange juice le jus d'orange *zhoo do-roñzh*
pasta les pâtes *pat*
pepper le poivre *pwavr*
rice le riz *ree*
salt le sel *sel*
sugar le sucre *sookr*
stock cube le bouillon cube *boo-yoñ koob*
tea le thé *tay*
tomatoes *(tin)* la boîte de tomates *bwat duh to-mat*
tuna *(tin)* la boîte de thon *bwat duh toñ*
vinegar le vinaigre *vee-negr*
yoghurt le yaourt *ya-oort*

The best place to buy fresh fruit and vegetables is the local market. There is no market on Mondays.

Fruit les fruits *frwee*

apples les pommes *pom*
apricots les abricots *a-bree-ko*
bananas les bananes *ba-nan*
cherries les cerises *suh-reez*
figs les figues *feeg*
grapefruit le pamplemousse *poñ-pluh-moos*
grapes le raisin *ray-zañ*
lemon le citron *seet-roñ*
melon le melon *muh-loñ*
nectarines les nectarines *nek-ta-reen*
oranges les oranges *o-roñzh*
peaches les pêches *pesh*
pears les poires *pwahr*
pineapple l'ananas *ana-nass*
plums les prunes *proon*
raspberries les framboises *froñ-bwaz*
strawberries les fraises *frez*
watermelon la pastèque *pas-tek*

Vegetables les légumes *lay-goom*

artichokes les artichauts *ar-tee-shoh*
aubergines les aubergines *oh-ber-zheen*
asparagus les asperges *asperzh*
carrots les carottes *ka-rot*
cauliflower le chou-fleur *shoo-fluhr*
celery le céleri *say-luh-ree*
courgettes les courgettes *koor-zhet*
cucumber le concombre *koñ-kombr*
French beans les haricots verts *a-ree-koh vehr*
garlic l'ail *eye*
leeks les poireaux *pwa-roh*
lettuce la laitue *lay-too*
mushrooms les champignons *shoñ-pee-nyoñ*
onions les oignons *on-yoñ*
peas les petits pois *puh-tee pwa*
peppers les poivrons *pwa-vroñ*
potatoes les pommes de terre *pom duh ter*
radishes les radis *ra-dee*
spinach les épinards *ay-pee-nar*
spring onions les ciboules *see-bool*
tomatoes les tomates *to-mat*
turnip les navets *na-vay*

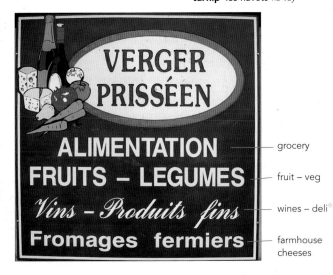

VERGER
PRISSÉEN

ALIMENTATION — grocery
FRUITS – LEGUMES — fruit – veg
Vins – Produits fins — wines – deli
Fromages fermiers — farmhouse cheeses

*There are a number of good French department stores. Look out for **Printemps**, **Monoprix** and **Galeries Lafayette**. They are generally open from about 9.30am to 7pm, Monday to Saturday with late-night shopping on Thursdays.*

— everything must go

— sales

Department store:
Printemps

special offers

keywords keywords keywords

grand magasin
groñ ma-ga-zañ
department store

sous-sol
soo-sol
basement

rez-de-chaussée
ray-duh-shoh-say
ground floor

premier étage
pruhm-yehr ay-tazh
first floor

rayon
ray-oñ
department

électroménager
el-ek-troh-meh-na-zhay
electrical goods

bijouterie
bee-zhoo-tree
jewellery

femme
fam
ladies'

homme
om
men's

enfant
oñ-foñ
children's

which floor is...?
à quel étage est...?
a kel ayt-azh ay...

the lingerie department
le rayon lingerie
luh ray-oñ loñzh-ree

the shoe department
le rayon chaussures
luh ray-oñ shoh-soor

the food department
le rayon alimentation
luh ray-oñ a-lee-moñ-tass-yoñ

talking

Women's clothes sizes

UK/Australia	8	10	12	14	16	18	20	22
Europe	36	38	40	42	44	46	48	50
US/Canada	6	8	10	12	14	16	18	20

Men's clothes sizes (suits)

UK/US/Canada	36	38	40	42	44	46
Europe	46	48	50	52	54	56
Australia	92	97	102	107	112	117

Shoes

UK/Australia	2	3	4	5	6	7	8	9	10	11
Europe	35	36	37	38	39	41	42	43	45	46
US/Canada women	4	5	6	7	8	9	10	11	12	-
US/Canada men	3	4	5	6	7	8	9	10	11	12

Children's Shoes

UK/US/Canada	0	1	2	3	4	5	6	7	8	9	10	11
Europe	15	17	18	19	20	22	23	24	26	27	28	29

talking talking

do you have size...?
est-ce que vous avez la taille...?
ess kuh vooz a-vay la tye...

do you have this in my size?
est-ce que vous avez ça dans ma taille?
ess kuh vooz a-vay sa doñ ma tye

it is too big
c'est trop grand
say troh groñ

I'm just looking
je regarde seulement
zhuh ruh-gard suhl-moñ

do you have a smaller/larger size?
vous l'avez en plus petit/grand?
voo lav-ay oñ ploo puh-tee/groñ

can I try this on?
est-ce que je peux l'essayer?
ess kuh zhuh puh leh-say-ay

shoe size...
la pointure...
la pwañ-toor...

I take size...
je fais du...
zhuh fay doo...

it is too small
c'est trop petit
say troh puh-tee

where are the changing rooms?
où sont les cabines d'essayage?
oo soñ lay ka-been deh-say-yazh

do you have it in other colours?
vous avez ça dans d'autres coloris?
vooz a-vay sa doñ dotr ko-lo-ree

*You can buy stamps at the **tabac** or at the post office. In Paris and big towns, the post office is open 8am to 7pm Monday to Friday and until 12pm on Saturdays. In smaller towns the hours may be reduced, so the morning is the best time to go.*

Logo of the French Post Office.

French postboxes are yellow.

Postboxes often have two slots.

last collection
4pm weekdays

1pm Saturday

Paris & region
(local mail)

elsewhere in
France & abroad

where is the post office?
où est la poste?
oo ay la post

do you sell stamps?
est-ce que vous vendez des timbres?
ess kuh voo voñ-day day tañbr

five 55-cent stamps, please
cinq timbres de cinquante-cinq centimes, s'il vous plaît
sañk tañbr duh sañ-koñt-sañk soñ-teem seel voo play

10 stamps please
dix timbres s'il vous plaît
dee tañbr seel voo play

for postcards
pour cartes postales
poor kart pos-tal

for letters
pour lettres
poor letr

to Europe
pour l'Europe
poor luh-rop

to America
pour les États-Unis
poor layz ay-ta zoo-nee

to Australia
pour l'Australie
poor lo-stra-lee

I want to send this parcel
je voudrais envoyer ce colis
zhuh voo-dray oñ-vwa-yay suh ko-lee

I want to send this registered
je voudrais l'envoyer en recommandé
zhuh voo-dray loñ-vwa-yay oñ ruh-kom-oñ-day

fast/air mail
poste prioritaire
post pree-o-ree-tehr

surface
par voie normale
par vwa nor-mal

talking talking talking

keywords

pellicule
pay-lee-kool
film

pile
peel
battery

en mat
oñ mat
mat

en brillant
oñ bree-yoñ
glossy

caméscope
kam-ay-skop
camcorder

cassettes
kas-set
tapes

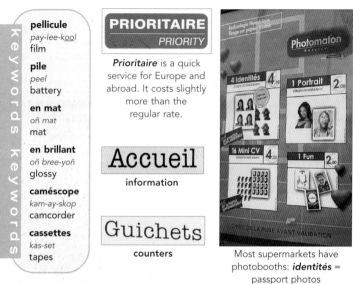

PRIORITAIRE
PRIORITY

Prioritaire is a quick service for Europe and abroad. It costs slightly more than the regular rate.

Accueil
information

Guichets
counters

Most supermarkets have photobooths: *identités* = passport photos

talking

I want to buy film
je voudrais acheter des pellicules
zhuh voo-dray ash-tay day pay-lee-kool

tapes for this camcorder
des cassettes pour ce caméscope
day kass-et poor suh kam-e-skop

a colour film
une pellicule couleur
oon pay-lee-kool koo-luhr

with ... pictures
de ... vues
duh ... voo

24
vingt-quatre
vañt-katr

36
trente-six
troñt-sees

a slide film
une pellicule pour diapositives
oon pay-lee-kool poor dee-a-po-zee-teev

can you develop this film?
est-ce que vous pouvez développer cette pellicule?
ess kuh voo poo-vay dayv-lo-pay set pay-lee-kool

when will the photos be ready?
quand est-ce que les photos seront prêtes?
koñt ess kuh lay foh-toh suh-roñ pret

can we take pictures here?
est-ce qu'on peut prendre des photos ici?
ess koñ puh proñdr day foh-toh ee-see

could you take a picture of us?
est-ce que vous pourriez nous prendre en photo?
ess kuh voo poo-ree-ay noo proñdr oñ foh-toh

I'd like to save my photos onto a CD-Rom
je voudrais archiver mes photos sur CD-Rom
zhuh voo-dray arh-shee-vay may foh-toh soor say-day-rom

Phones

Coin phones are extremely scarce. The numerous phone boxes all operate with a phonecard, **une télécarte**, which you can buy in metro stations, in **tabacs** or at the Post Office. Cheap rates with French Telecom are from 7pm to 8am during the week, and all day Saturday and Sunday (you get 50% extra time).

15	SAMU
17	POLICE
18	SAPEURS-POMPIERS

emergency numbers
ambulance
fire brigade

public phone
Many public phones also work with credit cards.

When buying a phonecard, you will be asked how many units you want.

Télécarte 50

do you sell phonecards?
est-ce que vous vendez des télécartes?
ess kuh voo voñ-day day te-le-kart

50 units
de cinquante unités
duh sañ-koñt oo-nee-tay

Mr Lebrun please
Monsieur Lebrun s'il vous plaît
muh-syuh luh-bruñ seel voo play

can I speak to Paul?
je peux parler à Paul?
zhuh puh par-lay a paul

I'd like an outside line please
je voudrais une ligne s'il vous plaît
zhuh voo-dray oon leen-yuh seel voo play

I'd like to make a reverse charge call
je voudrais téléphoner en PCV
zhuh voo-dray te-le-fo-nay oñ pay-say-vay

what is your phone number?
quel est votre numéro de téléphone?
kel ay votr noo-may-ro duh te-le-fon

a phonecard please
une télécarte s'il vous plaît
oon te-le-kart seel voo play

120 units
de cent vingt unités
duh soñ vañt oo-nee-tay

extension...
le poste...
luh post...

this is Caroline
c'est Caroline à l'appareil
say caroline a la-pa-ray

hello? (on phone)
allô?
a-loh

my number is...
voici mon numéro...
vwa-see moñ noo-may-ro...

talking talking talking talking

k e y w o r d s   k e y w o r d s

télécarte
te-le-kart
phonecard

numéro vert
noo-may-ro vert
freephone

indicatif
uñ-dee-ka-teef
dialling code

renseignements
roñ-sen-yuh-moñ
directory
enquiries

pages jaunes
pazh zhohn
yellow pages

annuaire
a-noo-ehr
phone directory

Instructions for use and emergency numbers
are translated into English at some call boxes.
You can make phone calls and also receive them.
The number of the phonebox is on the top line.

01	44	79	04	57
zéro un	quarante-quatre	soixante-dix-neuf	zéro quatre	cinquante-sept

French phone numbers are given in 2 digits.

décrochez
pick up

*swipe your
credit card
here*

*insert your
phonecard
here*

Pick up the receiver first then insert
a phonecard or credit card, or dial
the free emergency number.

Mobile
phones
allowed.

Switch off
mobile
phones.

t a l k i n g

I will call back...
je vais rappeler...
je vay rap-lay...

later
plus tard
ploo tar

tomorrow
demain
duh-mañ

do you have a mobile?
vous avez un portable?
vooz a-vay uñ por-tabl

when can I call you?
quand est-ce que je peux vous téléphoner?
koñt ess kuh zhuh puh voo te-le-fo-nay

what is your mobile number?
quel est votre numéro de portable?
kel ay votr noo-may-roh duh por-tabl

my mobile number is...
mon numéro de portable est...
moñ noo-may-roh duh por-tabl ay...

Internet cafés are not very common. You generally pay by the hour. There are internet consoles in some post offices and at RER stations.

CYBERCAFÉ @

Le MARGUERITE BISTROT
Vous propose Le
Wi-Fi

Free Access

LA CONNEXION INTERNET
HAUT DEBIT SANS FIL

haut debit = broadband
sans fil = wireless

internet café
You go in and pay for time online.

keywords keywords keywords

aide
ed
help

ordinateur
or-dee-na-tuhr
computer

mot de passe
mo duh pass
password

cliquez ici
klee-kay ee-see
click here

écran
ay-krañ
screen

arrobase
a-ro-baz
at (@)

---

what is your e-mail address?
quelle est votre adresse e-mail?
kel ay votr ad-ress ee-mehl

my e-mail address is...
mon adresse e-mail est...
moñ ad-ress ee-mehl ay...

caroline.smith@anycompany.co.uk
caroline point smith arrobase anycompany point co point uk
caroline pwañ smith a-ro-baz anycompany pwañ say oh pwañ oo kah

can I send an e-mail?
je peux envoyer un e-mail?
zhuh puh oñ-vwa-yay uñ ee-mehl

it is not working
ça ne marche pas
sa nuh marsh pa

did you get my e-mail?
est-ce que vous avez reçu mon e-mail?
ess-kuh vooz av-ay ruh-soo moñ ee-mehl

how much is it for one hour?
c'est combien pour une heure?
say koñ-byañ poor oon uhr

talking talking talking

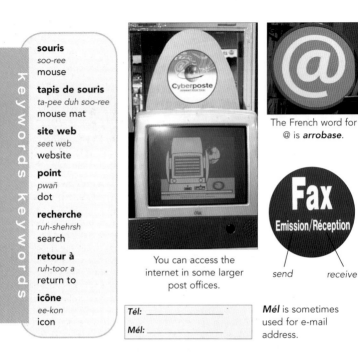

souris
soo-ree
mouse

tapis de souris
ta-pee duh soo-ree
mouse mat

site web
seet web
website

point
pwañ
dot

recherche
ruh-shehrsh
search

retour à
ruh-toor a
return to

icône
ee-kon
icon

You can access the
internet in some larger
post offices.

The French word for
@ is **arrobase**.

send   receive

| Tél: _____ |
| Mél: _____ |

Mél is sometimes
used for e-mail
address.

I want to send a fax
je voudrais envoyer un fax
zhuh voo-dray oñ-vwa-yay uñ faks

do you have a fax?
est-ce que vous avez un fax?
ess-kuh vooz av-ay uñ faks

can I send a fax from here?
est-ce que je peux envoyer un fax d'ici?
ess kuh zhuh puh oñ-vwa-yay uñ faks dee-se

can I receive a fax here?
je peux recevoir un fax ici?
zhuh puh ruh-suh-vwar uñ faks ee-see

how much is it to send a fax?
c'est combien pour envoyer un fax?
say koñ-byañ poor oñ-vwa-yay uñ faks

what is your fax number?
quel est votre numéro de fax?
kel ay votr noo-may-roh duh faks

there is a problem with your fax
il y a un problème avec votre fax
eel ee a uñ prob-lehm a-vek votr faks

did you get my fax?
est-ce que vous avez reçu mon fax?
ess kuh vooz av-ay ruh-soo moñ faks

Out & About

> *Tourist offices are known as* **Offices de Tourisme** *and* **Syndicats d'initiative**. *Most towns will have one and they can help with accommodation, what is on in the area, local transport and places to eat.*

tourist information

Paris sign indicating place of historic interest.

wine route

EXPOSITION

exhibition

Municipal museums close on Mondays. National museums close on Tuesdays (except Musée d'Orsay, Trianon Palace and Versailles), so check before you set off. For national museums there is an entrance fee (sometimes they are free on Sundays). They are free for under 18s and there are reductions for 18–25-year-olds and for over 60s. Most towns have municipal museums offering free Sunday admission. Under 7s and over 60s go free.

tasting sales

cave means *cellar*, not *cave!*

Most towns have a guide to the area. It is full of useful information such as emergency numbers for police, doctor, dentist, etc., as well as details of hotels, restaurants, shops, sporting activities, etc.

keywords keywords keywords keywords

animation
a-nee-mass-yoñ
show

exposition
eks-poh-zee-syoñ
exhibition

randonnée
roñ-don-ay
trek, ramble

dégustation
deh-goo-stass-yoñ
wine tasting

foire
fwar
fair

église
ay-gleez
church

cathédrale
ka-tay-dral
cathedral

château
sha-toh
castle

hôtel de ville
oh-tel duh veel
town hall

museum card

In Paris, the Parisian transport authority (RATP) organizes bicycle rentals and guided rides at many metro stations.

In Paris you can go on a sightseeing trip on the Seine by *bateau-mouche* or *batobus*.

St-Germain-des-Prés

talking talking talking

where is the tourist office?
où est le syndicat d'initiative?
oo ay luh sañ-dee-ka dee-nees-ya-teev

do you have...?
vous avez...?
vooz a-vay...

a town guide/map
un plan de la ville
uñ ploñ duh la veel

leaflets in English
des brochures en anglais
day broh-shoor on oñ-glay

we want to visit...
nous voudrions visiter...
noo vood-ree-yoñ vee-zee-tay...

is it open to the public?
c'est ouvert au public?
sayt oo-vehr oh poob-leek

when can we visit the...?
quand est-ce qu'on peut visiter...?
koñt ess koñ puh vee-zee-tay...

when does it close?
ça ferme à quelle heure?
sa fehrm a kel uhr

are there any sightseeing tours?
est-ce qu'il y a des visites guidées?
ess keel ee a day vee-zeet gee-day

*You will be able to find out about sporting activities from the local tourist office. They will also be listed in the local **Guide pratique et touristique**.*

☂	**Baignade**	swimming
	Pêche	fishing
	Piscine découverte	open-air pool
🎾	**Tennis**	tennis
🐎	**Equitation**	horse-riding
🚶	**Randonnée pédestre**	trekking
⛷	**Ski de fond**	cross-country skiing
🛶	**Canoë-kayak**	canoeing
🧗	**Escalade**	rock climbing
🔦	**Spéléologie**	potholing

Leaflets detail local sporting facilities.

Beaches that have no lifeguards don't generally have showers or many facilities.

PLAGE
NON SURVEILLEE
A VOS RISQUES
ET PERILS

S.O.S
POMPIERS ☎ 18
POLICE ☎ 17

unpatrolled beach   at your own risk

Initiation
beginners

location
for hire

Piscine
swimming pool

details of swimming facilities

PISCINE ....
Boulevard de l'Europe   ☎ 03 84 24 27 94
Bassin couvert, bassin olympique en plein air, pataugeoire et fosse à plongeons.

covered pool | open-air olympic pool | paddling pool | diving pool

where can we...?
où est-ce qu'on peut...?
oo ess koñ puh...

how much is it to...?
c'est combien pour...?
say koñ-byañ poor...

per hour/day
par heure/jour
par uhr/zhoor

is there a swimming pool?
est-ce qu'il y a une piscine?
ess keel ee a oon pee-seen

where can we...?
où est-ce qu'on peut faire...?
oo ess koñ puh fehr...

play tennis
jouer au tennis
zhoo-ay oh ten-eess

hire bikes
louer des vélos
loo-ay day vay-loh

can we hire skis?
on peut louer des skis?
oñ puh loo-ay day skee

is it dangerous to swim here?
c'est dangereux de nager ici?
say doñ-zhuh-ruh duh na-zhay ee-see

windsurf
du surf
doo suhrf

play golf
jouer au golf
zhoo-ay oh golf

go riding
faire du cheval
fehr doo shuh-val

waterski
du ski nautique
doo skee noh-teek

where can we hire a beach umbrella?
où est-ce qu'on peut louer un parasol?
oo ess koñ puh loo-ay uñ pa-ra-sol

talking talking

VENTE BILLETS

tickets sales

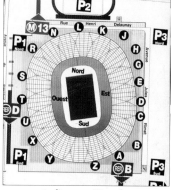

stadium seating plan

LE PLUS BEAU LIEU DE RENCONTRE'

ENTREE ACREDITES

season ticket entrance

OBJETS INTERDITS
ARMES
COUTEAUX
BOUTEILLES EN VERRE
ET TOUS OBJETS CONTONDANTS

forbidden objects:
weapons, knives, glass bottles

Stade de France

---

talking

we'd like to go to a football match
nous voudrions aller à un match de football
noo vood-ree-yoñ a-lay a uñ match duh foot-bol

who is playing?
qui joue?
kee zhoo

where can we get tickets?
où est-ce qu'on peut avoir des billets?
oo ess koñ puh av-war day bee-yay

how do we get to the stadium?
pour aller au stade?
poor a-lay oh stad

what time is the match?
à quelle heure commence le match?
a kel uhr koh-moñss luh match

Accommodation

*French hotels operate a star system (1- to 4-star, and luxury). You can get great value from 1-star hotels. Increasingly, there is bed & breakfast (**chambre d'hôte** or **chambres chez l'habitant**).*

The number 2000 indicates that this hotel has received classification for that particular year.

You won't have to hand in your passport, but you may be asked to fill in a **fiche d'étranger** form giving your passport number.

FICHE D'ÉTRANGER	
CH. N°	
NOM : Name in capital letters Name in Druckschrift	*(écrire en majuscules)*
Nom de jeune fille : Maiden Name Mädchenname	
Prénoms : Christian Names Vornamen	
Date de naissance : Date of birth Geburtsdatum	
Lieu de naissance : Place of birth Geburtsort	
Domicile habituel : Permanent address Gewöhnlicher Wohnort	
Profession : Occupation Beruf	
Nationalité : Nationality Nationalität	
Passeport n° : Pass Ausweis	
Date d'arrivée en France : Date of arrival in France Einreisedatum in Frankreich	
Date probable de sortie : Probable date of your way out Voraussichtliches Ausreisedatum	

Booking in advance

You can contact the hotel direct but you will be required to pay a deposit (**arrhes**) of approximately 25% of the bill. This is non-refundable if you cancel your booking.

I would like to book a room
je voudrais réserver une chambre
zhuh vood-ray ray-zayr-vay <u>oo</u>n shoñbr

a single/a double
pour une personne/deux personnes
poor <u>oo</u>n pehr-son/duh pehr-son

for ... nights
pour ... nuits
poor ... nwee

from ... to...
du ... au...
d<u>oo</u> ... oh...

I will fax to confirm
je confirmerai par fax
zhuh koñ-feerm-ray par faks

my name is ...
je m'appelle ...
zhuh ma-pel...

my credit card number is...
voici le numéro de ma carte de crédit...
vwa-see luh n<u>oo</u>-may-ro duh ma kart duh kray-dee...

I will arrive at...
j'arrive à...
zha-reev a...

Hotels display the prices outside.

Taxe de Séjour: 0,53 €		
Hôtel Pacific		
62100 Calais		
Chambres 2-3 :		
Douche	29 €	1-2 pers.
Chambres 8-11-12 :		
Douche WC	35 €	1-2 pers.
Chambres 5-16-19 :	40 €	1-2 pers.
Douche WC	44 €	3pers.Twin
Chambres 4-9-7-17 :	40 €	1-2 pers.
Bain WC	44 €	3pers.Twin
Chambre 10-15:		
Douche ou Bain WC	40 €	Twin
Chambres 1-14 Familiale:		
Douche WC	54 €	4 pers.
Petit.Déjeuner:5,5 € Garage: 4 € Lit BB: 3,5 €		
Forfait VRP : 36 € (chambre + petit déj.)		

taxe de séjour = tourist tax
chambre = room
douche = shower
bain = bath
familiale = family

petit déjeuner = breakfast
Lit BB = cot
Forfait VRP = special rate
for sales people

Chambre d'hôte is bed and breakfast.

❖❖❖❖❖	2 chambres agréables, de 2 et 3 personnes avec sanitaires privés	2 pleasant rooms, for 2 and 3 people, with private facilities
Chambres d'hôte	Tarifs d'une chambre, petit déjeuner inclus: 1 personne: 2 personnes: 3 personnes:	price per room, breakfast included
❖❖❖❖❖		

talking talking talking

do you have a room for tonight?
est-ce que vous avez une chambre pour ce soir?
ess kuh vooz av-ay <u>oon</u> shoñbr poor suh swar

with twin beds
à deux lits
a duh lee

a single room
pour une personne
poor <u>oon</u> pehr-son

a double room
pour deux personnes
poor duh pehr-son

a family room
pour une famille
poor <u>oon</u> fa-meey

with ensuite bath
avec bain
a-vek bañ

with shower
avec douche
a-vek doosh

with a double bed
avec un grand lit
a-vek uñ groñ lee

for tonight
pour ce soir
poor suh swar

for one night
pour une nuit
poor <u>oon</u> nwee

for... nights
pour ... nuits
poor ... nwee

how much is it per night?
c'est combien par nuit?
say koñ-byañ par nwee

is breakfast included?
le petit déjeuner est compris?
luh puh-tee day-zhuh-nay ay koñ-pree

how much is half board?
c'est combien la demi-pension?
say koñ-byañ la duh-mee poñ-syoñ

I'd like to see the room
je voudrais voir la chambre
zhuh voo-dray vwar la shoñbr

what time should we check out?
à quelle heure est-ce qu'il faut quitter la chambre?
a kel uhr ess-keel foh kee-tay la shoñbr

	• 16 appartements
	1 à 4 personnes
low season — per week	Basse saison : 299 € la semaine
high season — per week	Haute saison : 336 € la semaine

A LOUER MEUBLES — to let — furnished
TOUT CONFORT — all mod cons

CHAMBRES DISPONIBLES

rooms available

You will find all sorts of accommodation on offer in tourist areas.

LOCATION

for hire
Don't be fooled into thinking it is the same word as in English! In French it is pronounced *loh-ka-syoñ*.

Rubbish is collected from street bins daily. Recycling bins are often available.

chambres d'hôtes means *bed and breakfast*. Note the symbol of *Gîtes de France*, the *B&B association*.

B.& B.
CHAMBRES
D'HÔTES
1ère A Gauche
Tel. 02.35.90.66.73

1st on left

Youth hostels (*Auberges de la Jeunesse*)
are signposted locally.

The symbol of the French Youth
Hostel Federation.

Douche

shower

Salle de bain

bathroom

information/
reception

accueil

chaud

hot

froid

cold

DOUCHES
8ᴴ30 A 10ᴴ30
17ᴴ30 A 19ᴴ30

showers
8.30am to 10.30am
5.30pm to 7.30pm

can you show me how this works?
est-ce que vous pouvez me montrer comment ça marche?
ess kuh voo poo-vay muh moñ-tray koh-moñ sa marsh

how does ... work?
comment fonctionne...?
ko-moñ foñks-yon...

the cooker
la cuisinière
la kwee-zeen-yehr

the washing machine
la machine à laver
la ma-sheen a la-vay

the dishwasher
le lave-vaisselle
luh lav-vay-sel

the microwave
le micro-ondes
luh mee-kro-oñd

who do we contact if there are problems?
qui faut-il contacter s'il y a un problème?
kee foht-eel koñ-tak-tay seel ee a uñ prob-lem

there is/are no...
il n'y a pas de...
eel nee a pa duh...

the sink is blocked
l'évier est bouché
lay-vyay ay boo-shay

where do I leave the rubbish?
où est-ce que je dois mettre la poubelle?
oo ess kuh zhuh dwa metr la poo-bel

we'd like an extra key
nous voudrions une autre clé
noo voo-dree-oñ oon otr klay

what is the security code?
quel est le code d'entrée?
kel ay luh kod doñ-tray

talking talking talking talking

Camping

camping on the farm

Campsites display prices and are star-rated.

Camping Le Provencal
Arrêté Préfectoral n° 94/450
Capacité Accueil 200 empl.

TARIFS		
Du **01/07** au **25/08**		— tariffs
Forfait T.T.C.		
2 P.+auto+empl	21.20	— 2 people & car & pitch
Personne supl.	5	— extra person
Enfant -5 ans	3,65	— child under 5
Voiture supl.	4,25	— extra car
Chien	2,75	— dog
Electricité 6A.	3	— electricity
Taxe séjour adulte	0,45	— tourist tax per day
Visiteur	5	— visitor
Instal. supl.	4,25	

COMPLET

full

keywords keywords keywords

emplacement
oñ-plas-moñ
pitch

lessive
less-eev
washing powder

ouvre-boîtes
oovr-bwat
tin-opener

tire-bouchon
teer-boo-shoñ
corkscrew

allumettes
a-loo-met
matches

bougies
boo-zhee
candles

bouteille de gaz
boo-tay duh gaz
gas cylinder

---

is there a campsite near here?
est-ce qu'il y a un camping près d'ici?
ess keel ee a uñ koñ-peeng pray dee-see

have you any vacancies?
est-ce que vous avez des places?
ess kuh vooz av-ay day plass

we want to stay for ... nights
nous voudrions rester ... nuits
noo voo-dree-oñ res-tay ... nwee

how much is it...?
c'est combien...?
say koñ-byañ...

per tent
pour une tente
poor oon toñt

per caravan
pour une caravane
poor oon ka-ra-van

is there a restaurant on the campsite?
est-ce qu'il y a un restaurant dans le camping?
ess keel ee a uñ res-to-roñ doñ luh koñ-peeng

can we have a more sheltered site?
est-ce qu'on peut avoir un emplacement plus abrité?
ess koñ puh av-war un oñ-plass-moñ plooz ab-ree-tay

can we camp here overnight?
est-ce qu'on pourrait camper ici cette nuit?
ess koñ poo-ray koñ-pay ee-see set nwee

talking talking talking

blanc
bloñ
whites

prélavage
pray-la-vazh
prewash

lavage
la-vazh
wash

rinçage
rañ-sazh
rinse

amidonnage
a-mee-don-azh
starching

essorage
ess-o-razh
spin

launderette self-service

Most launderettes are self-service and entirely automatic; there is no-one to attend to the customer. There is generally a central point/machine to pay at.

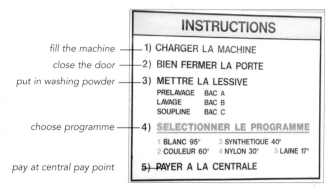

INSTRUCTIONS

fill the machine ⎯ 1) CHARGER LA MACHINE

close the door ⎯ 2) BIEN FERMER LA PORTE

put in washing powder ⎯ 3) METTRE LA LESSIVE

PRELAVAGE	BAC A
LAVAGE	BAC B
SOUPLINE	BAC C

choose programme ⎯ 4) SELECTIONNER LE PROGRAMME

1 BLANC 95°	3 SYNTHETIQUE 40°
2 COULEUR 60°	4 NYLON 30° 5 LAINE 17°

pay at central pay point ⎯ 5) PAYER A LA CENTRALE

Special Needs

Facilities for the disabled are gradually improving, but it is still quite difficult to get around using public transport.

Are you sure these places are reserved for you?

disabled parking

disabled toilet

Reduced tariffs for disabled (**handicapé**) and children (**enfants**)

disabled access

are there any disabled toilets?
est-ce qu'il y a des toilettes pour handicapés?
ess keel ee a day twa-let poor oñ-dee-ka-pay

is there a wheelchair-accessible entrance?
est-ce qu'il y a une entrée pour les fauteuils roulants?
ess keel ee a oon oñ-tray poor lay foh-tuhy roo-loñ

is it possible to visit ... with a wheelchair?
est-ce qu'on peut visiter ... en fauteuil roulant?
ess koñ puh vee-zee-tay ... oñ foh-tuhy roo-loñ

is there a reduction for the disabled?
est-ce qu'il y a une réduction pour les handicapés?
ess keel ee a oon ray-dooks-yoñ poor lay oñ-dee-ka-pay

I need a bedroom on the ground floor
j'ai besoin d'une chambre au rez-de-chaussée
zhay buhz-wañ doon shoñbr oh ray-duh-shoh-say

I use a wheelchair
je suis en fauteuil roulant
zhuh swee oñ foh-tuhy roo-loñ

where is the lift?
où est l'ascenseur?
oo ay lass-oñ-suhr

talking talking

With Kids

In general, French children tend to go to bed early because they start school early in the morning. Public transport is free for under 4s; between 4 and 12, children pay half fare.

Key to minimum age for play areas.

2 years   3 years   6 years   11 years

keywords

enfant
oñ-foñ
child

siège pour bébés
syehzh poor bay-bay
baby seat

chaise de bébé
shez duh bay-bay
high chair

lit d'enfant
lee doñ-foñ
cot

aire de jeux
ehr duh zhuh
play park

play park

talking talking talking

is it safe for children?
c'est sans danger pour les enfants?
say soñ doñ-zhay poor layz oñ-foñ

where can I change the baby?
où est-ce que je peux changer le bébé?
oo ess kuh zhuh puh soñ-zhay luh bay-bay

do you have...? est-ce que vous avez...? *ess kuh vooz a-vay...*	**a high chair** une chaise de bébé *oon shehz duh bay-bay*	**a cot** un lit d'enfant *uñ lee doñ-foñ*
do you sell...? est-ce que vous vendez...? *ess kuh voo voñ-day...*	**baby wipes** des lingettes *day lañ-zhet*	**nappies** des couches *day koosh*

is there a children's menu?
est-ce que vous avez un menu pour les enfants?
ess kuh vooz av-ay uñ muh-noo poor layz oñ-foñ

is there a play park near here?
est-ce qu'il y a une aire de jeux près d'ici?
ess keel ee a oon ehr duh zhuh pray dee-see

Health

*The old E111 form has been replaced with a new European Health Insurance card – apply at the post office or online at **www.dh.gov.uk**. If you require treatment look for a doctor who is **conventionné** (i.e. working within the French national health system). You must get a signed statement of your treatment in order to reclaim expenses. Remember the pharmacist is also qualified to give advice.*

Pharmacies operate a night duty rota. You can get details from pharmacies themselves, or if you are unable to find one, the police will be able to give details.

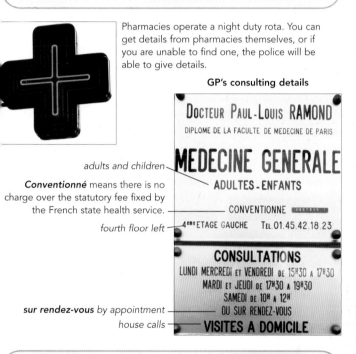

GP's consulting details

DOCTEUR PAUL-LOUIS RAMOND
DIPLOME DE LA FACULTE DE MEDECINE DE PARIS

MEDECINE GENERALE
ADULTES - ENFANTS

adults and children

Conventionné means there is no charge over the statutory fee fixed by the French state health service.

CONVENTIONNE

fourth floor left

4ᵉᵐᵉ ETAGE GAUCHE   TEL.01.45.42.18.23

CONSULTATIONS
LUNDI MERCREDI ET VENDREDI DE 15ʰ30 A 17ʰ30
MARDI ET JEUDI DE 17ʰ30 A 19ʰ30
SAMEDI DE 10ʰ A 12ʰ
OU SUR RENDEZ-VOUS

sur rendez-vous by appointment

house calls

VISITES A DOMICILE

---

where is the nearest chemist?
où est la pharmacie la plus proche?
oo ay la far-ma-see la ploo prosh

this bite is infected
cette piqûre est infectée
set pee-koor ay añ-fek-tay

have you something for...?
est-ce que vous avez quelque chose contre...?
ess kuh vooz av-ay kel-kuh shohz koñtr...

sunburn
les coups de soleil
lay koo duh so-lay

diarrhoea
la diarrhée
la dee-ar-ay

a headache
le mal de tête
luh mal duh tet

flu
la grippe
la greep

I need aspirin
j'ai besoin d'aspirine
zhay buh-swañ das-pee-reen

I have a temperature
j'ai de la fièvre
zhay duh la fyehvr

talking

Consultations are the *surgery times*. Check if you need to make an appointment, *un rendez-vous*. The waiting room is *la salle d'attente*.

I feel ill
je me sens mal
zhuh muh soñ mal

he/she feels ill
il/elle se sent mal
eel/el suh soñ mal

I need a doctor
j'ai besoin d'un médecin
zhay buhz-wañ duñ mayd-sañ

we need a doctor to come out
il faut que le médecin vienne
eel foh kuh luh mayd-sañ vyen

can you call a doctor?
vous pouvez appeler un médecin?
voo poo-vay ap-lay uñ mayd-sañ

my child is ill
mon enfant est malade
mon oñ-foñ ay ma-lad

I have a pain here
j'ai mal ici
zhay mal ee-see

I am on this medication
je prends ces médicaments
zhuh proñ say may-dee-ka-moñ

I am pregnant
je suis enceinte
zhuh swee oñ-sañt

I am on the pill
je prends la pilule
zhuh proñ la pee-lool

I am breastfeeding
j'allaite mon enfant
zha-let moñ oñ-foñ

I have cystitis
j'ai une cystite
zhay oon sees-teet

I have high blood pressure
j'ai de la tension
zhay duh la toñss-yoñ

I am allergic to...
je suis allergique à...
zhuh sweez al-ehr-zheek a...

my blood group is...
mon groupe sanguin est...
moñ groop soñ-gañ ay...

I am O negative
je suis O négatif
zhuh swee oh nay-ga-teef

A positive
A positif
ah poh-zee-teef

I need a receipt for my insurance
il me faut un reçu pour mon assurance
eel muh foh uñ ruh-soo poor moñ a-soo-roñss

I'm diabetic
je suis diabétique
zhuh swee dee-a-beh-teek

I need a dentist
j'ai besoin d'un dentiste
zhay buhz-wañ duñ doñ-teest

I have toothache
j'ai mal aux dents
zhay mal oh doñ

my filling has come out
le plombage est parti
luh ploñ-bazh ay par-tee

can you repair my dentures?
vous pouvez réparer mon dentier?
voo poo-vay ray-pa-ray moñ doñt-yay

I need a temporary filling
j'ai besoin d'un plombage provisoire
zhay buhz-wañ duñ ploñ-bazh pro-veez-wahr

I have an abscess
j'ai un abcès
zhay un ab-seh

talking talking talking talking talking talking talking

If you require hospital treatment your Health Insurance card should cover you for 75% of the cost. You pay the balance and also a fixed daily hospital charge. (These are not refundable.)

accident & emergency
Calls for an ambulance are free from any phone, so you can phone from a phonebox, even if it accepts only cards. Just lift the receiver and dial 15.

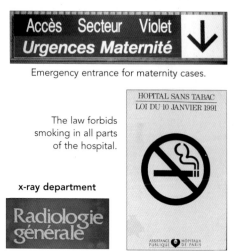

Emergency entrance for maternity cases.

The law forbids smoking in all parts of the hospital.

x-ray department

If you need to go to hospital

will I/he/she have to go to hospital?
est-ce qu'il faudra aller à l'hôpital?
ess keel foh-dra a-lay a lop-ee-tal

to the hospital please
à l'hôpital s'il vous plaît
a lop-ee-tal seel voo play

I need to go to casualty
je dois aller aux urgences
zhuh dwa a-lay ohz oor-zhoñss

must I stay in bed?
est-ce que je dois rester au lit?
ess kuh zhuh dwa res-tay oh lee

when are the visiting hours?
quelles sont les heures de visite?
kel soñ layz uhr duh vee-zeet

can you explain what is the matter?
vous pouvez m'expliquer le problème?
voo poo-vay meks-plee-kay luh prob-lehm

where is the hospital?
où est l'hôpital?
oo ay lop-ee-tal

which ward?
quel service?
kel sehr-veess

Emergency

i The emergency number is 17. You will see either **Police** or **Gendarmerie** (in smaller towns and villages). You should report all thefts or crimes to them.

police station

fire station

Gendarmerie

local police

talking talking talking talking talking

help!
au secours!
oh suh-koor

can you help me?
vous pouvez m'aider?
voo poo-vay mah-day

please call...
s'il vous plaît! appelez...
seel voo play ap-lay...

the police
la police
la po-leess

an ambulance
une ambulance
oon oñ-boo-loñss

fire!
au feu!
oh fuh

please call the fire brigade!
s'il vous plaît! appelez les pompiers!
seel voo play ap-lay lay poñ-pyay

my ... has been stolen
on m'a volé mon/ma...
oñ ma vo-lay moñ/ma...

I want to report a theft
je veux signaler un vol
zhuh vuh seen-ya-lay uñ vol

here are my insurance details
voici mon assurance
vwa-see moñ a-soo-roñss

please give me your insurance details
votre assurance s'il vous plaît
votr a-soo-roñss seel voo play

where is the police station?
où est la gendarmerie?
oo ay la zhoñ-darm-ree

I would like to phone...
je voudrais appeler...
zhuh voo-dray ap-lay...

my car has been broken into
on a forcé ma voiture
on a for-say ma vwa-toor

I need a report for my insurance
il me faut un constat pour mon assurance
eel muh foh uñ koñ-sta poor mon a-soo-roñss

Food
&
Drink

French Food

i The French take their food very seriously, and what they eat largely depends upon what is available locally and in season. In Brittany you find fresh fish and superb seafood. In Normandy, the abundance of dairy produce means that the cooking is rich in butter and cream. And many of the dishes make use of the locally grown apples: either in the form of cider or **calvados** (brandy made from apples). You can get an idea of the different dishes from the map on pages 92-93. Some of the greatest chefs have come from France and French cuisine is very much sauce-based. It is worth trying to familiarise yourself with the various sauces as they will appear time and time again on menus.

Some restaurants offer set-price menus. This is a lunchtime menu (*du midi*), available from Monday to Friday (*du Lundi au Vendredi*).
entrée starter
plat main dish
café coffee

where can we have a snack?
où est-ce qu'on peut manger un petit quelque chose?
oo ess koñ puh moñ-zhay puh-tee kel-kuh shoz

can you recommend a good local restaurant?
pouvez-vous nous recommander un bon restaurant?
poo-vay voo noo ruh-ko-moñ-day uñ boñ res-toh-roñ

are there any vegetarian restaurants?
est-ce qu'il y a des restaurants végétariens?
ess keel ee a day res-toh-roñ vay-zhay-ta-ryañ

do we need to book?
est-ce qu'il faut réserver une table?
ess keel foh ray-zehr-vay oon tabl

what do you recommend?
qu'est-ce que vous me recommandez?
kess kuh voo muh ruh-ko-moñ-day

how do we get to the restaurant?
pour aller au restaurant?
poor a-lay oh res-toh-roñ

talking talking talking

'Brekkie' menu Breakfast is
le petit déjeuner.

Croissants and Danish pastries, etc,
are known as *Viennoiseries*.

La boulangerie (*baker's*) is a great place for snacks. Bakers
bake bread at least twice a day and with a bit of luck you will
be able to get your **baguette** or **ficelle** fresh from the oven.

pâté

rillettes
pork pâté

croque-monsieur
*toasted ham
and cheese*

œuf au plat
fried egg

hot dog

cooked ham

crudités
raw vegetables

croque-madame
*toasted ham & cheese
topped with fried egg*

omelettes

**cornichons
supplément**
gherkins extra

Types of sandwiches available in a French café.

i *Bars often serve food, perhaps a dish of the day, **plat du jour** (served only at lunchtime), toasted cheese-and-ham sandwiches, **croque-monsieur** (**croque-madame** has a fried egg on top) or sandwiches. Food is usually reasonably priced and available throughout the day.*

You can buy sweet and savoury pastries from the **boulangerie** as well as sandwiches and drinks, since many **boulangeries** are also **pâtisseries** (cake shops).

Y. Cadot PATISSIER CHOCOLATIER

Cake shops often have a tearoom (**Salon de thé**), serving mouth-watering cakes and generally weak tea with lemon. Try **chocolat chaud** (hot chocolate).

I'd like a ... please
je voudrais un/une ... s'il vous plaît
zhuh voo-dray uñ/<u>oo</u>n ... seel voo pleh

a white coffee
un crème
uñ krem

a decaff coffee
un déca
uñ day-ka

a tea with milk
un thé au lait
uñ tay oh lay

an orange juice
un jus d'orange
uñ zh<u>oo</u> do-roñzh

a red wine
un vin rouge
uñ vañ roozh

a bottle of mineral water
une bouteille d'eau minérale
<u>oo</u>n boo-tay doh mee-nay-ral

an espresso
un café
uñ ka-fe

a large white coffee
un grand crème
uñ groñ krem

a hot chocolate
un chocolat chaud
uñ sho-ko-la shoh

a half of lager
un demi
uñ duh-mee

an apple juice
un jus de pomme
uñ zh<u>oo</u> duh pom

a white wine
un vin blanc
uñ vañ bloñ

sparkling   **still**
gazeuse   plate
gaz-uhz   *plat*

talking talking talking talking

GAUFRES — waffles
CREPES — crêpes
SAUCISSES CHAUDES — cold sausage
PANINI — panini
CROQUE MONSIEUR — **croque monsieur** (ham and cheese toastie)
GLACES — ice-cream
BOISSONS FRAICHES — cold drinks

a snack board

ice cream parlour

If you want a cone, ask for *un cornet*. One scoop is *une boule*, two scoops are *deux boules*.

You can generally buy fresh bread from the *alimentation générale*.

keywords keywords keywords keywords

menthe
moñt
mint

framboise
fromb-waz
raspberry

fraise
frez
strawberry

cassis
ka-sees
blackcurrant

citron
see-troñ
lemon

ananas
a-na-nass
pineapple

pêche
pesh
peach

pistache
pee-stash
pistacchio

noisette
nwa-zet
hazelnut

citron vert
see-troñ vehr
lime

talking talking talking

can we eat here?
est-ce qu'on peut manger ici?
ess koñ puh moñzhay ee-see

what can we eat?
qu'est-ce qu'on peut manger?
kess koñ puh moñ-zhay

do you have a dish of the day?
est-ce que vous avez un plat du jour?
ess kuh vooz avay uñ pla doo zhoor

what is the dish of the day?
quel est le plat du jour?
kel ay luh pla doo zhoor

what sandwiches do you have?
qu'est-ce que vous avez comme sandwichs?
kess kuh vooz avay kom soñd-weech

I'd like an ice cream
je voudrais une glace
zhuh voo-dray oon glass

what flavours do you have?
qu'est-ce que vous avez comme parfums?
kess kuh vooz a-vay kom par-fuñ

i Sunday lunch is often a time for families to eat out. You should book to be sure of getting a table. In smaller towns, restaurants tend to shut on Sunday evenings.

Opening times in a restaurant window. Note that it is closed on Sunday (*fermé le dimanche*).

59 € 50

Boisson non comprise

Drink not included
Check what is and is not included in the price of your meal.

Kids' meal served in a supermarket café.

à la cafétéria
Spécial enfants
menu

hamburger or — 1 steak haché ou
3 fish fingers — 3 bâtonnets de colin pané,
chips, 1 dessert — des frites, 1 dessert,
1 drink — 1 boisson,
1 toy — 1 gadget,
1 surprise — 1 surprise !

Bôîtakado

3 € 80

GRATUIT LE MARDI SOIR

free on Tuesday evenings

I would like to book a table
je voudrais réserver une table
zhuh voo-dray ray-zehr-vay <u>oo</u>n tabl

for tonight
pour ce soir
poor suh swar

for lunch
pour le déjeuner
poor luh day-zhuh-nay

at 19.30
à dix-neuf heures trente
a dees nuhf uhr troñt

in the name of Smart
au nom de Smart
oh noñ duh Smart

for 4 people
pour quatre personnes
poor katr pehr-son

for tomorrow night
pour demain soir
poor duh-mañ swar

at 12.30
à midi et demi
a mee-dee ay duh-mee

at 8 o'clock
à vingt heures
a vañt uhr

smoking/non-smoking
fumeur/non-fumeur
<u>foo</u>-muhr/noñ-<u>foo</u>-muhr

bank card payment terminal
In shops, supermarkets and restaurants, French people key in their PIN number. British bank card holders may be asked to sign a receipt.

restaurant bill

RESTAURANT
LE SAINT CHARLES
47, place d'Armes
62100 CALAIS
03 21 96 02 96
Fax 03 21 96 81 31

le Lundi 18 février 2002

3	*aperitif*	6 30
3	*menus 14*	42 00
3	*suppl log vin*	6 90
2	*suppl dessert*	3 85
1	*cuvée rouge*	10 70
2	*cafés*	3 70
	Merci	
Tl	TOTAL	74 05

3 set-price menus

suppl extra

cuvée rouge
bottle house red

---

the menu please
le menu s'il vous plaît
luh muh-noo seel voo pleh

the wine list please
la carte des vins s'il vous plaît
la kart day vañ seel voo play

I'd like the menu at ... euros
je voudrais le menu à ... euros
zhuh voo-dray luh muh-noo a ... uh-roh

do you have a children's menu?
est-ce que vous avez un menu enfants?
ess kuh vooz avay uñ muh-noo oñ-foñ

for a main dish I will have...
comme plat principal je prends...
kom pla prañ-see-pal zhuh proñ...

what vegetarian dishes do you have?
qu'est-ce que vous avez comme plats végétariens?
kes kuh vooz a-vay kom pla vay-zhay-ta-ryañ

what cheeses do you have?
qu'est-ce que vous avez comme fromages?
kes kuh vooz a-vay kom fromazh

what desserts do you have?
qu'est-ce que vous avez comme desserts?
kess kuh vooz a-vay kom day-sehr

some tap water please
de l'eau s'il vous plaît
duh loh seel voo play

some more bread please
encore du pain s'il vous plaît
oñ-kor doo pañ seel voo play

the bill please
l'addition s'il vous plaît
la-dee-syoñ seel voo play

talking talking talking talking talking talking

Carte *Menu*
POTAGES *soups*

ENTRÉES *starter*

POISSONS *fish*

FRUITS DE MER
seafood

VIANDES *meat*

GIBIER et VOLAILLE
game and poultry

LÉGUMES *vegetables*

FROMAGES *cheeses*

DESSERTS *sweet*

BOISSONS *drinks*

The various courses you will
find on any restaurant menu.

dish of the day
fish
or meat
or poultry
garnis
with vegetables & French fries

Plat du Jour à 7€⁵⁰
poisson ⎫
ou viande ⎬ garnis
ou volaille ⎭

Menu 1 à 15€
au choix:
Pâté croûte avec crudité
Crudités de Saison
Pâté de Campagne et crud
Spaghetti à la forestièr
Salade Portugaise

starter

au choix:

Poulet rôti
Boeuf Bourguignon
Côte de Porc grillée
Saucisse sicilienne
ou
Plat du Jour

main course

dish of the day

Tous ces plats sont ga

Plateau de Fromage
ou
Dessert du Jour

cheese platter
or
dessert of the day

En supplément pour vos fins de repas:
Café, Infusion, Alc

to end the meal
(not included in the price)

Menu à prix fixe
set-price menu

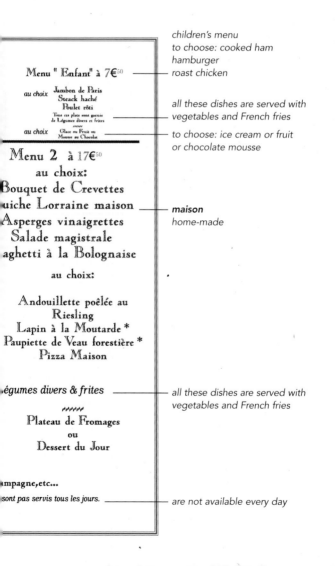

*By law, restaurants have to exhibit their menus outside. There are often two or three menus at different prices and a list of à la carte dishes. It is more expensive to select from the à la carte menu. The service charge is 15%. Service is included unless you see it stated (**service non compris**).*

Menu " Enfant" à 7€⁵⁰

children's menu
to choose: cooked ham
hamburger
roast chicken

au choix   Jambon de Paris
           Steack haché
           Poulet rôti
           Tous ces plats sont garnis
           de Légumes divers et frites

all these dishes are served with vegetables and French fries

au choix   Glace ou Fruit ou
           Mousse au Chocolat

to choose: ice cream or fruit or chocolate mousse

Menu 2   à 17€⁵⁰
au choix:
Bouquet de Crevettes
uiche Lorraine maison
Asperges vinaigrettes
Salade magistrale
aghetti à la Bolognaise

maison
home-made

au choix:

Andouillette poêlée au
Riesling
Lapin à la Moutarde *
Paupiette de Veau forestière *
Pizza Maison

.égumes divers & frites

all these dishes are served with vegetables and French fries

Plateau de Fromages
ou
Dessert du Jour

mpagne,etc...

sont pas servis tous les jours.

are not available every day

Wine

*France is awash with cheap wine, some of it as low as 1,25 euro a bottle. Walk right on past these, because the very best tactic in France is to stick to what you would pay at home rather than going for the cheapies; superb wine can be had for around 7 euro. The best advice for bargain hunters is to find a reputable local **cave** (winery shop), where it's possible to taste before buying; it's usually safer to spend around 4 euro a bottle here. If in doubt, stick to reds for safety, and pick out the **domaine**- or **château**-bottled wines.*

This label is marked **Appellation Contrôlée**. This is the French system that guarantees the origin of a wine from a demarcated area – in this case, Côtes de Bourg.

1996
Château de Passedieu
CÔTES DE BOURG
APPELLATION CÔTES DE BOURG CONTRÔLÉE

JEAN-PIERRE DUBOIS, PROPRIÉTAIRE — A BAYON · GIRONDE · FRANCE
MIS EN BOUTEILLE AU CHATEAU
12 % vol.   PAR S.V. GRANDSCHATEAUX 33560 FRANCE   75 cl
PRODUCE OF FRANCE

alcohol content 12%
11.5% is average;
14% is a pretty heavy wine

bottled at the château

Côtes de Bourg is a Bordeaux wine. Be sceptical about bargains from the Bordeaux region unless you really know your onions. Avoid fancy labels at low prices, particularly from the Médoc. For earlier drinking and lower prices look out for St Emilion, Côtes de Castillon, Côtes de Blaye, Côtes de Francs and Côtes de Bourg (above). Nearby ACs Côtes de Duras and Pecharmant (Bergerac) are also good. For whites choose Pessac-Léognan; for sweet whites St Croix du Mont.

keywords keywords keywords

cuvée
koo-vay
vintage

rouge
roozh
red

blanc
bloñ
white

mousseux
moo-suh
sparkling

brut
broot
very dry

sec
sek
dry

demi-sec
duh-mee sek
sweet

doux
doo
very sweet

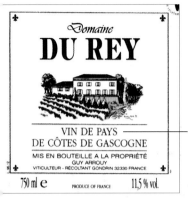

verre
vehr
glass

ballon
ba-loñ
large glass

pichet
pee-shay
carafe

Vin de pays simply means the wine has come from one area and has not been blended. ***Vin de table*** or ***vin ordinaire*** indicates that the wine has been blended. These wines are often sold in plastic bottles.

Rhône has some snob ACs, but on the whole is still seriously underrated. Herby, sunkissed Syrah blends can match the reds of Burgundy and Bordeaux at about half the price. Alongside the famous names like Hermitage and Côte-Rôtie are others which dipped out of favour but have now cleaned up their act and in many cases taken on New World methods. Châteauneuf-du-Pape is one of these though there are still too many overcooked, tired and flabby examples on sale. Côtes du Rhone Villages is increasingly reliable. Try also: Vacqueyras, Gigondas. White is very risky unless it's Hermitage or Condrieu.

the wine list please
la carte des vins s'il vous plaît
la kart day vañ seel voo play

can you recommend a good wine?
vous pouvez nous recommander un bon vin?
voo poo-vay noo ruh-ko-moñ-day uñ boñ vañ

a bottle of wine	**red**	**white**	**rosé**
une bouteille de vin	rouge	blanc	rosé
oon boo-tay duh vañ	*roozh*	*bloñ*	*ro-zay*

a carafe of wine	**a glass of wine**
un pichet de vin	un verre de vin
uñ pee-shay duh vañ	*uñ vehr duh vañ*

what liqueurs do you have?
qu'est-ce que vous avez comme liqueurs?
kess kuh vooz a-vay kom lee-kuhr

Champagne is good value on home ground and the supermarkets all have a good selection.

Calvados, apple brandy from Normandy. This regional speciality is used for cooking as well as drinking. See page 92–93.

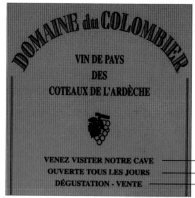

Wine tasting is a fun way of buying wine. Try a sample or two and buy a bottle or case (if you really like it), but don't feel you have to.

VENEZ VISITER NOTRE CAVE — come and visit our cellars
OUVERTE TOUS LES JOURS — open every day
DÉGUSTATION – VENTE — wine tasting – sale

Cave
wine cellar

*When you ask for a **bière** in France, you will be served lager. If you want an ale or bitter, you should ask for **bière brune**. Draught beer will come as a **demi** (half pint approx.); you would not normally get a pint of beer in France as they tend to drink in halves. It can be quite expensive to drink out in France.*

There are a number of smallish brewers in the northern-most part of France near to Belgium. **Bière de Garde** is the term used to refer to them because they were traditionally unfiltered and designed to mature further in the bottle when laid down in the cellar.

Ch'ti: pale-coloured with a fruity aroma.

(à la) pression
(a la) pres-syoñ
draught

bière blonde
byehr blond
lager

bière brune
byehr broon
ale

grande
groñd
large

petite
puh-teet
small

keywords

Jenlain: light red colour with a sharp aroma; a full-bodied, slightly tart beer.

half a pint of lager
un demi
uñ duh-mee

a French lager
une bière française
oon byehr froñ-sez

do you have any ales?
est-ce que vous avez des bières brunes?
ess kuh vooz a-vay day byehr broon

talking

Flavours of France

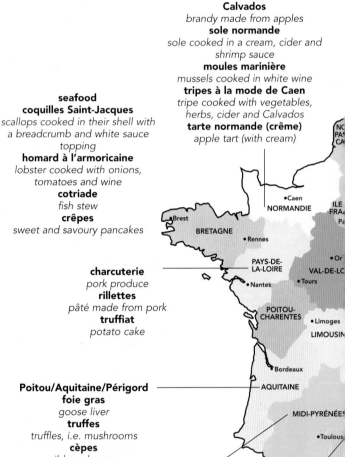

Calvados
brandy made from apples
sole normande
*sole cooked in a cream, cider and
shrimp sauce*
moules marinière
mussels cooked in white wine
tripes à la mode de Caen
*tripe cooked with vegetables,
herbs, cider and Calvados*
tarte normande (crême)
apple tart (with cream)

seafood
coquilles Saint-Jacques
*scallops cooked in their shell with
a breadcrumb and white sauce
topping*
homard à l'armoricaine
*lobster cooked with onions,
tomatoes and wine*
cotriade
fish stew
crêpes
sweet and savoury pancakes

charcuterie
pork produce
rillettes
pâté made from pork
truffiat
potato cake

Poitou/Aquitaine/Périgord
foie gras
goose liver
truffes
truffles, i.e. mushrooms
cèpes
wild mushrooms
anguilles
eels

perdreau à la catalane
*partridge cooked in orange juice
and peppers*
cassoulet
*bean stew with pork or mutton
and sausages*

tourte à la viande
veal or pork pie
potée auvergnate
cabbage and meat stew (pork)
truffade
*mashed potatoes with garlic and
cheese*

NORMANDIE
•Caen
•Brest
BRETAGNE
• Rennes
PAYS-DE-
LA-LOIRE
• Nantes
POITOU-
CHARENTES
•Limoges
LIMOUSIN
•Tours
VAL-DE-LO
•Or
ILE
FRA
Pa
NC
PA
CA
•Bordeaux
AQUITAINE
MIDI-PYRÉNÉE
•Toulous

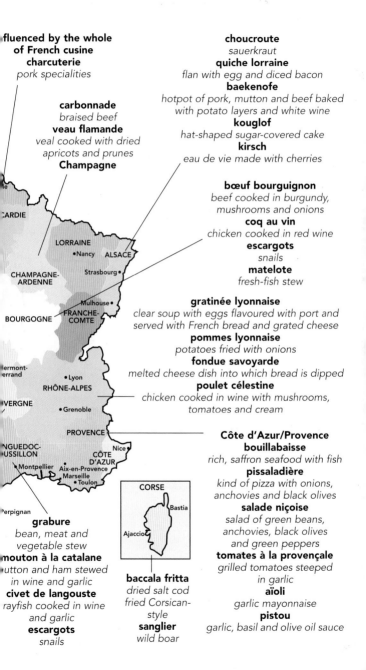

influenced by the whole
of French cusine
charcuterie
pork specialities

carbonnade
braised beef
veau flamande
*veal cooked with dried
apricots and prunes*
Champagne

choucroute
sauerkraut
quiche lorraine
flan with egg and diced bacon
baekenofe
*hotpot of pork, mutton and beef baked
with potato layers and white wine*
kouglof
hat-shaped sugar-covered cake
kirsch
eau de vie made with cherries

bœuf bourguignon
*beef cooked in burgundy,
mushrooms and onions*
coq au vin
chicken cooked in red wine
escargots
snails
matelote
fresh-fish stew

gratinée lyonnaise
*clear soup with eggs flavoured with port and
served with French bread and grated cheese*
pommes lyonnaise
potatoes fried with onions
fondue savoyarde
melted cheese dish into which bread is dipped
poulet célestine
*chicken cooked in wine with mushrooms,
tomatoes and cream*

Côte d'Azur/Provence
bouillabaisse
rich, saffron seafood with fish
pissaladière
*kind of pizza with onions,
anchovies and black olives*
salade niçoise
*salad of green beans,
anchovies, black olives
and green peppers*
tomates à la provençale
*grilled tomatoes steeped
in garlic*
aïoli
garlic mayonnaise
pistou
garlic, basil and olive oil sauce

PICARDIE

LORRAINE
• Nancy   ALSACE
CHAMPAGNE-
ARDENNE   Strasbourg •
Mulhouse •
BOURGOGNE   FRANCHE-
COMTÉ

Clermont-
Ferrand
• Lyon
RHÔNE-ALPES
AUVERGNE
• Grenoble

PROVENCE
LANGUEDOC-
ROUSSILLON   Nice •
CÔTE
• Montpellier   D'AZUR
Aix-en-Provence
Marseille
• Toulon

Perpignan
grabure
*bean, meat and
vegetable stew*
mouton à la catalane
*mutton and ham stewed
in wine and garlic*
civet de langouste
*rayfish cooked in wine
and garlic*
escargots
snails

CORSE
Bastia
Ajaccio

baccala fritta
*dried salt cod
fried Corsican-
style*
sanglier
wild boar

If you cannot eat certain things, it is as well warning the waiter before making your choice.

talking talking talking talking talking talking talking

I'm vegetarian
je suis végétarien(ne)
zhuh swee vay-zhay-tay-ryañ(-ryeñ)

I don't eat meat/pork
je ne mange pas de viande/porc
zhuh nuh moñzh pa duh vyoñd/por

I don't eat fish
je ne mange pas de poisson
zhuh nuh moñzh pa duh pwa-soñ

I'm allergic to shellfish
je suis allergique aux crustacés
zhuh swee a-lehr-zheek oh kroos-ta-say

I am allergic to peanuts
je suis allergique aux cacahuètes
zhuh swee a-lehr-zheek oh ka-ka-wet

I can't eat raw eggs
je ne peux pas manger d'œufs crus
zhuh nuh puh pa moñ-zhay duh kroo

I am on a diet
je suis au régime
zhuh swee oh ray-zheem

I can't eat liver
je ne peux pas manger de foie
zhuh nuh puh pa moñ-zhay duh fwah

I don't drink alcohol
je ne bois pas d'alcool
zhuh nuh bwa pa dal-kol

what is in this?
quels sont les ingrédients?
kel soñ lay añ-gra-dyoñ

is it raw?
c'est cru?
say kroo

is it made with unpasteurised milk?
c'est fait avec du lait cru?
say fay a-vek doo lay kroo

frit
free
fried

en croûte
oñ kroot
in pastry

darne
darn
steak or fillet

rôti
ro-tee
roast

en daube
oñ dohb
casseroled

farci
far-see
stuffed

grillé
gree-yay
grilled

fumé
foo-may
smoked

fricassé
free-ka-say
stewed

mariné
ma-ree-nay
marinated

hâché
a-shay
minced

au four
oh foor
baked

garni
gar-nee
served with veg

bleu
bluh
very rare

Menu Reader

...à la/à l'/au/aux... 'in the style of...', or 'with...'
  au feu de bois cooked over a wood fire
  au four baked
  au porto in port
abats offal, giblets
abricot apricot
Abricotine liqueur brandy with apricot flavouring
agneau lamb
agrumes citrus fruit
aïado roast shoulder of lamb stuffed with garlic and other ingredients
aïgo bouïdo garlic soup
ail garlic
aile wing
aïoli rich garlic mayonnaise originated in the south and gives its name to the dish it is served with: cold steamed fish and vegetables. The mayonnaise is served on the side
airelles bilberries, cranberries
aligot puréed potato with cheese
allumettes very thin chips
amande almond
amuse-bouche nibbles
arlésienne, à l' with tomatoes, onions, aubergines, potatoes and rice
armagnac fine grape brandy from the Landes area
armoricaine, ...à l' cooked with brandy, wine, tomatoes and onions
ananas pineapple
anchoïade anchovy paste usually served on grilled French bread
anchois anchovies
andouille (eaten cold), **andouillette** (eaten hot) spicy tripe sausage
anglaise, ...à l' poached or boiled
anguille eel
anis aniseed
arachide peanut (uncooked)
araignée de mer spider crab

artichaut artichoke
  artichauts à la barigoule artichokes in wine, with carrots, garlic, onions
asperge asparagus
aspic de vollaille chicken in aspic
assiette dish, platter
  assiette anglaise plate of assorted cold meats
  assiette de charcuterie plate of assorted pâtés and salami
  assiette de crudités selection of raw vegetables served with a dip
  assiette du pêcheur assorted fish or seafood
aubergine aubergine
  aubergines farcies stuffed aubergines
auvergnate, ...à l' with cabbage, sausage and bacon
avocat avocado
babas au rhum rum baba
baccala frittu dried salt cod fried Corsica style
Badoit mineral water, very slightly sparkling
baekenofe hotpot of pork, mutton and beef baked in white wine with potato layers from Alsace
baguette stick of French bread
banane banana
  bananes flambées bananas flambéed in brandy
bar sea-bass
barbue brill
bardatte cabbage stuffed with rabbit or hare
barquette small boat-shaped flan
basilic basil

blanquette de veau

baudroie *fish soup with vegetables, garlic and herbs, monkfish*

bavarois *moulded cream and custard pudding, usually served with fruit*

Béarnaise, à la *sauce similar to mayonnaise but flavoured with tarragon and white wine. Traditionally served with steak*

bécasse *woodcock*

béchamel *classic white sauce made with milk, butter and flour*

beignets *fritters, doughnuts*

Bénédictine *herb liqueur on a brandy base*

betterave *beetroot*

beurre *butter*
  beurre blanc, ...à la *sauce of white wine and shallots with butter*

bien cuit *well done*

bière *beer*
  bière pression *draught beer*
  bière blonde *lager*
  bière brune *bitter*

bifteck *steak*

bigorneau *periwinkle*

biologique *organic*

bis *wholemeal (of bread or flour)*

biscuit de Savoie *sponge cake*

bisque *smooth rich seafood soup*
  bisque de homard *lobster soup*

blanquette *white meat stew served with a creamy white sauce*
  blanquette de veau *veal stew in white sauce*
  blanquette de volaille *chicken stew in white sauce*

blé *wheat*

blette *Swiss chard*

bleu *very rare*

bœuf *beef*
  bœuf bourguignon *beef in burgundy, onions and mushrooms*
  bœuf en daube *rich beef stew with wine, olives, tomatoes and herbs*

bombe *moulded ice cream dessert*

bonite *bonito, small tuna fish*

bonne femme, ...à la *cooked in white wine with mushrooms*

bordelaise, ...à la *cooked in a sauce of red wine, shallots and herbs*

bouchée *vol-au-vent*
  bouchée à la reine *vol-au-vent filled with chicken or veal and mushrooms in a white sauce*

bœuf bourguignon

boudin pudding
boudin blanc white pudding
boudin noir black pudding
bouillabaisse rich seafood dish flavoured with saffron originally from Marseilles
bouilleture d'anguilles eels cooked with prunes and red wine
bouilli boiled
bouillon stock
bouillon de légumes vegetable stock
bouillon de poule chicken stock
boulangère, ...à la baked with potatoes and onions
boulettes meatballs
bourgeoise, ...à la with carrots, onions, bacon, celery and braised lettuce
bourguignonne, ...à la cooked in red wine, with onions, bacon and mushrooms
bourride fish stew traditionally served with garlic mayonnaise (aïoli)
brandade de morue dried salt cod puréed with potatoes and olive oil
brème bream
brioche sweet bun
brioche aux fruits sweet bun with glacé fruit
brochet pike
brochette kebab
brocoli broccoli
brugnon nectarine
bugnes doughnuts from the Lyons area
bulot whelk
cabillaud fresh cod
cacahuète peanut
café coffee
café au lait coffee with hot milk
café crème white coffee
café décaféiné decaffeinated coffee
café express espresso coffee
café glacé iced coffee
café irlandais Irish coffee
café noir black coffee
caille quail
caille sur canapé quail served on toast

bouillabaisse

caillettes rolled liver stuffed with spinach
cajou, noix de cashew nut
calisson almond sweet
calmar (or **calamar**) squid
calvados apple brandy made from apples (Normandy)
canard duck
canard à l'orange roast duck with orange sauce
canard périgourdin roast duck with prunes, pâté de **foie gras** and truffles
canard Rouennais stuffed roast duck covered in red wine sauce
caneton duckling
cannelle cinnamon
câpres capers
carbonnade de bœuf braised beef
cardon cardoon
cari curry
carotte carrot
carottes Vichy carrots cooked in butter and sugar
carpe carp
carpe farcie carp stuffed with mushrooms or **foie gras**
carré persillé roast lamb Normandy style (with parsley)
carrelet plaice
carte des vins wine list

cassoulet

cassis *blackcurrant, blackcurrant liqueur*
cassoulet *bean stew with pork or mutton, confit and sausages. There are many regional variations*
caviar *caviar*
  caviar blanc *mullet roe*
  caviar niçois *a paste made with anchovies and olive oil*
cédrat *large citrus fruit, similar to a lemon*
céleri *celery; celeriac*
  céleri rémoulade *celeriac in a mustard and herb dressing*
céleri-rave *celeriac*
cèpes *boletus mushrooms, wild mushrooms*
  cèpes marinés *wild mushrooms marinated in oil, garlic and herbs*
cerfeuil *chervil*
cerise *cherry*
cervelas *smoked pork sausages, saveloy*
cervelle *brains (usually lamb or calf)*

cervelle de Canut *savoury dish of fromage frais, goat's cheese, herbs and white wine*
champignon *mushroom*
  champignons à la grècque *mushrooms cooked in wine, olive oil, herbs and tomato*
  champignons de Paris *button mushrooms*
  champignons périgourdine *mushrooms with truffles and foie gras*
chanterelle *chanterelle (wild golden-coloured mushroom)*
chantilly *whipped cream*
charlotte *custard and fruit in lining of almond fingers*
Chartreuse *aromatic herb liqueur made by Carthusian monks*
chasseur *literally hunter-style, cooked with white wine, shallots mushrooms and herbs*
châtaigne *chestnut*
châteaubriand *thick fillet steak*
châtelaine, ...à la *with artichoke hearts*
chaud(e) *hot*
chaudrée
  rochelaise *a selection of fish stewed in red wine*
chauffé *heated*
chausson *a pasty filled with meat or seafood*
  chausson aux pommes *apple turnover*
cheval, à *topped with a fried egg*
chèvre *goat*
chevreuil *venison*
chichi *doughnut shaped in a stick*
chicorée *chicory, endive*
chocolat *chocolate*
  chocolat chaud *hot chocolate*
chou *cabbage*
choucroute *sauerkraut*
  choucroute garnie *sauerkraut with various types of sausages*

chou-fleur *cauliflower*
choux brocolis *broccoli*
choux de Bruxelles *Brussels sprouts*
ciboule (or cive) *spring onions*
ciboulette *chives*
cidre *cider, sparkling (bouché)
or still, quite strong*
cidre brut *dry cider*
cidre doux *sweet cider*
citron *lemon*
citron pressé *freshly squeezed
lemon juice with water and sugar*
citron vert *lime*
citrouille *pumpkin*
civet *thick stew*
civet de langouste *crayfish in
wine sauce*
civet de lièvre *hare stewed in
wine, onions and mushrooms*
clafoutis *cherry pudding*
clou de girofle *clove*
cochon *pig*
coco *coconut*
cocotte, en *cooked in a small
earthenware casserole*
cœur *heart*
cœurs d'artichauts *artichoke hearts*
cœurs de palmier *palm hearts*
cognac *high quality white grape brandy*
coing *quince*
Cointreau *orange-flavoured liqueur*
colbert,...à la *fried, with a coating of egg and breadcrumbs*
colin *hake*
compote de fruits *mixed stewed fruit*
concombre *cucumber*
condé *rich rice pudding with fruits*

coq au vin

confit *pieces of meat preserved
in fat*
confit d'oie *goose meat
preserved in its own fat*
confit de canard *duck meat
preserved in its own fat*
confiture *jam*
confiture d'oranges *marmalade*
congre *conger eel*
consommé *clear soup, generally
made from meat
or fish stock*
contre-filet *sirloin fillet (beef)*
coq au vin *chicken and
mushrooms cooked in red wine*
coquelet *cockerel*
coques *cockles*
coquillages *shellfish*
coquilles Saint-Jacques *scallops*
coquilles Saint-Jacques à la
Bretonne *scallops cooked in
shell with a bread-crumb and
white sauce topping*
coquilles Saint-Jacques à la
provençale *scallops with garlic
sauce*
coquillettes *pasta shells*
cornichon *gherkin*
côtelette *cutlet*
côtelettes d'agneau *lamb cutlets*
côte *rib, chop*
côtes de porc *pork chops*

crudités

cotriade *fish stew (Brittany)*
cou *neck*
coulibiac *salmon cooked in puff pastry*
coulis *puréed fruit sauce*
coupe *goblet with ice cream*
courge *marrow*
cousinat *chestnut and cream soup*
crabe *crab*
craquelots *smoked herring*
crémant *sparkling wine*
crème *cream*
  crème anglaise *fresh custard*
  crème au beurre *butter cream with egg yolks and sugar*
  crème brûlée *rich custard with caramelised sugar on top*
  crème caramel *baked custard with caramelised sugar sauce*
  crème chantilly *slightly sweetened whipped cream*
  crème fraîche *sour cream*
  crème pâtissière *thick fresh custard used in tarts and desserts*
  crème renversée *(or* crème caramel*) custard with a caramelised top*
crème de *cream of... (soup)*
  crème d'Argenteuil *white asparagus soup*
  crème de cresson *watercress soup*
  crème de marrons *chestnut purée*

crème de menthe *peppermint-flavoured liqueur*
crêpes *sweet and savoury pancakes*
  crêpes fourrées *filled pancakes*
  crêpes Suzette *pancakes with a Cointreau or Grand Marnier sauce usually flambéed*
crépinette *type of sausage*
crevette *prawn*
  crevette grise *shrimp*
  crevette rose *large prawn*
croque-madame *grilled cheese and bacon, sausage, chicken or egg sandwich*
croque-monsieur *grilled gruyère cheese and ham sandwich*
croûte, en *in pastry*
croûtes, croûtons, ...aux *served with cubes of toasted or fried bread*
cru *raw*

crudités *assortment of raw vegetables (grated carrots, sliced tomatoes, etc) served as a starter*
crustacés *shellfish*
cuisses de grenouille *frogs' legs*
cuit *cooked*
culotte *rump steak*
Curaçao *orange-flavoured liqueur*
darne *fish steak*
datte *date*
daube *casserole with wine, herbs, garlic, tomatoes and olives*
dauphinoise, ...à la *baked in milk*
daurade *sea bream*
diable, ...à la *strong mustard seasoning*
diabolo menthe *mint cordial and lemonade*
dinde *turkey*
diots au vin blanc *pork sausages in white wine*
duxelles *fried mushrooms and shallots with cream*
eau *water*
  eau de Seltz *soda water*
  eau-de-vie *brandy (often made from plum, pear, etc)*
  eau minérale *mineral water*
  eau minérale gazeuse *sparkling mineral water*
  eau du robinet *tap water*
échalote *shallot*
échine *loin of pork*
écrevisse *freshwater crayfish*
églefin *haddock*
emballé *wrapped*
  en brochette *cooked like a kebab (on a skewer)*
  encornet *squid*
  endive *chicory*
  entrecôte *rib steak*
  entrées *starters*
  entremets *sweets (desserts)*

escargots

épaule *shoulder*
éperlan *whitebait*
épice *spice*
épinards *spinach*
escalope *escalope*
escargots *snails (generally cooked with strong seasonings)*
  escargots à la bourguignonne *snails with garlic butter*
espadon *swordfish*
estouffade de boeuf *beef stew cooked in red wine, herbs, onions, mushrooms and diced bacon*
estragon *tarragon*
esturgeon *sturgeon*
faisan *pheasant*
far aux pruneaux *prune cake from Brittany*
farci(e) *stuffed*
farigoule *thyme (in provençal dialect)*
faux-filet *sirloin*
fenouil *fennel*
feuille *leaf*
feuilleté *in puff pastry*
fèves *broad beans*
fiadone *ewe's cheese and lemon dish from Corsica*
figue *fig*
filet *fillet steak*
  filet de bœuf en croûte *steak in pastry*
  filet de bœuf *tenderloin*
  filet mignon *small pork fillet steak*

fondue savoyarde

financière, ...à la *rich sauce made with Madeira wine and truffles*

fine de claire *type of oyster*

fines herbes *mixed, chopped herbs*

flageolet *type of small green haricot bean*

flamande, ...à la *served with potatoes, cabbage, carrots and pork*

flambé(e) *doused with brandy or another spirit and set alight, usually cooked at your table*

flammenküche *onion, bacon and cream tartlet from Alsace*

flétan *halibut*

flocons d'avoine *oat flakes*

florentine *with spinach, usually served with mornay sauce*

foie *liver (usually calf's)*
  foie de volailles *chicken livers*

foie gras *goose liver*

fond d'artichaut *artichoke heart*

fondue *a shared dish which is served in the middle of the table. Each person uses a long fork to dip their bread or meat into the pot*

fondue (au fromage) *melted cheeses with white wine into which chunks of bread are dipped*

fondue bourguignonne *small chunks of beef dipped into boiling oil and eaten with different sauces. The meat equivalent to cheese fondue*

forestière, ...à la *with bacon and mushroom*

fougasse *type of bread with various fillings (olives, anchovies)*

fourré(e) *stuffed*

frais (fraîche) *fresh*

fraise *strawberry*
  fraises des bois *wild strawberries*

framboise *raspberry*

frappé *iced*

fricassée *a stew, usually chicken or veal, and vegetables*

frisée *curly endive*

frit(e) *fried*

friture *fried food, usually small fish*

froid(e) *cold*

fromage *cheese*
  fromage blanc *soft white cheese*
  fromage frais *creamy fresh cheese*

froment *wheat*

fruit *fruit*
  fruit de la passion *passion fruit*
  fruits de mer *shellfish, seafood*

fumé(e) smoked
fumet fish stock
galantine meat in aspic
galette savoury buckwheat pancake
gambas large prawns
ganache chocolate cream filling
garbure thick vegetable and meat soup
gargouillau pear tart
garni(e) garnished i.e. served with something (vegetables)
garnitures side dishes
gâteau cake, gateau
  gâteau Saint-Honoré choux pastry cake filled with custard
gaufres waffles (often cream-filled)
gazeuse sparkling
gelée jelly, aspic
genièvre juniper berry
génoise sponge cake
germes de soja bean sprouts
gésier gizzard
gibier game
gigot d'agneau leg of lamb
gigot de mer large fish baked whole
gingembre ginger
glace ice cream
gougères choux pastry with cheese
goyave guava
Grand Marnier tawny-coloured, orange-flavoured liqueur
gratin, au topped with cheese and breadcrumb and grilled
gratin dauphinois potatoes cooked in cream, garlic and Swiss cheese
gratinée Lyonnaise clear soup with eggs flavoured with Port wine and served with toasted french bread and grated cheese

grenade pomegranate
grecque, ...à la cooked in olive oil, garlic, tomatoes and herbs, can be served hot or cold
grenouilles frogs' legs
  grenouilles meunière frogs' legs cooked in butter and parsley
grillade grilled meat
grillé(e) grilled
groseille redcurrant
groseille à maquereau gooseberry
hachis mince
hareng herring
haricots beans
  haricots beurre butter beans
  haricots blancs haricot beans
  haricots rouges red kidney beans
  haricots verts green beans, French beans
herbes (fines herbes) herbs
hollandaise, sauce sauce made of butter, egg yolks and lemon juice, served warm
homard lobster
  homard à l'armoricaine lobster cooked with onions, tomatoes and wine
  homard thermidor lobster served in cream sauce, topped with parmesan
hors d'œuvre variés selection of appetizers
huile oil
huile d'arachide groundnut oil
huile de tournesol sunflower oil
huître oyster
îles flottantes soft meringues floating on fresh custard
Izarra vert green-coloured herb liqueur
jambon ham
jambon de Bayonne cured raw ham from the Basque country
jambon de Paris boiled ham

jardinière, ...à la with peas and carrots, or other fresh vegetables
julienne vegetables cut into fine strips
jus juice, meat-based glaze or sauce
jus de pomme apple juice
jus d'orange orange juice
kig-ha farz meat stew from Brittany
kir white wine and **cassis** aperitif
kirsch a kind of **eau-de-vie** made from cherries (Alsace)
kouglof hat-shaped sugar-covered cake from Alsace
kouing amann cake from Brittany
lait milk
lait demi-écrémé semi-skimmed milk
lait écrémé skimmed milk
lait entier full-cream milk
laitue lettuce
lamproie à la bordelaise lamprey in red wine
langouste crayfish (saltwater)
langouste froide crayfish served cold with mayonnaise and salad
langoustines scampi (large)
langue tongue (veal, beef)
lapin rabbit
lard fat, streaky bacon
lard fumé smoked bacon
lardon strip of fat, diced bacon
laurier bayleaf
légumes vegetables
lentilles lentils
levure yeast
lièvre hare
limande lemon sole
limousine, ...à la cooked with chestnuts and red cabbage
lotte monkfish
loup de mer sea-bass
Lyonnaise, ...à la with onions
macaron macaroon
macédoine (de fruits) fresh fruit salad
macédoine de légumes mixed cooked vegetables
madeleine small sponge cake
magret de canard duck breast
maïs, maïs doux maize, sweetcorn

moules marinière

mange-tout sugar peas
mangue mango
maquereau mackerel
marcassin young wild boar
marinière, ...à la a sauce of white wine, onions and herbs (mussels or clams)
marmite casserole
marjolaine marjoram
marron chestnut
marrons glacés candied chestnuts
marrons Mont Blanc chestnut purée and cream
matelote fresh-fish stew
matelote à la normande sea-fish stew with cider, calvados and cream
médaillon thick, medal-sized slices of meat
melon melon
menthe mint, mint tea
merguez spicy, red sausage
meringues à la chantilly meringues filled with whipped cream
merlan whiting
merluche hake
mérou grouper
merveilles fritters flavoured with brandy
mignonnette small fillet of lamb

mijoté *stewed*

mille-feuille *thin layers of pastry filled with custard*

mirabelle *small yellow plum, plum brandy from Alsace*

mont-blanc *pudding made with chestnuts and cream*

Mornay, sauce *béchamel and cheese sauce*

morue *dried salt cod*

moules *mussels*

  moules marinière *mussels cooked in white wine*

  moules poulette *mussels in wine, cream and mushroom sauce*

mourtairol *beef, chicken, ham and vegetable soup*

mousse au chocolat *chocolate mousse*

mousseline *mashed potatoes with cream and eggs*

moutarde *mustard*

mouton *mutton or sheep*

mûre *blackberry*

muscade *nutmeg*

myrtille *bilberry*

navet *turnip*

nectarine *nectarine*

niçoise, ...à la *with garlic and tomatoes*

noisette *hazelnut*

noisettes d'agneau *small round pieces of lamb*

noix *walnut, general term for a nut*

nouilles *noodles*

œuf *egg*

  œufs à la coque *soft-boiled eggs*

  œufs au plat *fried eggs*

  œufs Bénédicte *poached eggs on toast, with ham and hollandaise sauce*

  œufs brouillés *scrambled eggs*

œufs durs *hard-boiled eggs*

œufs en cocotte *eggs baked in individual containers with wine*

œufs frits *fried eggs and bacon*

oie *goose*

  oie farci aux pruneaux *goose stuffed with prunes*

oignon *onion*

olive *olive*

omelette *omelette*

  omelette brayaude *cheese and potato omelette*

  omelette nature *plain omelette*

  omelette norvégienne *baked Alaska*

onglet *cut of beef (steak)*

orange *orange*

orangeade *orangeade*

orge *barley*

os *bone*

oseille *sorrel*

oursin *sea urchin*

pain *bread, loaf of bread*

  pain au chocolat *croissant with chocolate filling*

  pain bagnat *bread roll with egg, olives, salad, tuna, anchovies and olive oil*

  pain bis *brown bread*

  pain complet *wholemeal bread*

pain d'épices ginger cake
pain de mie white sliced loaf
pain de seigle rye bread
pain grillé toast
palmier caramelized puff pastry
palombe wood pigeon
palourde clam
pamplemousse grapefruit
panais parsnip
pané(e) with breadcrumbs
panini toasted Italian sandwich
panisse thick chickpea flour pancake
pannequets au fromage pancakes filled with white sauce and cheese (Brittany)
papillote, en in filo pastry
parfait rich home-made ice cream
Paris Brest ring-shaped cake filled with praline-flavoured cream
parisienne, ...à la sautéed in butter with white wine, sauce and shallots
parmentier with potatoes
pastèque watermelon
pastis aniseed-based aperitif
patate douce sweet potato
pâté pâté
　pâté de foie de volailles chicken liver pâté
　pâté en croûte pâté encased in pastry
pâtes pasta
　pâtes fraîches fresh pasta
patranque central France dish of bread cubes, garlic and cheese
paupiettes meat slices stuffed and rolled
pavé thick slice
pays d'auge, ...à la cream and cider or Calvados
paysanne, ...à la cooked with diced bacon and vegetables
pêche peach
　pêches melba poached peaches

served with a raspberry sauce and vanilla ice cream or whipped cream
perche perch (fish)
　perche du Menon perch cooked in champagne
perdreau (perdrix) partridge, grouse
Périgueux, sauce with truffles
Pernod aperitif with aniseed flavour (**pastis**)
persil parsley
persillé(e) with parsley
petit-beurre butter biscuit
petits farcis stuffed tomatoes, aubergines, courgettes and peppers
petit pain roll
petits fours bite-sized cakes and pastries
petits pois small peas
petit-suisse thick fromage frais
pieds et paquets mutton or pork tripe and trotters
pigeon pigeon
pignons pine nuts
pilon drumstick (chicken)
piment chilli
　piment doux sweet pepper
　piment fort chilli
　pimenté peppery hot
pintade/pintadeau guinea fowl
pipérade tomato, pepper and onion omelette
piquant spicy
pissaladière a kind of pizza made mainly in the Nice region, filled with onions, anchovies and black olives
pistache pistachio
pistou garlic, basil and olive oil sauce from Provence – similar to **pesto**.
plat dish
　plat principal main course
plate still

poires belle hélène

plie *plaice*
poché(e) *poached*
poêlé *pan-fried*
pimenté *peppery hot*
point, ...à *medium rare*
poire *pear*
  poires belle Hélène *poached pears with vanilla ice cream and chocolate sauce*
poireau *leek*
pois *peas*
pois cassés *split peas*
pois-chiches *chickpeas*
poisson *fish*
poitrine *breast (lamb or veal)*
poivre *pepper*
poivron *sweet pepper*
  poivron rouge *red pepper*
  poivron vert *green pepper*
pomme *apple*
pomme (de terre) *potato*
  pommes à l'anglaise *boiled potatoes*
  pommes à la vapeur *steamed potatoes*
  pommes allumettes *match-stick chips*
  pommes dauphine *potato croquettes*

  pommes duchesse *potato mashed then baked in the oven*
  pommes frites *fried potatoes*
  pommes Lyonnaise *potatoes fried with onions*
  pommes mousseline *potatoes mashed with cream*
  pommes rissolées *small potatoes deep-fried*
pompe aux grattons *pork flan*
porc *pork*
pot au feu *beef and vegetable stew*
potage *soup, generally creamed or thickened*
potée auvergnate *cabbage and meat soup*
potiron *type of pumpkin*
poularde *fattened chicken*
poulet *chicken*
  poulet basquaise *chicken stew with tomatoes, mushrooms and peppers*
  poulet célestine *chicken cooked in white wine with mushrooms and onion*
  poulet Vallée d'Auge *chicken cooked with cider, calvados, apples and cream*
poulpe à la niçoise *octopus in tomato sauce*

pousses de soja *bean sprouts*
poussin *baby chicken*
poutargue *mullet roe paste*
praire *clam*
praliné *hazelnut flavoured*
primeurs *spring vegetables*
provençale, ...à la *cooked with tomatoes, peppers, garlic and white wine*
prune *plum, plum brandy*
pruneau *prune, damson (Switz.)*
purée *mashed potatoes; purée*
quatre-quarts *cake made with equal parts of butter, flour, sugar and eggs*
quenelles *poached fish or meat mousse balls served in a sauce*
quenelles de brochet *pike mousse in cream sauce*
quetsch *type of plum*
queue de bœuf *oxtail*
quiche Lorraine *flan with egg, fresh cream and diced back bacon*
râble *saddle*
radis *radishes*
ragoût *stew, casserole*
raie *skate*
raifort *horseradish*
raisin *grape*
raisin sec *sultana, raisin*
raïto *red wine, olive, caper, garlic and shallot sauce*
ramier *wood pigeon*
râpé(e) *grated*
rascasse *scorpion fish*
ratatouille *tomatoes, aubergines, courgettes and garlic cooked in olive oil*
rave *turnip*
raviolis *pasta parcels of meat*
reine-claude *greengage*
rillettes *coarse pork pâté*
rillettes de canard *coarse duck pâté*
ris de veau *calf sweetbread*
riz *rice*
rognon *kidney*
rognons blancs *testicles*

ratatouille

rognons sautés sauce madère *sautéed kidneys served in Madeira sauce*
romaine *cos lettuce*
romarin *rosemary*
rond de gigot *large slice of leg of lamb*
rosbif *roast beef*
rôti *roast*
rouget *red mullet*
rouille *spicy version of garlic mayonnaise (aïoli) served with fish stew or soup*
roulade *meat or fish, stuffed and rolled*
roulé *sweet or savoury roll*
rumsteak *rump steak*
rutabaga *swede*
sabayon *dessert made with egg yolks, sugar and Marsala wine*
sablé *shortbread*
safran *saffron*
saignant *rare*
Saint-Hubert *game consommé flavoured with wine*
salade *lettuce, salad*
salade aveyronnaise *cheese salad (made with Roquefort)*
salade de fruits *fruit salad*
salade de saison *mixed salad and/or greens in season*
salade lyonnaise *vegetable salad (cooked), dressed with eggs, bacon and croutons*
salade niçoise *many variations on a famous theme: the basic ingredients are green beans, anchovies, black olives, green peppers*

salade niçoise

salade russe *mixed cooked vegetables in mayonnaise*
salade verte *green salad*
salé *salted/spicy*
salsifis *salsify*
sandwich *sandwich*
sanglier *wild boar*
sarrasin *buckwheat*
sarriette *savoury (herb)*
sauce *sauce*
sauce piquante *gherkins, vinegar and shallots*
saucisse/saucisson *sausage*
saumon *salmon*
saumon fumé *smoked salmon*
saumon poché *poached salmon*
sauté(e) *sautéed*
sauté d'agneau *lamb stew*
savarin *a filled ring-shaped cake*
savoyarde, ...à la *with gruyère cheese*
scarole *endive, escarole*
sec *dry or dried*
seiche *cuttlefish*
sel *salt*
selle d'agneau *saddle of lamb*
semoule *semolina*
socca *thin chickpea flour pancake*
sole *sole*
sole Albert *sole in cream sauce with mustard*
sole cardinal *sole cooked in wine, served with lobster sauce*

sole Normande *sole cooked in a cream, cider and shrimp sauce*
sole Saint Germain *grilled sole with butter and tarragon sauce*
sole-limande *lemon sole*
soufflé *light fluffy dish made wih egg yolks and stiffly beaten egg whites combined with cheese, ham, fish, etc*
soufflé au Grand Marnier *soufflé flavoured with Grand Marnier liqueur*
soufflé au jambon *ham soufflé*
soupe *hearty and chunky soup*
soupe à l'oignon *onion soup usually served with a crisp chunk of French bread in the dish with grated cheese piled on top*
soupe à la bière *beer soup*
soupe au pistou *vegetable soup with garlic and basil*
soupe aux choux *cabbage soup with pork*
soupe de poisson *fish soup*
steak *steak*
steak au poivre *steak with peppercorns*
steak tartare *minced raw steak mixed with raw egg, chopped onion, tartare or worcester sauce, parsley and capers*
sucre *sugar*
sucré *sweet*

soupe à l'oignon

tarte tatin

suprême de volaille *breast of chicken in cream sauce*
tajine *North African casserole*
tapenade *olive paste*
tarte *open tart, generally sweet*
  tarte aux fraises *strawberry tart*
  tarte aux pommes *apple tart*
  tarte flambée *thin pizza-like pastry topped with onion, cream and bacon (Alsace)*
  tarte Normande *apple tart*
  tarte tatin *upside down tart with caramelized apples or pears*
  tarte tropézienne *sponge cake filled with custard cream topped with almonds*
tartiflette *cheese, cured ham and potato dish from the Savoie*
tartine *open sandwich*
terrine *terrine, pâté*
  terrine de campagne *pork and liver terrine*
  terrine de porc et gibier *pork and game terrine*
tête de veau *calf's head*
thé *tea*
  thé au citron *tea with lemon*
  thé au lait *tea with milk*
  thé sans sucre *tea without sugar*
thermidor *lobster grilled in its shell with cream sauce*
thon *tuna fish*

tian provençal *baked tomatoes and courgettes with cheese*
tilleul *lime tea*
timbale *round dish in which a mixture of usually meat or fish is cooked. Often lined with pastry and served with a rich sauce*
  timbale d'écrevisses *crayfish in a cream, wine and brandy sauce*
  timbale de fruits *pastry base covered with fruits*
tiramisu *mascarpone cheese, coffee, chocolate and cream*
tisane *herbal tea*
tomate *tomato*
  tomates à la provençale *grilled tomatoes steeped in garlic*
  tomates farcies *stuffed tomatoes*
tomme *type of cheese*
tournedos *thick fillet steak*
  tournedos Rossini *thick fillet steak on fried bread with goose liver and truffles on top*
tourte à la viande *meat pie usually made with veal and pork*
tripe *tripe*
  tripes à la mode de Caen *tripe cooked with vegetables, herbs, cider and calvados*
tripoux *mutton tripe*
truffade *sautéed potatoes with cheese and bacon (central France)*
truffe *truffle*
truffiat *potato cake*
truite *trout*
  truite aux amandes *trout covered with almonds*
turbot *turbot*
vacherin *large meringue filled with cream, ice cream and fruit*
vapeur, …à la *steamed*
veau *calf, veal*
  veau sauté Marengo *veal cooked in a casserole with white wine, garlic, tomatoes and mushrooms*
velouté *thick creamy white sauce made with fish, veal or chicken stock. Also used in soups*
venaison *venison*
verdure, en *garnished with green vegetables*

tournedos rossini

verjus *juice of unripe grapes*
vermicelle *vermicelli*
verveine *herbal tea made with verbena*
viande *meat*
viande séchée *thin slices of cured beef*
vichyssoise *leek and potato soup, served cold*
viennoise *fried in egg and breadcrumbs*
vin *wine*

vin blanc *white wine*
vin de pays *local regional wine*
vin de table *table wine*
vin rosé *rosé wine*
vin rouge *red wine*
vinaigrette *French dressing of oil and vinegar*
vinaigre *vinegar*
violet *sea squirt*
volaille *poultry*
yaourt *yoghurt*
zewelwai *onion flan*

A

a(n) un *(m)*/une *(f)*
abbey l'abbaye *(f)*
able: to be able to pouvoir
abortion l'avortement *(m)*
about *(approximately)* vers ; environ
  (concerning) au sujet de
  about 100 francs environ cent francs
  about 10 o'clock vers dix heures
above au-dessus (de)
  above the bed au-dessus du lit
  above the farm au-dessus de la ferme
abroad à l'étranger
abscess l'abcès *(m)*
accelerator l'accélérateur *(m)*
accent l'accent *(m)*
to accept accepter
  do you accept this card? vous acceptez
  cette carte?
access l'access *(m)*
accident l'accident *(m)*
accident & emergency department
  les urgences
accommodation le logement
to accompany accompagner
account le compte
account number le numéro de compte
to ache faire mal
  it aches ça fait mal
acid l'acide *(m)*
actor l'acteur *(m)*, l'actrice *(f)*
adaptor *(electrical)* l'adaptateur *(m)*
address l'adresse *(f)*
  here's my address voici mon adresse
  what is the address? quelle est
  l'adresse?
address book le carnet d'adresse
admission charge l'entrée *(f)*
to admit *(to hospital)* hospitaliser
adult *m/f* l'adulte
  for adults pour adultes
advance: in advance à l'avance
advertisement *(in paper)* l'annonce *(f)*
  (on TV) la publicité
to advise conseiller
A&E les urgences
aeroplane l'avion *(m)*
aerosol l'aérosol *(m)*
afraid: to be afraid of avoir peur de
after après
afternoon l'après-midi *(m)*
  in the afternoon l'après-midi
  this afternoon cet après-midi
  tomorrow afternoon demain après-midi
aftershave l'après-rasage *(m)*

again encore
against contre
age l'âge *(m)*
agency l'agence *(f)*
ago: a week ago il y a une semaine
to agree être d'accord
agreement l'accord *(m)*
AIDS le SIDA
air ambulance l'hélicoptère médical *(m)*
airbag *(in car)* l'airbag *(m)*
airbed le matelas pneumatique
air-conditioning la climatisation
air-conditioning unit le climatisatiseur
air freshener le désodorisant
airline la ligne aérienne
air mail: by airmail par avion
airplane l'avion *(m)*
airport l'aéroport *(m)*
airport bus la navette pour l'aéroport
air ticket le billet d'avion
aisle le couloir
alarm l'alarme *(f)*
alarm clock le réveil
alcohol l'alcool *(m)*
alcohol-free sans alcool
alcoholic drink la boisson alcoolisée
all tout(e)/tous/toutes
allergic allergique
  I'm allergic to... je suis allergique à…
allergy l'allergie *(f)*
to allow permettre
  it's not allowed c'est interdit
all right *(agreed)* d'accord
  are you all right? ça va?
almost presque
alone tout(e) seul(e)
Alps les Alpes
already déjà
also aussi
altar l'autel *(m)*
always toujours
a.m. du matin
am: I am je suis
amber *(traffic light)* orange
ambulance l'ambulance *(f)*
America l'Amérique *(f)*
American américain(e)
amount *(total)* le montant
anaesthetic l'anesthésique *(m)*
  a local anaesthetic une anesthésie
  locale
  a general anaesthetic une anesthésie
  générale
anchor l'ancre *(f)*

and et
angina l'angine de poitrine (f)
angry fâché(e)
animal l'animal (m)
aniseed l'anis (m)
ankle la cheville
anniversary l'anniversaire (m)
to announce annoncer
announcement l'annonce (f)
annual annuel(-elle)
another un(e) autre
  another beer une autre bière
answer la réponse
to answer répondre à
answerphone le répondeur
antacid le comprimé contre les brûlures
  d'estomac
antibiotic l'antibiotique (m)
antifreeze l'antigel (m)
antihistamine l'antihistaminique (m)
antiques les antiquités
antique shop le magasin d'antiquités
antiseptic l'antiseptique (m)
any de (du/de la/des)
  have you any apples? vous avez des
  pommes?
anyone quelqu'un/personne
anything quelque chose/rien
anywhere quelque part
apartment l'appartement (m)
appendicitis l'appendicite (f)
apple la pomme
application form le formulaire
appointment le rendez-vous
  I have an appointment j'ai rendez-vous
approximately environ
April avril
architect m/f l'architecte
architecture l'architecture (f)
are: you are vous êtes
  we are nous sommes
  they are ils/elles sont
arm le bras
armbands (for swimming) les bracelets
  gonflables
armchair le fauteuil
to arrange arranger
to arrest arrêter
arrival l'arrivée (f)
to arrive arriver
art l'art (m)
art gallery le musée
arthritis l'arthrite (f)
artificial artificiel

artist l'artiste (m/f)
ashtray le cendrier
to ask demander
  to ask a question poser une question
aspirin l'aspirine (f)
asthma l'asthme (m)
  I have asthma je suis asthmatique
at à
  at my/your home chez moi/vous
  at 8 o'clock à huit heures
  at once tout de suite
  at night la nuit
Atlantic Ocean l'Océan atlantique (m)
attack (mugging) l'agression (f)
  (medical) la crise
to attack agresser
attic le grenier
attractive séduisant(e)
auction la vente aux enchères
audience le public
August août
aunt la tante
au pair la jeune fille au pair
Australia l'Australie (f)
Australian australien(ne)
author l'écrivain ; l'auteur (m)
automatic automatique
automatic car la voiture à boîte
  automatique
auto-teller le distributeur automatique
  (de billets)
autumn l'automne (m)
available disponible
avalanche l'avalanche (f)
avenue l'avenue (f)
average moyen(ne)
to avoid éviter
awake: I was awake all night je n'ai
  pas dormi de toute la nuit
awful affreux(-euse)
awning (for caravan etc) l'auvent (m)
axle (car) l'essieu (m)

B

baby le bébé
baby food les petits pots
baby milk (formula) le lait maternisé
baby's bottle le biberon
baby seat (car) le siège pour bébés
babysitter le/la babysitter
baby wipes les lingettes
back (of body) le dos
backpack le sac à dos
bacon le bacon ; le lard

bad *(food, weather)* mauvais(e)
badminton le badminton
bag le sac
  (suitcase) la valise
baggage les bagages
baggage allowance le poids (de bagages) autorisé
baggage reclaim la livraison des bagages
bait *(for fishing)* l'appât *(m)*
baked au four
baker's la boulangerie
balcony le balcon
bald *(person)* chauve
  (tyre) lisse
ball *(large: football, etc)* le ballon
  (small: golf, tennis, etc) la balle
ballet le ballet
balloon le ballon
banana la banane
band *(music)* le groupe
bandage le pansement
bank *(money)* la banque
  (river) la rive ; le bord
bank account le compte en banque
banknote le billet de banque
bar le bar
bar of chocolate la tablette de chocolat
barbecue le barbecue
  to have a barbecue faire un barbecue
barber's le coiffeur
to bark aboyer
barn la grange
barrel *(wine, beer)* le tonneau
basement le sous-sol
basil le basilic
basket le panier
basketball le basket-ball
bat *(baseball, cricket)* la batte
  (animal) la chauve-souris
bath le bain
  to have a bath prendre un bain
bathing cap le bonnet de bain
bathroom la salle de bains
  with bathroom avec salle de bains
battery *(for car)* la batterie
  (for radio, camera, etc) la pile
bay *(along coast)* la baie
B&B la chambre d'hôte
to be être
beach la plage
  private beach la plage privée
  sandy beach la plage de sable
  nudist beach la plage de nudistes
beach hut la cabine

bean le haricot
beard la barbe
beautiful beau (belle)
beauty salon le salon de beauté
because parce que
to become devenir
bed le lit
  double bed le grand lit ; le lit de deux personnes
  single bed le lit d'une personne
  sofa bed le canapé-lit
  twin beds les lits jumeaux
bed clothes les draps et couvertures
bedroom la chambre à coucher
bee l'abeille *(f)*
beef le bœuf
beer la bière
before avant
to begin commencer
behind derrière
beige beige
Belgian belge
Belgium la Belgique
to believe croire
bell *(church, school)* la cloche
  (doorbell) la sonnette
to belong to appartenir à
below sous
belt la ceinture
bend *(in road)* le virage
berth *(train, ship, etc)* la couchette
beside *(next to)* à côté de
  beside the bank à côté de la banque
best le/la meilleur(e)
bet le pari
to bet on faire un pari sur
better meilleur(e)
  better than meilleur que
between entre
bib *(baby's)* le bavoir
bicycle la bicyclette ; le vélo
bicycle pump la pompe à vélo
bicycle repair kit la trousse de réparation (pour vélo)
bidet le bidet
big grand(e), gros(se)
bike *(pushbike)* le vélo
  (motorbike) la moto
bike lock l'antivol *(m)*
bikini le bikini
bill *(restaurant)* l'addition *(f)*
  (hotel) la note
  (for work done) la facture
bin *(dustbin)* la poubelle
bin liner le sac poubelle

binoculars les jumelles
bird l'oiseau *(m)*
biro le stylo
birth la naissance
birth certificate l'acte de naissance *(m)*
birthday l'anniversaire *(m)*
  happy birthday! bon anniversaire!
  my birthday is on... mon anniversaire c'est le...
birthday card la carte d'anniversaire
birthday present le cadeau d'anniversaire
biscuits les biscuits
bit: a bit (of) un peu (de)
bite *(animal)* la morsure
  (insect) la piqûre
to bite *(animal)* mordre
  (insect) piquer
bitten *(by animal)* mordu(e)
  (by insect) piqué(e)
bitter amer(-ère)
black noir(e)
black ice le verglas
blank *(disk, tape)* vierge
blanket la couverture
bleach l'eau de Javel *(f)*
to bleed saigner
blender *(for food)* le mixeur
blind *(person)* aveugle
blind *(for window)* le store
blister l'ampoule *(f)*
block of flats l'immeuble *(m)*
blocked bouché(e)
  the sink is blocked l'évier est bouché
blond *(person)* blond(e)
blood le sang
blood group le groupe sanguin
blood pressure la tension (artérielle)
blood test l'analyse de sang *(f)*
blouse le chemisier
blow-dry le brushing
blowout *(of tyre)* l'éclatement *(m)*
blue bleu(e)
  dark blue bleu foncé
  light blue bleu clair
boar *(wild)* le sanglier
to board *(plane, train, etc)* embarquer
boarding card la carte d'embarquement
boarding house la pension (de famille)
boat le bateau
  (rowing) la barque
boat trip l'excursion en bateau *(f)*
body le corps
to boil faire bouillir
boiled bouilli(e)

boiler la chaudière
bomb la bombe
bone l'os *(m)*
  (fish) l'arête *(f)*
bonfire le feu
book le livre
to book *(reserve)* réserver
booking la réservation
booking office le bureau de location
bookshop la librairie
boots les bottes
  (short) les bottillons
border *(of country)* la frontière
boring ennuyeux(-euse)
born: to be born naître
to borrow emprunter
boss le chef
both les deux
bottle la bouteille
  a bottle of wine une bouteille de vin
  a bottle of water une bouteille d'eau
  a half-bottle une demi-bouteille
bottle opener l'ouvre-bouteilles *(m)*
bottom *(of pool, etc)* le fond
bowl *(for soup, etc)* le bol
bow tie le nœud papillon
box la boîte
box office le bureau de location
boxer shorts le caleçon
boy le garçon
boyfriend le copain
bra le soutien-gorge
bracelet le bracelet
brain le cerveau
brake(s) le(s) frein(s)
to brake freiner
brake cable le câble de frein
brake fluid le liquide de freins
brake lights les feux de stop
brake pads les plaquettes de frein
branch *(of tree)* la branche
  (of company, etc) la succursale
brand *(make)* la marque
brass le cuivre
brave courageux(-euse)
bread le pain
  (French stick) la baguette
  (thin French stick) la ficelle
  sliced bread le pain de mie en tranches
bread roll le petit pain
to break casser
breakable fragile
breakdown *(car)* la panne
  (nervous) la dépression

breakdown van la dépanneuse
breakfast le petit déjeuner
breast le sein
to breast-feed allaiter
to breathe respirer
brick la brique
bride la mariée
bridegroom le marié
bridge le pont
briefcase la serviette
Brillo® pad le tampon Jex®
to bring apporter
Britain la Grande-Bretagne
British britannique
broadband le haut débit
brochure la brochure ; le dépliant
broken cassé(e)
  my leg is broken je me suis cassé la jambe
broken down *(car, etc)* en panne
bronchitis la bronchite
bronze le bronze
brooch la broche
broom *(brush)* le balai
brother le frère
brother-in-law le beau-frère
brown marron
bruise le bleu
brush la brosse
bubble bath le bain moussant
bucket le seau
buffet car *(train)* la voiture-buffet
to build construire
building l'immeuble *(m)*
bulb *(light)* l'ampoule *(f)*
bumbag la banane
bumper *(on car)* le pare-chocs
bunch *(of flowers)* le bouquet
  (of grapes) la grappe
bungee jumping le saut à l'élastique
bureau de change le bureau de change
burger le hamburger
burglar le/la cambrioleur(-euse)
burglar alarm le système d'alarme
to burn brûler
bus le bus
  (coach) le car
bus pass la carte de bus
bus station la gare routière
bus stop l'arrêt de bus *(m)*
bus ticket le ticket de bus
business les affaires
  on business pour affaires
business card la carte de visite

business centre le centre des affaires
business class la classe affaires
businessman/woman l'homme/ la femme d'affaires
business trip le voyage d'affaires
busy occupé(e)
but mais
butcher's la boucherie
butter le beurre
button le bouton
to buy acheter
by *(via)* par
  (beside) à côté de
  by bus en bus
  by car en voiture
  by ship en bateau
  by train en train
bypass *(road)* la rocade

C

cab *(taxi)* le taxi
cabaret le cabaret
cabin *(on boat)* la cabine
cabin crew l'équipage *(m)*
cablecar le téléphérique ; la benne
café le café
  internet café le cybercafé
cafetière la cafetière
cake *(large)* le gâteau
  (small) la pâtisserie ; le petit gâteau
cake shop la pâtisserie
calculator la calculatrice
calendar le calendrier
call *(telephone)* l'appel *(m)*
to call *(speak, phone)* appeler
calm calme
camcorder le caméscope
camera l'appareil photo *(m)*
camera case l'étui *(m)*
camera phone le téléphone portable appareil-photo
camera shop le magasin de photo
to camp camper
camping gas le butane
camping stove le camping-gaz®
campsite le camping
can *(to be able to)* pouvoir
  (to know how to) savoir
  I can je peux/sais
  we can nous pouvons/savons
can la boîte
can opener l'ouvre-boîtes *(m)*
Canada le Canada
Canadian canadien(ne)
canal le canal

to cancel annuler
cancellation l'annulation (f)
cancer le cancer
candle la bougie
canoe le kayak
canoeing: to go canoeing faire du
  canoë-kayak
cap (hat) la casquette
  (contraceptive) le diaphragme
capital (city) la capitale
car la voiture
car alarm l'alarme de voiture (f)
car ferry le ferry
car hire la location de voitures
car insurance l'assurance automobile (f)
car keys les clés de voiture
car park le parking
car parts les pièces pour voiture
car phone le téléphone de voiture
car port l'auvent (m)
car radio l'autoradio (m)
car seat (for child) le siège pour enfant
carwash le lavage automatique
carafe le pichet
caravan la caravane
carburettor le carburateur
card la carte
  birthday card la carte
  d'anniversaire
  business card la carte de visite
  playing cards les cartes à jouer
cardboard le carton
cardigan le gilet
careful: to be careful faire attention
  careful! attention!
carpet (rug) le tapis
  (fitted) la moquette
carriage (railway) la voiture
carrot la carotte
to carry porter
carton (cigarettes) la cartouche
  (milk, juice) le brick
case (suitcase) la valise
cash l'argent liquide (m)
to cash (cheque) encaisser
cash desk la caisse
cash dispenser (ATM) le distributeur
  automatique (de billets)
cashier le/la caissier(-ière)
cashpoint le distributeur automatique
  (de billets)
casino le casino
casserole dish la cocotte
cassette la cassette
cassette player le magnétophone

castle le château
casualty department les urgences
cat le chat
cat food la nourriture pour chats
catalogue le catalogue
catch (bus, train) prendre
cathedral la cathédrale
Catholic catholique
cave la grotte
cavity (in tooth) la carie
CD le CD
CD player le lecteur de CD
CD ROM le CD-Rom
ceiling le plafond
cellar la cave
cellphone le téléphone cellulaire
cemetery le cimetière
centimetre le centimètre
central central(e)
central heating le chauffage central
central locking le verrouillage central
centre le centre
century le siècle
ceramic la céramique
cereal la céréale
certain (sure) certain(e)
certificate le certificat
chain la chaîne
chair la chaise
chairlift le télésiège
chalet le chalet
chambermaid la femme de chambre
champagne le champagne
change (small coins) la monnaie
to change changer
  to change money changer de l'argent
  to change clothes se changer
  to change bus changer d'autobus
  to change train changer de train
changing room la cabine d'essayage
Channel (English) la Manche
chapel la chapelle
charcoal le charbon de bois
charge (fee) le prix
charge: I've run out of charge je n'ai
  plus de batterie
to charge prendre
to charge recharger: I need to charge
  my phone j'ai besoin de recharger
  mon téléphone
charge card la carte de paiement
charger (battery) le chargeur
charter flight le vol charter
chatroom (internet) le forum

117

cheap bon marché
cheaper moins cher
cheap rate (phone) le tarif réduit
to check vérifier
to check in enregistrer
check-in (desk) l'enregistrement
  des bagages (m)
  (at hotel) la réception
cheek la joue
cheers! santé!
cheese le fromage
chef le chef de cuisine
chemist's la pharmacie
cheque le chèque
cheque book le carnet de chèques
cheque card la carte d'identité bancaire
chest (body) la poitrine
chewing gum le chewing-gum
chicken le poulet
chickenpox la varicelle
child l'enfant (m)
child safety seat (car) le siège pour
  enfant
children les enfants
  for children pour enfants
chilli (fruit) le piment ; ·
  (dish) le chili con carne
chimney la cheminée
chin le menton
china la porcelaine
chips les frites
chiropodist le/la pédicure
chocolate le chocolat
  drinking-chocolate le chocolat
  en poudre
  hot chocolate le chocolat chaud
chocolates les chocolats
choir la chorale
to choose choisir
chop (meat) la côtelette
chopping board la planche à découper
christening le baptême
Christian name le prénom
Christmas Noël (m)
  merry Christmas! joyeux Noël!
Christmas card la carte de Noël
Christmas Eve la veille de Noël
church l'église (f)
cigar le cigare
cigarette la cigarette
cigarette lighter le briquet
cigarette paper le papier à cigarette
cinema le cinéma
circle (theatre) le balcon

circuit breaker le disjoncteur
circus le cirque
cistern (toilet) le réservoir de chasse
  d'eau
city la ville
city centre le centre-ville
class la classe
  first-class de première classe
  second-class de seconde classe
clean propre
to clean nettoyer
cleaner (person) la femme de ménage
cleanser (for face) le démaquillant
clear clair(e)
client le client/la cliente
cliff (along coast) la falaise
  (in mountains) l'escarpement (m)
to climb (mountain) faire de la montagne
climbing boots les chaussures de
  montagne
Clingfilm® le Scellofrais®
clinic la clinique
cloakroom le vestiaire
clock l'horloge (f)
close by proche
to close fermer
closed (shop, etc) fermé(e)
cloth (rag) le chiffon
  (fabric) le tissu
clothes les vêtements
clothes line la corde à linge
clothes pegs les pinces à linge
clothes shop le magasin de vêtements
cloudy nuageux(-euse)
club le club
clutch (in car) l'embrayage (m)
coach (bus) le car ; l'autocar (m)
coach station la gare routière
coach trip l'excursion en car (f)
coal le charbon
coast la côte
coastguard le garde-côte
coat le manteau
coat hanger le cintre
cockroach le cafard
cocktail le cocktail
cocktail bar le cocktail-bar
cocoa le cacao
code le code
coffee le café
  white coffee le café au lait
  black coffee le café noir
  cappuccino le cappuccino
  decaffeinated coffee le café
  décaféiné

coil *(IUD)* le stérilet
coin la pièce de monnaie
Coke® le Coca®
colander la passoire
cold froid
  I'm cold j'ai froid
  it's cold il fait froid
cold water l'eau froide *(f)*
cold *(illness)* le rhume
  I have a cold j'ai un rhume
cold sore le bouton de fièvre
collar le col
collar bone la clavicule
colleague le/la collègue
to collect *(someone)* aller chercher
collection la collection
colour la couleur
colour-blind daltonien(ne)
colour film *(for camera)* la pellicule
  couleur
comb le peigne
to come venir
  (to arrive) arriver
  to come back revenir
  to come in entrer
  come in! entrez!
comedy la comédie
comfortable confortable
company *(firm)* la compagnie ; la société
compartment le compartiment
compass la boussole
to complain faire une réclamation
complaint la plainte
to complete remplir
compulsory obligatoire
computer l'ordinateur *(m)*
computer disk *(floppy)* la disquette
computer game le jeu électronique
computer program le programme
  informatique
concert le concert
concert hall la salle de concert
concession la réduction
concussion la commotion (cérébrale)
conditioner l'après-shampooing *(m)*
condom le préservatif
conductor *(in orchestra)* le chef
  d'orchestre
conference la conférence
to confirm confirmer
confirmation la confirmation
confused: *I am confused* je m'y perds
congratulations félicitations!
connection *(train, bus, etc)*
  la correspondance

constipated constipé(e)
consulate le consulat
to consult consulter
to contact contacter
contact lenses les verres de contact
contact lens cleaner le produit pour
  nettoyer les verres de contact
to continue continuer
contraceptive le contraceptif
contract le contrat
convenient: *it's not convenient* ça ne
  m'arrange pas
convulsions les convulsions
to cook *(be cooking)* cuisiner
  to cook a meal préparer un repas
cooked cuisiné
cooker la cuisinière
cool frais (fraîche)
cool-bag *(for picnic)* le sac isotherme
cool-box *(for picnic)* la glacière
copper le cuivre
copy *(duplicate)* la copie
to copy copier
cordless phone le téléphone sans fil
cork le bouchon
corkscrew le tire-bouchon
corner le coin
cornflakes les corn-flakes
corridor le couloir
cortisone la cortisone
cosmetics les produits de beauté
cost le coût
to cost coûter
  how much does it cost? ça coûte
  combien?
costume *(swimming)* le maillot (de bain)
cot le lit d'enfant
cottage la maison de campagne
cotton le coton
cotton bud le coton-tige®
cotton wool le coton hydrophile
couchette la couchette
cough la toux
to cough tousser
cough mixture le sirop pour la toux
cough sweets les pastilles pour
  la gorge
counter *(shop, bar, etc)* le comptoir
country *(not town)* la campagne
  (nation) le pays
countryside le paysage
couple *(two people)* le couple
  a couple of... deux ...
courgette la courgette

courier service le service de messageries
course *(syllabus)* le cours
  (of meal) le plat
cousin le/la cousin(e)
cover charge *(restaurant)* le couvert
cow la vache
craft fair le marché d'artisanat
crafts les objets artisanaux
craftsperson l'artisan(e)
cramps *(period pain)* les règles
  douloureuses
cranberry juice le jus de cranberry
crash *(car)* l'accident *(m)* ; la collision
crash helmet le casque
cream *(food, lotion)* la crème
  soured cream la crème fermentée
  whipped cream la crème fouettée
credit *(on mobile phone)* les unités *(fpl)*
credit card la carte de crédit
crime le crime
crisps les chips
croissant le croissant
cross la croix
to cross *(road, sea, etc)* traverser
cross-country skiing le ski de fond
cross-channel ferry le ferry qui traverse
  la Manche
crossing *(by sea)* la traversée
crossroads le carrefour ; le croisement
crossword puzzle les mots croisés
crowd la foule
crowded bondé(e)
crown la couronne
cruise la croisière
crutches les béquilles
to cry *(weep)* pleurer
crystal le cristal
cucumber le concombre
cufflinks les boutons de manchette
cul-de-sac le cul-de-sac
cup la tasse
cupboard le placard
currant le raisin sec
currency la devise ; la monnaie
current *(air, water, etc)* le courant
curtain le rideau
cushion le coussin
custom *(tradition)* la tradition
customer le/la client(e)
customs la douane
  (duty) les droits de douane
customs declaration la déclaration
  de douane
to cut couper

cut la coupure
cutlery les couverts
to cycle faire du vélo
cycle track la piste cyclable
cycling le cyclisme
cyst le kyste
cystitis la cystite

D

daily *(each day)* tous les jours
dairy produce les produits laitiers
dam le barrage
damage les dégâts
damp humide
dance le bal
to dance danser
danger le danger
dangerous dangereux(-euse)
dark l'obscurité *(f)*
  after dark la nuit tombée
date la date
date of birth la date de naissance
daughter la fille
daughter-in-law la belle-fille ; la bru
dawn l'aube *(f)*
day le jour
  per day par jour
  every day tous les jours
dead mort(e)
deaf sourd(e)
dear *(expensive, in letter)* cher (chère)
debit card la carte de paiement
debts les créances
decaffeinated décaféiné(e)
  decaffeinated coffee le café décaféiné
December décembre
deckchair la chaise longue
to declare déclarer
  nothing to declare rien à déclarer
deep profond(e)
deep freeze le congélateur
deer le cerf
to defrost décongeler
to de-ice *(windscreen)* dégivrer
delay le retard
  how long is the delay? il y a combien
  de retard?
delayed retardé(e)
delicatessen l'épicerie fine *(f)*
delicious délicieux(-euse)
demonstration la manifestation
dental floss le fil dentaire
dentist le/la dentiste
dentures le dentier

deodorant le déodorant
to depart partir
department le rayon
department store le grand magasin
departure le départ
departure lounge la salle
　d'embarquement
deposit les arrhes
to describe décrire
description la description
desk *(furniture)* le bureau
　(information) l'accueil *(m)*
dessert le dessert
details les détails
detergent le détergent
detour la déviation
to develop *(photos)* faire développer
diabetes le diabète
diabetic diabétique
　I'm diabetic je suis diabétique
to dial *(a number)* composer
dialling code l'indicatif *(m)*
dialling tone la tonalité
diamond le diamant
diapers les couches (pour bébé)
diaphragm le diaphragme
diarrhoea la diarrhée
diary l'agenda *(m)*
dice le dé
dictionary le dictionnaire
to die mourir
diesel le gas-oil
diet le régime
　I'm on a diet je suis au régime
　special diet le régime spécial
different différent(e)
difficult difficile
to dilute diluer ; ajouter de l'eau à
dinghy le canot
dining room la salle à manger
dinner *(evening meal)* le dîner
　to have dinner dîner
diplomat le diplomate
direct *(train, etc)* direct(e)
directions les indications
　to ask for directions demander
　le chemin
directory *(telephone)* l'annuaire *(m)*
directory enquiries (le service des)
　renseignements
dirty sale
disability: *to have a disability*
　être handicapé(e)
disabled *(person)* handicapé(e)

to disagree ne pas être d'accord
to disappear disparaître
disaster la catastrophe
disco la discothèque
discount le rabais
to discover découvrir
disease la maladie
dish le plat
dishtowel le torchon à vaisselle
dishwasher le lave-vaisselle
disinfectant le désinfectant
disk *(floppy)* la disquette
to dislocate *(joint)* disloquer
disposable jetable
distant lointain(e)
distilled water l'eau distillée *(f)*
district *(of town)* le quartier
to disturb déranger
to dive plonger
diversion la déviation
divorced divorcé(e)
DIY shop le magasin de bricolage
dizzy pris(e) de vertige
to do faire
doctor le médecin
documents les papiers
dog le chien
dog food la nourriture pour chiens
dog lead la laisse
doll la poupée
dollar le dollar
domestic flight le vol intérieur
donor card la carte de donneur
　d'organes
door la porte
doorbell la sonnette
double double
double bed le grand lit
double room la chambre pour deux
　personnes
doughnut le beignet
down: *to go down* descendre
downstairs en bas
Down's syndrome la trisomie
　he/she has Down's syndrome
　il/elle est trisomique
drain *(house)* le tuyau d'écoulement
draught *(of air)* le courant d'air
　there's a draught il y a un courant
　d'air
draught lager la bière pression
drawer le tiroir
drawing le dessin
dress la robe

to dress s'habiller
dressing *(for food)* la vinaigrette
(for wound) le pansement
dressing gown le peignoir
drill *(tool)* la perceuse électrique
drink la boisson
to drink boire
drinking water l'eau potable *(f)*
to drive conduire
driver *(of car)* le conducteur/
la conductrice
driving licence le permis de conduire
drought la sécheresse
to drown se noyer
drug *(medicine)* le médicament
(narcotics) la drogue
drunk ivre ; soûl(e)
dry sec (sèche)
to dry sécher
dry-cleaner's le pressing
dummy *(for baby)* la tétine
during pendant
dust la poussière
duster le chiffon
dustpan and brush la pelle et
la balayette
duty-free hors taxe
duvet la couette
duvet cover la housse de couette
DVD le DVD
DVD player le lecteur de DVD
dye la teinture
dynamo la dynamo

E

each chacun/chacune
ear l'oreille *(f)*
earlier plus tôt
early tôt
to earn gagner
earphones le casque
earplugs les boules Quiès®
earrings les boucles d'oreille
earth la terre
earthquake le tremblement de terre
east l'est *(m)*
Easter Pâques
happy Easter! joyeuses Pâques!
easy facile
to eat manger
ecological écologique
economy *(class)* économique
eco-tourism l'écotourisme *(m)*

egg l'œuf *(m)*
fried eggs les œufs sur le plat
hard-boiled egg l'œuf dur
scrambled eggs les œufs brouillés
soft-boiled egg l'œuf à la coque
either ... or soit ... soit
elastic band l'élastique *(m)*
elastoplast® le sparadrap
elbow le coude
electric électrique
electric blanket la couverture chauffante
electric toothbrush la brosse à dents
électrique
electric razor le rasoir électrique
electrician l'électricien *(m)*
electricity l'électricité *(f)*
electricity meter le compteur
électrique
electronic électronique
electronic organizer l'agenda
électronique *(m)*
elevator l'ascenseur *(m)*
e-mail le e-mail
to e-mail sb envoyer un e-mail à qn
e-mail address l'adresse éléctronique ;
(on forms) le mél
embassy l'ambassade *(f)*
emergency l'urgence *(f)*
emergency exit la sortie de secours
empty vide
end la fin
engaged *(to be married)* fiancé(e)
(phone, toilet, etc) occupé(e)
engine le moteur
England l'Angleterre *(f)*
English anglais(e)
(language) l'anglais *(m)*
Englishman/-woman l'Anglais(e) *(m/f)*
to enjoy aimer
I enjoy swimming j'aime nager
I enjoy dancing j'aime danser
enjoy your meal! bon appétit!
enough assez
that's enough ça suffit
enquiry desk les renseignements
to enter entrer
entertainment les divertissements
entrance l'entrée *(f)*
entrance fee le prix d'entrée
envelope l'enveloppe *(f)*
epileptic épileptique
epileptic fit la crise d'épilepsie
equipment l'équipement *(m)*
equal égal
eraser la gomme

error l'erreur (f)
escalator l'escalator (m)
to escape s'échapper
essential indispensable
estate agency l'agence immobilière (f)
Euro (unit of currency) l'euro (m)
eurocheque l'eurochèque (m)
Europe l'Europe (f)
European européen(ne)
European Union l'Union européenne (f)
evening le soir
  this evening ce soir
  tomorrow evening demain soir
  in the evening le soir
  7 o'clock in the evening sept heures
  du soir
evening dress (man) la tenue de soirée
  (woman) la robe du soir
evening meal le dîner
every chaque
everyone tout le monde
everything tout
everywhere partout
examination l'examen (m)
example: *for example* par exemple
excellent excellent(e)
except sauf
excess baggage l'excédent de bagages
  (m)
exchange l'échange (m)
to exchange échanger
exchange rate le taux de change
exciting passionnant(e)
excursion l'excursion (f)
excuse: *excuse me!* excusez-moi!
  (to get by) pardon!
exercise l'exercice (m)
exhaust pipe le pot d'échappement
exhibition l'exposition (f)
exit la sortie
expenses les frais
expensive cher (chère)
expert m/f l'expert(e)
to expire (ticket, passport) expirer
to explain expliquer
explosion l'explosion (f)
to export exporter
express (train) le rapide
express (parcel, etc) en exprès
extension (electrical) la rallonge
extra (additional) supplémentaire
  (more) de plus
eye l'œil (m)
  eyes les yeux

eyebrows les sourcils
eye drops les gouttes pour les yeux
eyelashes les cils
eyeliner l'eye-liner (m)
eye shadow le fard à paupières

F

fabric le tissu
face le visage
face cloth/glove le gant de toilette
facial les soins du visage
facilities les installations
factor (sunblock) l'indice (m)
  factor 25 indice 25
factory l'usine (f)
to faint s'évanouir
fainted évanoui(e)
fair (hair) blond(e)
  (just) juste
fair (funfair) la fête foraine
fake faux (fausse)
fall (autumn) l'automne (m)
to fall tomber
  he has fallen il est tombé
false teeth le dentier
family la famille
famous célèbre
fan (handheld) l'éventail (m)
  (electric) le ventilateur
  (sports) le supporter
fan belt la courroie de ventilateur
fancy dress le déguisement
far loin
  is it far? c'est loin?
fare (bus, metro, etc) le prix du billet
farm la ferme
farmer le fermier
farmhouse la ferme
farmers' market le marché fermier
fashionable à la mode
fast rapide
  too fast trop vite
to fasten (seatbelt) attacher
fat gros (grosse)
  (noun) la graisse
father le père
father-in-law le beau-père
fault (defect) un défaut
  it's not my fault ce n'est pas de
  ma faute
favour le service
favourite préféré(e)
fax le fax
  by fax par fax
fax number le numéro de fax

to fax *(document)* faxer
(person) envoyer un fax à
February février
to feed nourrir
to feel sentir
I feel sick j'ai la nausée
I don't feel well je ne me sens pas bien
feet les pieds
felt-tip pen le feutre
female *(animal)* la femelle
ferry le ferry
festival le festival
to fetch aller chercher
fever la fièvre
few peu
a few quelques-un(e)s
fiancé(e) le fiancé/la fiancée
field le champ
to fight se battre
file *(computer)* le fichier
(for papers) le dossier
to fill remplir
to fill in *(form)* remplir
to fill up *(with petrol)* faire le plein
fill it up! *(car)* le plein!
fillet le filet
filling *(in tooth)* le plombage
film le film
(for camera) la pellicule
Filofax® le Filofax
filter *(on cigarette)* le filtre
to find trouver
fine *(penalty)* la contravention
finger le doigt
to finish finir
finished fini(e)
fire le feu ; l'incendie *(m)*
fire alarm l'alarme d'incendie *(f)*
fire brigade les pompiers
fire engine la voiture de pompiers
fire escape *(staircase)* l'échelle de secours *(f)*
fire exit la sortie de secours
fire extinguisher l'extincteur *(m)*
fireplace la cheminée
fireworks les feux d'artifice
firm la compagnie
first premier(-ière)
first aid les premiers secours
first aid kit la trousse de secours
first-class de première classe
first name le prénom
fish le poisson
to fish pêcher

fisherman le pêcheur
fishing la pêche
to go fishing aller à la pêche
fishing permit le permis de pêche
fishing rod la canne à pêche
fishmonger's le/la marchand(e) de poisson
fit *(medical)* l'attaque *(f)*
to fit: *it doesn't fit me* ça ne me va pas
to fix *(repair)* réparer
can you fix it? vous pouvez le réparer?
fizzy gazeux(-euse)
flag le drapeau
flames les flammes
flash *(for camera)* le flash
flashlight la lampe de poche
flask *(vacuum flask)* le Thermos®
flat *(appartment)* l'appartement *(m)*
flat *(level)* plat
(beer) éventé
flat tyre le pneu dégonflé
flavour le goût
(of ice cream) le parfum
flaw le défaut
fleas les puces
flesh la chair
flex *(electrical)* le fil
flight le vol
flip flops les tongs
flippers les palmes
flood l'inondation *(f)*
flash flood la crue subite
floor *(of room)* le sol
(storey) l'étage
(on the) ground floor (au) rez-de-chaussée
(on the) first floor (au) premier étage
(on the) second floor (au) deuxième étage
which floor? quel étage?
floorcloth la serpillère
floppy disk la disquette
florist's shop le magasin de fleurs
flour la farine
flower la fleur
flu la grippe
fly la mouche
to fly *(person)* aller en avion
(bird) voler
fly sheet le double toit
fog le brouillard
foggy: *it was foggy* il y avait du brouillard
foil le papier alu(minium)
to fold plier

to **follow** suivre
food la nourriture
food poisoning l'intoxication alimentaire *(f)*
foot le pied
  to go on foot aller à pied
football le football
football match le match de football
football pitch le terrain de football
football player le/la joueur(-euse) de football
footpath le sentier
for pour
  for me/you/us pour moi/vous/nous
  for him/her pour lui/elle
forbidden interdit(e)
forehead le front
foreign étranger(-ère)
foreign currency les devises étrangères
foreigner l'étranger(ère) *(m(f))*
forest la forêt
forever toujours
to **forget** oublier
fork *(for eating)* la fourchette
  (in road) l'embranchement *(m)*
form *(document)* le formulaire
  (shape, style) la forme
fortnight la quinzaine
forward en avant
foul *(football)* la faute
fountain la fontaine
four-wheel drive vehicle le quatre-quatre ; le 4 x 4
fox le renard
fracture la fracture
fragile fragile
fragrance le parfum
frame *(picture)* le cadre
France la France
  in/to France en France
free *(not occupied)* libre
  (costing nothing) gratuit(e)
free-range élevé(e) en plein air
freezer le congélateur
French français(e)
  (language) le français
French fries les frites
French people les Français
frequent fréquent(e)
fresh frais (fraîche)
fresh water *(not salt)* l'eau douce *(f)*
Friday vendredi
fridge le frigo
fried frit(e)
friend *m/f* l'ami(e)

frog la grenouille
frogs' legs les cuisses de grenouille
from de
  I'm from England je suis anglais(e)
  I'm from Scotland je suis écossais(e)
front le devant
  in front of... devant...
front door la porte d'entrée
frost le gel
frozen gelé(e)
  (food) surgelé(e)
fruit le fruit
  dried fruit les fruits secs
fruit juice le jus de fruit
fruit salad la salade de fruits
to **fry** frire
frying-pan la poêle
fuel le combustible
fuel gauge l'indicateur de niveau d'essence
fuel pump la pompe d'alimentation
fuel tank le réservoir d'essence
full plein(e)
  (occupied) complet(-ète)
full board la pension complète
fumes *(exhaust)* les gaz d'échappement
fun: to have fun s'amuser
funeral les obsèques
funfair la fête foraine
funny *(amusing)* amusant(e)
fur la fourrure
furnished meublé(e)
furniture les meubles
fuse le fusible
fuse box la boîte à fusibles
future l'avenir *(m)*

G

gallery la galerie
game le jeu
  (meat) le gibier
garage *(for petrol)* la station-service
  (for parking, repair) le garage
garden le jardin
garlic l'ail *(m)*
gas le gaz
gas cooker la gazinière
gas cylinder la bouteille de gaz
gastritis la gastrite
gate la porte
gay *(person)* homo
gear la vitesse
  in first gear en première
  in second gear en seconde
gearbox la boîte de vitesses

gear cable le câble d'embrayage
generous généreux(-euse)
gents (toilet) les toilettes pour hommes
genuine authentique
German allemand(e)
(language) l'allemand (m)
German measles la rubéole
Germany l'Allemagne (f)
to get (obtain) obtenir
(to fetch) aller chercher
to get in (vehicle) monter
to get off (bus, etc) descendre
gift le cadeau
gift shop la boutique de souvenirs
girl la fille
girlfriend la copine
to give donner
to give back rendre
glacier le glacier
glass le verre
a glass of water un verre d'eau
glasses (spectacles) les lunettes
glasses case l'étui à lunettes (m)
gloves les gants
glue la colle
gluten le gluten
GM-free sans OGM
to go aller
I'm going to... je vais ...
we're going to hire a car nous allons
louer une voiture
to go back retourner
to go in entrer
to go out (leave) sortir
goat la chèvre
God Dieu (m)
goggles (for swimming) les lunettes
de natation
gold l'or
is it gold? c'est en or?
golf le golf
golf ball la balle de golf
golf clubs les clubs de golf
golf course le terrain de golf
good bon (bonne)
(that's) good! (c'est) bien!
good afternoon bonjour
goodbye au revoir
good day bonjour
good evening bonsoir
good morning bonjour
good night bonne nuit
goose l'oie (f)

GPS (global positioning system) le systéme
de navigation GPS
gram le gramme
grandchildren les petits-enfants
granddaughter la petite-fille
grandfather le grand-père
grandmother la grand-mère
grandparents les grands-parents
grandson le petit-fils
grapes le raisin
grass l'herbe (f)
grated (cheese) râpé(e)
grater la râpe
greasy gras (grasse)
great (big) grand(e)
(wonderful) formidable
Great Britain la Grande-Bretagne
green vert(e)
green card (insurance) la carte verte
greengrocer's le magasin de fruits
et légumes
greetings card la carte de vœux
grey gris(e)
grill (part of cooker) le gril
grilled grillé(e)
grocer's l'épicerie (f)
ground la terre ; le sol
ground floor le rez-de-chaussée
on the ground floor au rez-de-
chaussée
groundsheet le tapis de sol
group le groupe
guarantee la garantie
guard (on train) le chef de train
guava la goyave
guest m/f (house guest) l'invité(e)
(in hotel) le/la client(e)
guesthouse la pension
guide (tourist guide) le/la guide
guidebook le guide
guided tour la visite guidée
guitar la guitare
gun (rifle) le fusil
(pistol) le pistolet
gym (gymnasium) le gymnase
gym shoes les chaussures de sport
gynaecologist le/la gynécologue

H

haemorrhoids les hémorroïdes
hail la grêle
hair les cheveux
hairbrush la brosse à cheveux
haircut la coupe (de cheveux)

hairdresser le/la coiffeur(-euse)
hairdryer le sèche-cheveux
hair dye la teinture pour les cheveux
hair gel le gel pour cheveux
hairgrip la pince à cheveux
hair mousse la mousse coiffante
hair spray la laque
half la moitié
  half an hour une demi-heure
half board la demi-pension
half fare le demi-tarif
half-price à moitié prix
ham (cooked) le jambon
  (cured) le jambon cru
hamburger le hamburger
hammer le marteau
hand la main
handbag le sac à main
hand luggage les bagages à main
hand-made fait main
handicapped handicapé(e)
handkerchief le mouchoir
handle la poignée
handlebars le guidon
hands-free kit (for phone) le kit mains-
  libres
handsome beau (belle)
hanger (coathanger) le cintre
hangover la gueule de bois
to hang up (telephone) raccrocher
hang-gliding le deltaplane
  to go hang-gliding faire du deltaplane
to happen arriver ; se passer
  what happened? qu'est-ce qui s'est
  passé?
happy heureux(-euse)
  happy birthday! bon anniversaire!
harbour le port
hard (not soft) dur(e)
  (not easy) difficile
hard disk le disque dur
hardware shop la quincaillerie
to harm someone faire du mal à
  quelqu'un
harvest (grape) les vendanges
hat le chapeau
to have avoir
to have to devoir
hay fever le rhume des foins
he il
head la tête
headache le mal de tête
  I have a headache j'ai mal à la tête
headlights les phares

headphones les écouteurs
head waiter le maître d'hôtel
health la santé
health food shop la boutique de
  produits diététiques
healthy sain(e)
to hear entendre
hearing aid la prothèse auditive
heart le cœur
heart attack la crise cardiaque
heartburn les brûlures d'estomac
heater l'appareil de chauffage (m)
heating le chauffage
to heat up faire chauffer
heavy lourd(e)
heel le talon
heel bar le talon-minute
height la hauteur
helicopter l'hélicoptère (m)
hello bonjour!
  (on telephone) allô?
helmet le casque
help! au secours!
to help aider
  can you help me? vous pouvez m'aider?
hem l'ourlet (m)
hepatitis l'hépatite (f)
her son/sa/ses
  her passport son passeport
  her room sa chambre
  her suitcases ses valises
herb l'herbe (f)
herbal tea la tisane
here ici
  here is... voici...
hernia la hernie
hi! salut!
to hide (something) cacher
  (oneself) se cacher
high haut(e)
high blood pressure la tension
high chair la chaise de bébé
high tide la marée haute
hill la colline
hill-walking la randonnée (de basse
  montagne)
him il ; lui
hip la hanche
hip replacement la pose d'une prothèse
  de la hanche
hire la location
  car hire la location de voitures
  bike hire la location de bicyclettes
  boat hire la location de bateaux
  ski hire la location de skis

to hire louer
hired car la voiture de location
his son/sa/ses
  his passport son passeport
  his room sa chambre
  his suitcases ses valises
historic historique
history l'histoire (f)
to hit frapper
to hitchhike faire du stop
HIV le VIH
hobby le passe-temps
to hold tenir
  (contain) contenir
hold-up *(in traffic)* l'embouteillage (m)
hole le trou
holiday les vacances
  on holiday en vacances
home la maison
  at my/your/our home chez
  moi/vous/nous
homeopathic *(remedy etc)*
  homéopathique
homeopathy l'homéopathie (f)
homesick: to be homesick avoir le
  mal du pays
  I'm homesick j'ai le mal du pays
homosexual homosexuel(le)
honest honnête
honey le miel
honeymoon la lune de miel
hood *(of car)* le capot
hook *(fishing)* l'hameçon (m)
to hope espérer
  I hope so/not j'espère que oui/non
horn *(of car)* le klaxon
hors d'œuvre le hors-d'œuvre
horse le cheval
horse racing les courses de chevaux
horse-riding: to go horse-riding
  faire du cheval
hosepipe le tuyau d'arrosage
hospital l'hôpital (m)
hostel *(youth hostel)* l'auberge de
  jeunesse (f)
hot chaud(e)
  I'm hot j'ai chaud
  it's hot (weather) il fait chaud
hot-water bottle la bouillotte
hotel l'hôtel (m)
hour l'heure (f)
  half an hour une demi-heure
  1 hour une heure
  2 hours deux heures
house la maison
househusband l'homme au foyer (m)

housewife la femme au foyer
house wine le vin en pichet
housework: to do the housework
  faire le ménage
hovercraft l'aéroglisseur (m)
how? *(in what way)* comment?
  how much/many? combien?
  how are you? comment allez-vous?
hungry: to be hungry avoir faim
  I'm hungry j'ai faim
to hunt chasser
hunting permit le permis de chasse
hurry: I'm in a hurry je suis pressé
to hurt: to hurt somebody faire du
  mal à quelqu'un
  that hurts ça fait mal
husband le mari
hut *(bathing/beach)* la cabine
  (mountain) le refuge
hydrofoil l'hydrofoil (m)
hypodermic needle l'aiguille
  hypodermique (f)

I

I je
ice la glace
  (cube) le glaçon
  with/without ice avec/sans glaçons
ice cream la glace
ice lolly l'esquimau (m)
ice rink la patinoire
to ice skate faire du patin (à glace)
ice skates les patins (à glace)
idea l'idée (f)
identity card la carte d'identité
if si
ignition l'allumage (m)
ignition key la clé de contact
ill malade
illness la maladie
immediately immédiatement
immersion heater le chauffe-eau
  électrique
immigration l'immigration (f)
immobilizer *(on car)* l'antivol (m)
immunisation l'immunisation (f)
to import importer
important important(e)
impossible impossible
to improve améliorer
in dans
  in 2 hours' time dans deux heures
  in France en France
  in Canada au Canada
  in London à Londres

in front of devant
included compris(e)
inconvenient gênant
to increase augmenter
indicator (car) le clignotant
indigestion l'indigestion (f)
indigestion tablets les comprimés pour les troubles digestifs
indoors à l'intérieur
infection l'infection (f)
infectious infectieux(-euse)
information les renseignements
information desk les renseignements
information office le bureau de renseignements
ingredients les ingrédients
inhaler l'inhalateur (m)
injection la piqûre
to injure blesser
injured blessé(e)
injury la blessure
inn l'auberge (f)
inner tube la chambre à air
inquiries les renseignements
inquiry desk le bureau de renseignements
insect l'insecte (m)
insect bite la piqûre (d'insecte)
insect repellent le produit antimoustiques
inside à l'intérieur
instant coffee le café instantané
instead of au lieu de
instructor le moniteur/la monitrice
insulin l'insuline (f)
insurance l'assurance (f)
insurance certificate l'attestation d'assurance (f)
to insure assurer
insured assuré(e)
to intend to avoir l'intention de
interesting intéressant(e)
international international(e)
internet l'internet (m)
   internet café le cybercafé
internet access l'accès internet (m)
   do you have internet access? avez-vous l'accès internet?
interpreter l'interprète (m/f)
interval (theatre) l'entracte (m)
interview l'entrevue (f)
   (TV, etc) l'interview (f)
into dans ; en
   into town en ville

to introduce présenter
invitation l'invitation (f)
to invite inviter
invoice la facture
iPod® l'iPod (m)
Ireland l'Irlande (f)
Irish irlandais(e)
iron (for clothes) le fer à repasser
   (metal) le fer
to iron repasser
ironing board la planche à repasser
ironmonger's la quincaillerie
is est
island l'île (f)
it il ; elle
Italian italien(ne)
Italy l'Italie (f)
to itch démanger
   it itches ça me démange
item l'article (m)
itemized bill la facture détaillée
IUD le stérilet

J

jack (for car) le cric
jacket la veste
   waterproof jacket l'anorak (m)
jam (food) la confiture
jammed (stuck) coincé(e)
January janvier
jar (honey, jam, etc) le pot
jaundice la jaunisse
jaw la mâchoire
jealous jaloux(-ouse)
jeans le jean
jellyfish la méduse
jet ski le jet-ski
jetty (landing pier) l'embarcadère (m)
Jew le Juif/la Juive
jeweller's la bijouterie
jewellery les bijoux
Jewish juif (juive)
job le travail ; l'emploi
to jog faire du jogging
to join (become member) s'inscrire
to join in participer
joint (body) l'articulation (f)
to joke plaisanter
joke la plaisanterie
journalist le/la journaliste
journey le voyage
judge le juge
jug le pichet
juice le jus

fruit juice le jus de fruit
orange juice le jus d'orange
a carton of juice un brick de jus
July juillet
to jump sauter
jumper le pull
jump leads les câbles de raccordement pour batterie
junction (road) le croisement ; le carrefour
June juin
just: *just two* deux seulement
  I've just arrived je viens d'arriver

K

to keep (retain) garder
kennel la niche
kettle la bouilloire
key la clé
  the car key la clé de la voiture
keyboard le clavier
keycard (electronic key) la carte-clé électronique
keyring le porte-clés
to kick donner un coup de pied à
kid (child) le gosse
kidneys (in body) les reins
kill tuer
kilo(gram) le kilo
kilometre le kilomètre
kind (person) gentil(-ille)
kind (sort) la sorte
kiosk (newsstand) le kiosque
  (phone box) la cabine
kiss le baiser
to kiss embrasser
kitchen la cuisine
kitchen paper l'essuie-tout (m)
kite (toy) le cerf-volant
kiwi fruit le kiwi
knee le genou
knickers la culotte
knife le couteau
to knit tricoter
to knock (on door) frapper
to knock down (in car) renverser
to knock over (vase, glass, etc) faire tomber
knot le nœud
to know (be aware of) savoir
  (person, place) connaître
  I don't know je ne sais pas
  I don't know Paris je ne connais pas Paris
to know how to do sth savoir faire quelque chose

to know how to swim savoir nager
kosher kascher

L

label l'étiquette (f)
lace la dentelle
laces (for shoes) les lacets
ladder l'échelle (f)
ladies (toilet) les toilettes pour dames
lady la dame
lager la bière
  bottled lager la bière en bouteille
  draught lager la bière pression
lake le lac
lamb l'agneau (m)
lamp la lampe
lamppost le réverbère
lampshade l'abat-jour (m)
to land atterrir
land la terre
landlady la propriétaire
landlord le propriétaire
landslide le glissement de terrain
lane la ruelle
  (of motorway) la voie
language la langue
language school l'école de langues (f)
laptop le portable
laptop bag la sacoche d'ordinateur portable
large grand(e)
last dernier(-ière)
  last month le mois dernier
  last night (evening/night-time) hier soir ; la nuit dernière
  last time la dernière fois
  last week la semaine dernière
  last year l'année dernière
  the last bus le dernier bus
  the last train le dernier train
late tard
  the train is late le train a du retard
  sorry we are late excusez-nous d'arriver en retard
later plus tard
to laugh rire
launderette la laverie automatique
laundry service le service de blanchisserie
lavatory les toilettes
lavender la lavande
law la loi
lawn la pelouse
lawyer m/f l'avocat(e)
laxative le laxatif

layby l'aire de stationnement (f)
lead (electric) le fil
lead (metal) le plomb
lead-free petrol l'essence sans plomb (f)
leaf la feuille
leak la fuite
to leak: it's leaking il y a une fuite
to learn apprendre
learning disability: he/she has a learning disability il a des difficultés d'apprentissage
lease (rental) le bail
leather le cuir
to leave (depart for) partir
   (depart from) quitter
   (to leave behind) laisser
   to leave for Paris partir pour Paris
   to leave London quitter Londres
left: on/to the left à gauche
left-handed (person) gaucher(-ère)
left-luggage (office) la consigne
left-luggage locker la consigne automatique
leg la jambe
legal légal(e)
leisure centre le centre de loisirs
lemon le citron
lemongrass la citronnelle
lemonade la limonade
to lend prêter
length la longueur
lens (of camera, etc) l'objectif (m)
   (contact lens) la lentille
lesbian la lesbienne
less moins
   less than moins de
lesson la leçon
to let (allow) permettre
   (to hire out) louer
letter la lettre
letterbox la boîte aux lettres
lettuce la laitue
level crossing le passage à niveau
library la bibliothèque
licence le permis
lid le couvercle
to lie down s'allonger
life belt la bouée de sauvetage
lifeboat le canot de sauvetage
lifeguard le maître nageur
life insurance l'assurance-vie (f)
life jacket le gilet de sauvetage
life raft le radeau de sauvetage
lift (elevator) l'ascenseur (m)

lift pass (on ski slopes) le forfait
light (not heavy) léger(-ère)
light la lumière
   have you got a light? avez-vous du feu?
light bulb l'ampoule (f)
lighter le briquet
lighthouse le phare
lightning les éclairs
like (preposition) comme
   like this comme ça
to like aimer
   I like coffee j'aime le café
   I don't like coffee je n'aime pas le café
   I'd like... je voudrais...
   we'd like... nous voudrions...
lilo® le matelas pneumatique
lime (fruit) le citron vert
line (mark) la ligne
   (row) la file
   (telephone) la ligne
linen le lin
lingerie la lingerie
lip la lèvre
lip-reading lire sur les lèvres
lip salve le baume pour les lèvres
lipstick le rouge à lèvres
liqueur la liqueur
list la liste
to listen to écouter
litre le litre
litter (rubbish) les ordures
little petit(e)
   a little... un peu de...
to live (in a place) vivre ; habiter
   I live in London j'habite à Londres
   he lives in a flat il habite dans un appartement
liver le foie
living room le salon
loaf le pain
local local(e)
lock la serrure
   the lock is broken la serrure est cassée
to lock fermer à clé
locker (for luggage) le casier
locksmith le serrurier
log (for fire) la bûche
logbook (of car) la carte grise
lollipop la sucette
London Londres
   to/in London à Londres
long long(ue)
   for a long time longtemps

long-sighted hypermétrope
to look after garder
to look at regarder
to look for chercher
loose *(not fastened)* desserré(e)
  it's come loose *(unscrewed)* ça s'est desserré
  (detached) ça s'est détaché
lorry le camion
to lose perdre
lost *(object)* perdu(e)
  I've lost… j'ai perdu…
  I'm lost je suis perdu(e)
lost property office le bureau des objets trouvés
lot: a lot of beaucoup de
lotion la lotion
lottery le loto
loud fort(e)
loudspeaker le haut-parleur
lounge *(in hotel, airport)* le salon
love l'amour
to love *(person)* aimer
  I love you je t'aime
  (food, activity, etc) adorer
  I love swimming j'adore nager
lovely beau (belle)
low bas (basse)
low-alcohol peu alcoolisé(e)
to lower baisser
low-fat allégé(e)
low tide la marée basse
luck la chance
lucky chanceux(-euse)
luggage les bagages
luggage allowance le poids maximum autorisé
luggage rack le porte-bagages
luggage tag l'étiquette à bagages *(f)*
luggage trolley le chariot (à bagages)
lump *(swelling)* la bosse
lunch le déjeuner
lunchbreak la pause de midi
lung le poumon
luxury le luxe

M

machine la machine
mad fou (folle)
magazine la revue
maggot l'asticot *(m)*
magnet l'aimant *(m)*
magnifying glass la loupe
maid la domestique

maiden name le nom de jeune fille
mail le courrier
  by mail par la poste
main principal(e)
mains *(electricity, water)* le secteur
main course *(of meal)* le plat principal
main road la route principale
to make faire
make-up le maquillage
male *(person)* masculin
mallet le maillet
man l'homme *(m)*
to manage *(to be in charge of)* gérer
manager le/la directeur(-trice)
mango la mangue
manicure la manicure
manual *(car)* manuel(le)
many beaucoup de
map la carte
  road map la carte routière
  street map le plan de la ville
March mars
margarine la margarine
marina la marina
mark *(stain)* la tache
market le marché
  where is the market? où est le marché?
  when is the market? le marché, c'est quel jour?
market place le marché
marmalade la marmelade d'oranges
married marié(e)
  I'm married je suis marié(e)
  are you married? vous êtes marié(e)?
marsh le marais
mascara le mascara
mass *(in church)* la messe
massage le massage
mast le mât
masterpiece le chef-d'œuvre
match *(game)* la partie
matches les allumettes
material *(cloth)* le tissu
to matter: it doesn't matter ça ne fait rien
  what's the matter? qu'est-ce qu'il y a?
mattress le matelas
May mai
mayonnaise la mayonnaise
mayor le maire
maximum le maximum
Mb *(megabyte)* Mo
me moi
meal le repas

to **mean** vouloir dire
  what does this mean? qu'est-ce que
  ça veut dire?
measles la rougeole
to **measure** mesurer
meat la viande
mechanic le mécanicien
medical insurance l'assurance maladie (f)
medical treatment les soins médicaux
medicine le médicament
Mediterranean Sea la Méditerranée
medium rare (meat) à point
to **meet** rencontrer
meeting la réunion
meeting point le point de rencontre
megabyte le mégaoctet
  128 megabytes 128 mégaoctets
to **melt** fondre
member (of club, etc) le membre
membership card la carte de membre
memory la mémoire
memory stick (for camera etc) le stick
  mémoire
men les hommes
to **mend** réparer
meningitis la méningite
menu (choices) le menu
  (card) la carte
message le message
metal le métal
meter le compteur
metre le mètre
metro le métro
metro station la station de métro
micro-brewery la mini-brasserie
microphone le micro(phone)
microwave oven le four à micro-ondes
midday midi
  at midday à midi
middle le milieu
middle-aged d'un certain âge
midge le moucheron
midnight minuit
  at midnight à minuit
migraine la migraine
  I have a migraine j'ai la migraine
mild (weather, cheese) doux (douce)
  (curry) peu épicé(e)
  (tobacco) léger(-ère)
milk le lait
  baby milk (formula) le lait maternisé
  fresh milk le lait frais
  full cream milk le lait entier
  hot milk le lait chaud
  long-life milk le lait longue conservation

powdered milk le lait en poudre
semi-skimmed milk le lait demi-écrémé
skimmed milk le lait écrémé
soya milk le lait de soja
UHT milk le lait UHT
with/without milk avec/sans lait
milkshake le milk-shake
millimetre le millimètre
mince (meat) la viande hachée
to **mind: do you mind if I...?** ça vous
  gêne si je...?
  I don't mind ça m'est égal
  do you mind? vous permettez?
mineral water l'eau minérale (f)
minibar le minibar
minidisk le minidisque
minimum le minimum
minister (church) le pasteur
minor road la route secondaire
mint (herb) la menthe
  (sweet) le bonbon à la menthe
minute la minute
mirror le miroir
  (in car) le rétroviseur
miscarriage la fausse couche
to **miss** (train, flight, etc) rater
Miss Mademoiselle
missing (disappeared) disparu(e)
mistake l'erreur (f)
misty brumeux(-euse)
misunderstanding le malentendu
to **mix** mélanger
mobile (phone) le mobile/le portable
mobile number le numéro de
  mobile/de portable
modem le modem
modern moderne
moisturizer la crème hydratante
mole (on skin) le grain de beauté
moment: at the moment en ce
  moment
monastery le monastère
Monday lundi
money l'argent (m)
  I have no money je n'ai pas d'argent
moneybelt la ceinture porte-monnaie
money order le mandat
month le mois
  this month ce mois-ci
  last month le mois dernier
  next month le mois prochain
monthly mensuel(-elle)
monument le monument
moon la lune
mooring (place) le mouillage

mop *(for floor)* le balai à franges
moped le vélomoteur
more encore
  more wine plus de vin
more than plus de
  more than 3 plus de trois
morning le matin
  in the morning le matin
  this morning ce matin
  tomorrow morning demain matin
morning-after pill la pilule du
  lendemain
mosque la mosquée
mosquito le moustique
mosquito bite la piqûre de moustique
mosquito coil la spirale anti-moustiques
mosquito net la moustiquaire
mosquito repellent le produit
  antimoustiques
most (of the) la plupart (de)
moth *(clothes)* la mite
mother la mère
mother-in-law la belle-mère
motor le moteur
motorbike la moto
motorboat le bateau à moteur
motorway l'autoroute *(f)*
mountain la montagne
mountain bike le VTT (vélo tout-terrain)
mountain rescue le sauvetage en
  montagne
mountaineering l'alpinisme *(m)*
mouse *(animal, computer)* la souris
moustache la moustache
mouth la bouche
mouthwash le bain de bouche
to move bouger
  it's moving ça bouge
movie le film
MP3 player le lecteur de MP3
Mr Monsieur
Mrs Madame
Ms Madame
much beaucoup
  too much trop
muddy boueux(-euse)
mug: *I've been mugged* je me suis
  fait agresser
mugging l'agression *(f)*
mumps les oreillons
muscle le muscle
museum le musée
mushrooms les champignons
music la musique
musical *(show)* la comédie musicale

Muslim musulman(e)
mussels les moules
must devoir
  I/we must go il faut que j'y aille/
  que nous y allions
  you must be there il faut que vous
  y soyez
mustard la moutarde
my mon/ma/mes
  my passport mon passeport
  my room ma chambre
  my suitcases mes valises

N

nail *(metal)* le clou
  (finger) l'ongle *(m)*
nailbrush la brosse à ongles
nail clippers le coupe-ongles
nail file la lime à ongles
nail polish le vernis à ongles
nail polish remover le dissolvant
nail scissors les ciseaux à ongles
name le nom
  my name is... je m'appelle...
  what is your name? comment vous
  appelez-vous?
nanny le/la baby-sitter
napkin la serviette de table
nappy la couche
narrow étroit(e)
national national(e)
nationality la nationalité
national park le parc national
natural naturel(le)
nature reserve la réserve naturelle
nature trail le sentier de grande
  randonnée
navy blue bleu marine
near près de
  near the bank près de la banque
  is it near? c'est près d'ici?
necessary nécessaire
neck le cou
necklace le collier
nectarine le brugnon
to need (to) avoir besoin de
  I need... j'ai besoin de...
  we need... nous avons besoin de...
  I need to phone j'ai besoin de
  téléphoner
needle l'aiguille *(f)*
  a needle and thread du fil et une
  aiguille
negative *(photography)* le négatif
neighbour le/la voisin(e)
nephew le neveu

net le filet
   the Net le net ; l'internet *(m)*
never jamais
   I never drink wine je ne bois jamais de vin
new nouveau(-elle)
news *(TV, radio, etc)* les informations
newsagent's le magasin de journaux
newspaper le journal
news stand le kiosque
New Year le Nouvel An
   happy New Year! bonne année!
New Year's Eve la Saint-Sylvestre
New Zealand la Nouvelle-Zélande
next prochain(e)
   (after) ensuite
   the next train le prochain train
   next month le mois prochain
   next week la semaine prochaine
   next Monday lundi prochain
   next to à côté de
   we're going to Paris next ensuite nous allons à Paris
nice beau (belle)
   (enjoyable) bon (bonne)
   (person) sympathique
niece la nièce
night *(night-time)* la nuit
   (evening) le soir
   at night la nuit/le soir
   last night hier soir
   tomorrow night (evening) demain soir
   tonight ce soir
nightclub la boîte de nuit
nightdress la chemise de nuit
night porter le gardien de nuit
no non
   (without) sans
   no problem pas de problème
   no thanks non merci
   no ice sans glaçons
   no sugar sans sucre
nobody personne
noise le bruit
   it's very noisy il y a beaucoup de bruit
non-alcoholic sans alcool
none aucun(e)
non-smoker: *I'm a non-smoker* je ne fume pas
non-smoking *(seat, compartment)* non-fumeurs
north le nord
Northern Ireland l'Irlande du Nord *(f)*
North Sea la mer du Nord
nose le nez
not ne ... pas
   I am not... je ne suis pas...

note *(banknote)* le billet
   (letter) le mot
note pad le bloc-notes
nothing rien
   nothing else rien d'autre
notice *(warning)* l'avis *(m)*
   (sign) le panneau
notice board le panneau d'affichage
novel le roman
November novembre
now maintenant
nowhere nulle part
nuclear nucléaire
number *(quantity)* le nombre
   (of room, house) le numéro
   phone number le numéro de téléphone
numberplate *(of car)* la plaque d'immatriculation
nurse *m/f* l'infirmier/l'infirmière
nursery la garderie
nursery slope la piste pour débutants
nut *(to eat)* la noix
   (for bolt) l'écrou *(m)*

O

oar l'aviron *(m)* ; la rame
oats l'avoine *(f)*
to obtain obtenir
occupation *(work)* l'emploi *(m)*
ocean l'océan *(m)*
October octobre
odd *(strange)* bizarre
of de
   a glass of... un verre de...
   made of... en...
off *(light)* éteint(e)
   (rotten) mauvais(e) ; pourri(e)
office le bureau
often souvent
oil *(for car, food)* l'huile *(f)*
oil filter le filtre à huile
oil gauge la jauge de niveau d'huile
ointment la pommade
OK! *(agreed)* d'accord!
old vieux (vieille)
   how old are you? quel âge avez-vous?
   I'm... years old j'ai... ans
old-age pensioner le/la retraité(e)
olive l'olive *(f)*
olive oil l'huile d'olive *(f)*
on *(light)* allumé(e)
   (engine, etc) en marche
   on the table sur la table
   on time à l'heure

once une fois
 at once tout de suite
one-way (street) à sens unique
onion l'oignon (m)
only seulement
open ouvert(e)
to open ouvrir
opera l'opéra (m)
operation (surgical) l'opération (f)
operator (phone) le/la standardiste
opposite en face de
 opposite the bank en face de la
 banque
 quite the opposite bien au contraire
optician m/f l'opticien/l'opticienne
or ou
orange (fruit) l'orange
 (colour) orange
orange juice le jus d'orange
orchestra l'orchestre (m)
order (in restaurant) la commande
 out of order en panne
to order (in restaurant) commander
organic biologique
to organize organiser
ornament le bibelot
other autre
 have you any others? vous en avez
 d'autres?
our (sing) notre
 (plural) nos
 our room notre chambre
 our passports nos passeports
 our baggage nos bagages
out (light) éteint(e)
 he's/she's out il/elle est sorti(e)
outdoor (pool, etc) en plein air
outside dehors
oven le four
ovenproof dish le plat qui va au four
over (on top of) au-dessus de
to overbook faire du surbooking
to overcharge faire payer trop cher
overdone (food) trop cuit(e)
overdose la surdose
to overheat surchauffer
to overload surcharger
to oversleep se réveiller en retard
to overtake (in car) doubler ; dépasser
to owe devoir
 you owe me... vous me devez...
to own posséder
owner le/la propriétaire
oyster l'huître (f)

P

pace le pas
pacemaker le stimulateur (cardiaque)
to pack (luggage) faire les bagages
package le paquet
package tour le voyage organisé
packet le paquet
padded envelope l'enveloppe
 matelassée
paddling pool la pataugeoire
padlock le cadenas
page la page
paid payé(e)
 I've paid j'ai payé
pain la douleur
painful douloureux(-euse)
painkiller l'analgésique (m)
to paint peindre
painting (picture) le tableau
pair la paire
palace le palais
pale pâle
palmtop computer l'ordinateur
 de poche (m)
pan (saucepan) la casserole
 (frying pan) la poêle
pancake la crêpe
panniers (for bike) les sacoches
panties la culotte
pants (underwear) le slip
panty liner le protège-slip
paper le papier
paper hankies les mouchoirs en papier
paper napkins les serviettes en papier
paragliding le parapente
paralysed paralysé(e)
paramedic l'urgentiste (m/f)
parcel le colis
pardon? comment?
 I beg your pardon! pardon!
parents les parents
Paris Paris
park le parc
to park garer (la voiture)
parking disk le disque de
 stationnement
parking meter le parcmètre
parking ticket le p.-v.
part: *spare parts* les pièces de
 rechange
partner (business) m/f l'associé(e)
 (boy/girlfriend) le compagnon/
 la compagne
party (group) le groupe

(celebration) la fête ; la soirée
(political) le parti
pass (bus, train) la carte
(mountain) le col
passenger le passager/la passagère
passionfruit le fruit de la passion
passport le passeport
passport control le contrôle des passeports
pasta les pâtes
pastry la pâte
(cake) la pâtisserie
path le chemin
patient (in hospital) le/la patient(e)
pavement le trottoir
to pay payer
I'd like to pay je voudrais payer
where do I pay? où est-ce qu'il faut payer?
payment le paiement
payphone le téléphone public
PDA l'organiseur PDA (m)
peace (after war) la paix
peak rate le plein tarif
peanut allergy l'allergie aux cacahuètes (f)
pear la poire
peas les petits pois
pedal la pédale
pedalo le pédalo®
pedestrian le/la piéton(ne)
pedestrian crossing le passage clouté
to pee faire pipi
to peel (fruit) peler
peg (for clothes) la pince à linge
(for tent) le piquet
pen le stylo
pencil le crayon
penfriend le/la correspondant(e)
penicillin la pénicilline
penis le pénis
penknife le canif
pensioner le/la retraité(e)
people les gens
pepper (spice) le poivre
(vegetable) le poivron
per par
per day par jour
per hour à l'heure
per person par personne
per week par semaine
100 km per hour 100 km à l'heure
perfect parfait(e)
performance (show) le spectacle
perfume le parfum

perhaps peut-être
period (menstruation) les règles
perm la permanente
permit le permis
person la personne
personal organizer l'agenda (m)
personal stereo le baladeur
pet l'animal domestique (m)
pet food les aliments pour animaux
pet shop la boutique d'animaux
petrol l'essence (f)
4-star le super
unleaded l'essence sans plomb
petrol cap le bouchon de réservoir
petrol pump la pompe à essence
petrol station la station-service
petrol tank le réservoir
pharmacist le/la pharmacien(ne)
pharmacy la pharmacie
phone le téléphone
by phone par téléphone
to phone téléphoner
phonebook l'annuaire (m)
phonebox la cabine (téléphonique)
phone call l'appel (m)
phonecard la télécarte
photocopier la photocopieuse
photocopy la photocopie
to photocopy photocopier
photograph la photo
to take a photograph prendre une photo
phrase book le guide de conversation
piano le piano
to pick (choose) choisir
(pluck) cueillir
pickpocket le pickpocket
picnic le pique-nique
to have a picnic pique-niquer
picnic hamper le panier à pique-nique
picnic rug la couverture
picture (painting) le tableau
(photo) la photo
pie (savoury) la tourte
piece le morceau
pier la jetée
pig le cochon
pill la pilule
I'm on the pill je prends la pilule
pillow l'oreiller (m)
pillowcase la taie d'oreiller
pilot le pilote
pin l'épingle (f)
pink rose

pint: *a pint of...* un demi-litre de...
pipe *(for water, gas)* le tuyau
 (smoking) la pipe
pitch *(place for tent/caravan)*
 l'emplacement *(m)*
pity: *what a pity* quel dommage
pizza la pizza
place l'endroit *(m)*
place of birth le lieu de naissance
plain *(unflavoured)* ordinaire
plait la natte
to plan prévoir
plan *(map)* le plan
plane *(aircraft)* l'avion *(m)*
plant *(in garden)* la plante
plaster *(sticking plaster)* le sparadrap
 (for broken limb, on wall) le plâtre
plastic *(made of)* en plastique
plastic bag le sac en plastique
plate l'assiette *(f)*
platform *(railway)* le quai
 which platform? quel quai?
play *(at theatre)* la pièce
to play *(games)* jouer
play park l'aire de jeux *(f)*
playroom la salle de jeux
pleasant agréable
please s'il vous plaît
pleased content(e)
 pleased to meet you! enchanté(e)!
plenty of beaucoup de
pliers la pince
plug *(electrical)* la prise
 (for sink) la bonde
to plug in brancher
plum la prune
plumber le plombier
plumbing la tuyauterie
plunger *(to clear sink)* le débouchoir
 à ventouse
p.m. de l'après-midi
poached poché(e)
pocket la poche
points *(in car)* les vis platinées
poison le poison
poisonous vénéneux
police *(force)* la police
policeman le policier
 (police woman) la femme policier
police station le commissariat ;
 la gendarmerie
polish *(for shoes)* le cirage
pollen le pollen
polluted pollué(e)

pony le poney
pony-trekking la randonnée à cheval
pool *(swimming)* la piscine
pool attendant le/la surveillant(e)
 de baignade
poor pauvre
popcorn le pop-corn
pop socks les mi-bas
popular populaire
pork le porc
port *(seaport)* le port
 (wine) le porto
porter *(for luggage)* le porteur
portion la portion
Portugal le Portugal
possible possible
post *(letters)* le courrier
 by post par courrier
to post poster
postbox la boîte aux lettres
postcard la carte postale
postcode le code postal
poster l'affiche *(f)*
postman/woman le facteur/la factrice
post office la poste
to postpone remettre à plus tard
pot *(for cooking)* la casserole
potato la pomme de terre
 baked potato la pomme de terre
 cuite au four
 boiled potatoes les pommes vapeur
 fried potatoes les pommes de terres
 sautées
 mashed potatoes la purée
 roast potatoes les pommes de terre
 rôties
 potato salad la salade de pommes
 de terre
pothole le nid de poule
pottery la poterie
pound *(money)* la livre
to pour verser
powder la poudre
powdered milk le lait en poudre
power *(electricity)* le courant
power cut la coupure de courant
pram le landau
to pray prier
to prefer préférer
pregnant enceinte
 I'm pregnant je suis enceinte
to prepare préparer
to prescribe prescrire
prescription l'ordonnance *(f)*
present *(gift)* le cadeau

preservative le conservateur
president le président
pressure la pression
 tyre pressure la pression des pneus
pretty joli(e)
price le prix
price list le tarif
priest le prêtre
print *(photo)* la photo
printer l'imprimante *(f)*
prison la prison
private privé(e)
prize le prix
probably probablement
problem le problème
professor le professeur d'université
programme *(TV, etc)* l'émission *(f)*
prohibited interdit(e)
promise la promesse
to promise promettre
to pronounce prononcer
 how's it pronounced? comment
 ça se prononce?
Protestant protestant(e)
to provide fournir
public public(-ique)
public holiday le jour férié
pudding le dessert
to pull tirer
 to pull a muscle se faire une
 élongation
to pull over *(car)* s'arrêter
pullover le pull
pump la pompe
puncture la crevaison
puncture repair kit la boîte de rustines®
puppet la marionnette
puppet show le spectacle de
 marionnettes
purple violet(-ette)
purpose le but
 on purpose exprès
purse le porte-monnaie
to push pousser
pushchair la poussette
to put *(place)* mettre
pyjamas le pyjama
Pyrenees les Pyrénées

Q

quality la qualité
quantity la quantité
quarantine la quarantaine
to quarrel se disputer

quarter le quart
quay le quai
queen la reine
query la question
question la question
queue la queue
to queue faire la queue
quick rapide
quickly vite
quiet *(place)* tranquille
quilt la couette
quite *(rather)* assez
 (completely) complètement
 quite good pas mal
 it's quite expensive c'est assez cher
quiz le jeu-concours

R

rabbit le lapin
rabies la rage
race *(people)* la race
 (sport) la course
race course le champ de courses
racket la raquette
radiator le radiateur
radio la radio
railcard la carte d'abonnement
 (de chemin de fer)
railway le chemin de fer
railway station la gare
rain la pluie
to rain: *it's raining* il pleut
raincoat l'imperméable *(m)*
rake le râteau
rape le viol
to rape violer
raped: *to be raped* être violé(e)
rare *(uncommon)* rare
 (steak) saignant(e)
rash *(skin)* la rougeur
rat le rat
rate *(price)* le tarif
rate of exchange le taux de change
raw cru(e)
razor le rasoir
razor blades les lames de rasoir
to read lire
ready prêt(e)
real vrai(e)
to realize (that ...) se rendre compte
 (que ...)
rearview mirror le rétroviseur
receipt le reçu
receiver *(of phone)* le récepteur

reception *(desk)* la réception
receptionist le/la réceptionniste
to recharge *(battery, etc)* recharger
recipe la recette
to recognize reconnaître
to recommend recommander
to record enregistrer
to recover *(from illness)* se remettre
to recycle recycler
red rouge
to reduce réduire
reduction la réduction
to refer to parler de
refill la recharge
to refund rembourser
to refuse refuser
regarding concernant
region la région
register le registre
to register *(at hotel)* se présenter
registered *(letter)* recommandé(e)
registration form la fiche
to reimburse rembourser
relation *(family)* le/la parent(e)
relationship les rapports
to remain rester
remember se rappeler
  I don't remember je ne m'en
  rappelle pas
remote control la télécommande
removal firm les déménageurs
to remove enlever
rent le loyer
to rent louer
rental la location
repair la réparation
to repair réparer
to repeat répéter
to reply répondre
report *(of theft, etc)* la déclaration
to report *(theft, etc)* déclarer
request la demande
to request demander
to require avoir besoin de
to rescue sauver
reservation la réservation
to reserve réserver
reserved réservé(e)
resident *m/f* l'habitant(e)
resort *(seaside)* la station balnéaire
  ski resort la station de ski
rest *(relaxation)* le repos
  (remainder) le reste
to rest se reposer

restaurant le restaurant
restaurant car le wagon-restaurant
retired retraité(e)
to return *(to a place)* retourner
  (to return something) rendre
return ticket le billet aller-retour
to reverse faire marche arrière
to reverse the charges appeler en PCV
reverse-charge call l'appel en PCV *(m)*
reverse gear la marche arrière
rheumatism le rhumatisme
rib la côte
ribbon le ruban
rice le riz
rich *(person, food)* riche
to ride *(horse)* faire du cheval
right *(correct)* exact(e)
right la droite
  on/to the right à droite
right of way la priorité
ring *(on finger)* la bague
to ring *(bell)* sonner
  it's ringing *(phone)* ça sonne
  to ring sb *(phone)* téléphoner à
  quelqu'un
ring road le périphérique
ripe mûr(e)
river la rivière
Riviera *(French)* la Côte d'Azur
road la route
road map la carte routière
road sign le panneau
roadworks les travaux
roast rôti(e)
roll *(bread)* le petit pain
roller blades les rollers
romantic romantique
roof le toit
roof-rack la galerie
room *(in house)* la pièce
  (in hotel) la chambre
  (space) la place
  double room la chambre pour deux
  personnes
  family room la chambre pour une
  famille
  single room la chambre pour une
  personne
room number le numéro de chambre
room service le service des chambres
root la racine
rope la corde
rose la rose
rosé wine le rosé
rotten *(fruit, etc)* pourri(e)

rough: *rough sea* la mer agitée
round rond(e)
roundabout *(traffic)* le rond-point
route la route ; l'itinéraire *(m)*
row *(theatre, etc)* la rangée
rowing *(sport)* l'aviron *(m)*
rowing boat la barque
rubber *(material)* le caoutchouc
  (eraser) la gomme
rubber band l'élastique *(m)*
rubber gloves les gants en caoutchouc
rubbish les ordures
rubella la rubéole
rucksack le sac à dos
rug *(carpet)* le tapis
ruins les ruines
ruler *(for measuring)* la règle
to run courir
rush hour l'heure de pointe *(f)*
rusty rouillé(e)

S

sad triste
saddle la selle
safe *(for valuables)* le coffre-fort
safe sûr ; sans danger
  is it safe? ce n'est pas dangereux?
safety belt la ceinture de sécurité
safety pin l'épingle de sûreté *(f)*
sail la voile
sailboard la planche à voile
sailing *(sport)* la voile
sailing boat le voilier
saint le/la saint(e)
salad la salade
  green salad la salade verte
  mixed salad la salade composée
  potato salad la salade de pommes
  de terre
  tomato salad la salade de tomates
salad dressing la vinaigrette
salami le salami
salary le salaire
sale la vente
sales *(reductions)* les soldes
salesman/woman le vendeur/
  la vendeuse
sales rep le/la représentant(e)
salt le sel
salt water l'eau salée
salty salé(e)
same même
sample l'échantillon *(m)*
sand le sable

sandals les sandales
sandwich le sandwich
  toasted sandwich le croque-monsieur
sanitary towel la serviette hygiénique
satellite dish l'antenne parabolique *(f)*
satellite TV la télévision par satellite
satnav *(satellite navigation system, for car)*
  le système de navigation satellite
Saturday samedi
sauce la sauce
saucepan la casserole
saucer la soucoupe
sauna le sauna
sausage la saucisse
to save *(life)* sauver
  (money) épargner ; économiser
savoury salé(e)
saw la scie
to say dire
scales *(for weighing)* la balance
scarf *(headscarf)* le foulard
  (woollen) l'écharpe *(f)*
scenery le paysage
schedule le programme
school l'école *(f)*
  primary school l'école primaire
  secondary school (11-15) le collège
  (15-18) le lycée
scissors les ciseaux
score *(of match)* le score
to score *(goal, point)* marquer
Scot *m/f* l'Écossais(e)
Scotland l'Écosse *(f)*
Scottish écossais(e)
scouring pad le tampon à récurer
screen *(computer, TV)* l'écran *(m)*
screen wash le lave-glace
screw la vis
screwdriver le tournevis
  phillips screwdriver le tournevis
  cruciforme
scuba diving la plongée sous-marine
sculpture la sculpture
sea la mer
seafood les fruits de mer
seam *(of dress)* la couture
to search fouiller
seasickness le mal de mer
seaside le bord de la mer
  at the seaside au bord de la mer
season *(of year, holiday time)* la saison
  in season de saison
seasonal saisonnier
season ticket la carte d'abonnement

seat *(chair)* le siège
  (in train) la place
  (cinema, theatre) le fauteuil
seatbelt la ceinture de sécurité
second second(e)
second *(time)* la seconde
second class seconde classe
second-hand d'occasion
secretary le/la secrétaire
security check les contrôles de sécurité *(mpl)*
security guard le/la vigile
sedative le calmant
to see voir
to seize saisir
self-catering flat l'appartement indépendant (avec cuisine)
self-employed: *to be self employed* travailler à son compte
self-service le libre-service
to sell vendre
  do you sell...? vous vendez...?
sell-by date la date limite de vente
Sellotape® le Scotch®
to send envoyer
senior citizen la personne du troisième âge
sensible raisonnable
separated séparé(e)
separately: *to pay separately* payer séparément
September septembre
serious grave
to serve servir
service *(church)* l'office *(m)*
  (in restaurant, shop, etc) le service
  is service included? le service est compris?
service charge le service
service station la station-service
set menu le menu à prix fixe
settee le canapé
several plusieurs
to sew coudre
sex le sexe
shade l'ombre *(f)*
  in the shade à l'ombre
to shake *(bottle, etc)* agiter
shallow peu profond(e)
shampoo le shampooing
shampoo and set le shampooing et la mise en plis
to share partager
sharp *(razor, knife)* tranchant
to shave se raser

shaver le rasoir électrique
shaving cream la crème à raser
shawl le châle
she elle
sheep le mouton
sheet *(for bed)* le drap
shelf le rayon
shell *(seashell)* le coquillage
sheltered abrité(e)
to shine briller
shingles *(illness)* le zona
ship le navire
shirt la chemise
shock le choc
shock absorber l'amortisseur *(m)*
shoe la chaussure
shoelaces les lacets
shoe polish le cirage
shoeshop le magasin de chaussures
shop le magasin
to shop faire du shopping
shop assistant le vendeur/la vendeuse
shop window la vitrine
shopping centre le centre commercial
shore le rivage
short court(e)
shortage le manque
short circuit le court-circuit
short cut le raccourci
shortly bientôt
shorts le short
short-sighted myope
shoulder l'épaule *(f)*
to shout crier
show le spectacle
to show montrer
shower *(wash)* la douche
  to take a shower prendre une douche
shower cap le bonnet de douche
shower gel le gel douche
to shrink *(clothes)* rétrécir
shut *(closed)* fermé(e)
to shut fermer
shutter *(on window)* le volet
shuttle service la navette
sick *(ill)* malade
  I feel sick j'ai envie de vomir
side le côté
side dish la garniture
sidelight le feu de position
sidewalk le trottoir
sieve la passoire
sightseeing le tourisme
  to go sightseeing faire du tourisme

sightseeing tour l'excursion touristique *(f)*
sign *(notice)* le panneau
to sign signer
signature la signature
signpost le poteau indicateur
silk la soie
silver l'argent *(m)*
SIM card la carte SIM
similar (to) semblable (à)
since depuis
to sing chanter
single *(unmarried)* célibataire
  (bed, room) pour une personne
single ticket l'aller simple *(m)*
sink *(washbasin)* l'évier *(m)*
sir Monsieur
sister la sœur
sister-in-law la belle-sœur
to sit s'asseoir
  sit down! asseyez-vous!
site *(website)* le site internet
size *(clothes)* la taille
  (shoe) la pointure
skates *(ice)* les patins à glace
  (roller) les patins à roulettes
to skate *(on ice)* patiner
  (roller) faire du patin à roulettes
skateboard le skate-board
  to go skateboarding faire du skate-board
ski le ski
to ski faire du ski
ski boots les chaussures de ski
skid le dérapage
to skid déraper
skiing le ski
ski instructor le/la moniteur(-trice) de ski
ski jump *(place)* le tremplin de ski
ski lift le remonte-pente
ski pants le fuseau
ski pass le forfait
ski pole le bâton (de ski)
ski run la piste
ski suit la combinaison de ski
ski tow le remonte-pente
skilled adroit(e) ; qualifié(e)
skin la peau
skirt la jupe
sky le ciel
slate l'ardoise *(f)*
sledge la luge
to sleep dormir
sleeper *(couchette)* la couchette
  (carriage) la voiture-lit
  (train) le train-couchettes

to sleep in faire la grasse matinée
sleeping bag le sac de couchage
sleeping car la voiture-lit
sleeping pill le somnifère
slice *(bread, cake, etc)* la tranche
sliced bread le pain de mie en tranches
slide *(photograph)* la diapositive
to slip glisser
slippers les pantoufles
slow lent(e)
to slow down ralentir
slowly lentement
small petit(e)
  smaller than plus petit(e) que
smell l'odeur *(f)*
  a bad smell une mauvaise odeur
smile le sourire
to smile sourire
smoke la fumée
to smoke fumer
  I don't smoke je ne fume pas
  can I smoke? on peut fumer?
smoke alarm le détecteur de fumée
smoked fumé(e)
smokers *(sign)* fumeurs
smooth lisse
SMS message le message SMS
snack le casse-croûte
  to have a snack casser la croûte
snack bar le snack-bar
snail l'escargot *(m)*
snake le serpent
snake bite la morsure de serpent
to sneeze éternuer
snorkel le tuba
snow la neige
to snow: *it's snowing* il neige
snowboard le snowboard
snowboarding le surf des neiges
  to go snowboarding faire du
  snowboard
snow chains les chaînes
snowed up enneigé(e)
snow tyres les pneus cloutés
soap le savon
soap powder *(detergent)* la lessive
sober: *to be sober* ne pas avoir bu
socket *(for plug)* la prise de courant
socks les chaussettes
soda water l'eau de Seltz *(f)*
sofa le canapé
sofa bed le canapé-lit
soft doux (douce)
soft drink le soda

software le logiciel
soldier le soldat
sole *(shoe)* la semelle
soluble soluble
some de (du/de la/des)
someone quelqu'un
something quelque chose
sometimes quelquefois
son le fils
son-in-law le gendre
song la chanson
soon bientôt
  as soon as possible dès que possible
sore douloureux(-euse)
sore throat: *to have a sore throat*
  avoir mal à la gorge
sorry: *I'm sorry!* excusez-moi!
sort la sorte
  what sort? de quelle sorte?
soup le potage ; la soupe
sour aigre
soured cream la crème fermentée
south le sud
souvenir le souvenir
spa la station thermale
space la place
spade la pelle
Spain l'Espagne *(f)*
spam *(email)* le spam
Spanish espagnol(e)
spanner la clé plate
spare parts les pièces de rechange
spare room la chambre d'amis
spare tyre le pneu de rechange
spare wheel la roue de secours
sparkling *(wine)* mousseux(-euse)
  (water) gazeux(-euse)
spark plug la bougie
to speak parler
  do you speak English? vous parlez
  anglais?
speaker *(loudspeaker)* le haut-parleur
special spécial(e)
specialist *(medical)* le/la spécialiste
speciality la spécialité
speeding l'excès de vitesse *(m)*
  a speeding ticket un p.-v. pour excès
  de vitesse
speed limit la limitation de vitesse
  to exceed speed limit dépasser la
  vitesse permise
speedboat le hors-bord
speedometer le compteur
SPF *(sun protection factor)* l'indice UVA *(m)*

to spell: *how is it spelt?* comment
  ça s'écrit?
to spend *(money)* dépenser
  (time) passer
spice l'épice *(f)*
spicy épicé(e)
spider l'araignée *(f)*
to spill renverser
spine la colonne vertébrale
spin dryer le sèche-linge
spirits *(alcohol)* les spiritueux
splinter *(in finger)* l'écharde *(f)*
spoke *(of wheel)* le rayon
sponge l'éponge *(f)*
spoon la cuiller
sport le sport
sports centre le centre sportif
sports shop le magasin de sports
spot *(pimple)* le bouton
sprain l'entorse *(f)*
spring *(season)* le printemps
  (metal) le ressort
square *(in town)* la place
squeeze presser
squid le calmar
stadium le stade
stage la scène
staff le personnel
stain la tache
stained glass window le vitrail
stairs l'escalier *(m)*
stale *(bread)* rassis(e)
stalls *(in theatre)* l'orchestre *(m)*
stamp le timbre
to stand *(get up)* se lever
  (be standing) être debout
star l'étoile *(f)*
  (celebrity) la vedette
to start commencer
starter *(in meal)* le hors d'œuvre
  (in car) le démarreur
station la gare
stationer's la papeterie
statue la statue
stay le séjour
  enjoy your stay! bon séjour!
to stay *(remain)* rester
  (reside for while) loger
  I'm staying at... je loge à...
steak le bifteck
to steal voler
steam la vapeur
steamed cuit(e) à la vapeur
steel l'acier *(m)*

steep raide
steeple le clocher
steering wheel le volant
step le pas
stepdaughter la belle-fille
stepfather le beau-père
stepmother la belle-mère
stepson le beau-fils
stereo la chaîne (stéréo)
sterling la livre sterling
steward le steward
stewardess l'hôtesse (f)
sticking-plaster le sparadrap
still: *still water* l'eau plate (f)
still (yet) encore
sting la piqûre
to sting piquer
stitches (surgical) les points de suture
stockings les bas
stolen volé(e)
stomach l'estomac (m)
stomachache: *to have a stomach-ache*
avoir mal au ventre
stomach upset l'estomac dérangé
stone la pierre
to stop arrêter
store (shop) le magasin
storey l'étage (m)
storm l'orage (m)
story l'histoire (f)
straightaway tout de suite
straight on tout droit
strange bizarre
straw (for drinking) la paille
strawberries les fraises
stream le ruisseau
street la rue
street map le plan des rues
strength la force
stress le stress
strike (of workers) la grève
string la ficelle
striped rayé(e)
stroke (haemorrhage) l'attaque
d'apoplexie
to have a stroke avoir une attaque
strong fort(e)
stuck bloqué(e)
student (male) l'étudiant
(female) l'étudiante
student discount le tarif étudiant
stuffed farci(e)
stung piqué(e)
stupid stupide

subscription l'abonnement (m)
subtitles les sous-titres
subway le passage souterrain
suddenly soudain
suede le daim
sugar le sucre
sugar-free sans sucre
to suggest suggérer
suit (man's) le costume
(woman's) le tailleur
suitcase la valise
sum la somme
summer l'été (m)
summer holidays les vacances d'été
summit le sommet
sun le soleil
to sunbathe prendre un bain de soleil
sunblock l'écran total (m)
sunburn le coup de soleil
suncream la crème solaire
Sunday le dimanche
sunflower le tournesol
sunglasses les lunettes de soleil
sunny: *it's sunny* il fait beau
sunrise le lever du soleil
sunroof le toit ouvrant
sunscreen (lotion) l'écran solaire (m)
sunset le coucher de soleil
sunshade le parasol
sunstroke l'insolation (f)
suntan le bronzage
suntan lotion le lait solaire
supermarket le supermarché
supper (dinner) le souper
supplement le supplément
to supply fournir
to surf faire du surf
to surf the Net surfer sur Internet
surfboard la planche de surf
surfing le surf
surgery (operation) l'opération
chirurgicale (f)
surname le nom de famille
surprise la surprise
to survive survivre
to swallow avaler
to sweat transpirer
sweater le pull
sweatshirt le sweat-shirt
sweet sucré(e)
sweetener l'édulcorant (m)
sweets les bonbons
to swell (bump, eye, etc) enfler
to swim nager

swimming pool la piscine
swimsuit le maillot de bain
swing (for children) la balançoire
swipecard la carte magnétique
Swiss suisse
switch le bouton
to switch off éteindre
to switch on allumer
Switzerland la Suisse
swollen enflé(e)
synagogue la synagogue
syringe la seringue

T

table la table
tablecloth la nappe
table tennis le tennis de table
table wine le vin de table
tablet le comprimé
to take (something) prendre
to take away (something) emporter
to take off (clothes) enlever
talc le talc
to talk (to) parler (à)
tall grand(e)
tampons les tampons hygiéniques
tangerine la mandarine
tank (petrol) le réservoir
  (fish) l'aquarium (m)
tap le robinet
tap water l'eau du robinet (f)
tape le ruban
  (cassette) la cassette
  adhesive tape le Scotch®
  video tape la cassette vidéo
tape measure le mètre à ruban
tape recorder le magnétophone
tart la tarte
taste le goût
to taste goûter
  can I taste some? je peux goûter?
tax l'impôt (m)
taxi le taxi
taxi driver le chauffeur de taxi
taxi rank la station de taxis
tea le thé
  herbal tea la tisane
  lemon tea le thé au citron
  tea with milk le thé au lait
teabag le sachet de thé
teapot la théière
teaspoon la cuiller à café
tea towel le torchon
to teach enseigner

teacher le professeur
team l'équipe (f)
tear (in material) la déchirure
teat (on bottle) la tétine
teenager l'adolescent(e)
teeth les dents
telegram le télégramme
telephone le téléphone
to telephone téléphoner
telephone box la cabine téléphonique
telephone call le coup de téléphone
telephone card la télécarte
telephone directory l'annuaire (m)
telephone number le numéro de téléphone
television la télévision
to tell dire
temperature la température
  to have a temperature avoir de la fièvre
temporary temporaire
tenant le/la locataire
tendon le tendon
tennis le tennis
tennis ball la balle de tennis
tennis court le court de tennis
tennis racket la raquette de tennis
tent la tente
tent peg le piquet de tente
terminal (airport) l'aérogare (f)
terrace la terrasse
terracotta la terre cuite
to test (try out) tester
testicles les testicules
tetanus injection la piqûre antitétanique
to text envoyer un SMS à
  I'll text you je t'enverrai un SMS
than que
to thank remercier
thank you merci
  thank you very much merci beaucoup
that cela
  that one celui-là/celle-là
the le/la/l'/les
theatre le théâtre
theft le vol
their (sing) leur
  (plural) leurs
them eux
there là
there is/are... il y a...
thermometer le thermomètre
these ces

these ones ceux-ci/celles-ci
ey ils/elles
ick (not thin) épais(se)
ief le voleur/la voleuse
igh la cuisse
in (person) mince
ing la chose
my things mes affaires
think penser
irsty: I'm thirsty j'ai soif
is ceci
this one celui-ci/celle-ci
orn l'épine (f)
ose ces
those ones ceux-là/celles-là
read le fil
roat la gorge
roat lozenges les pastilles pour
a gorge
rough à travers
umb le pouce
under le tonnerre
understorm l'orage (m)
ursday jeudi
yme le thym
cket le billet ; le ticket
a single ticket un aller simple
a return ticket un aller-retour
book of tickets le carnet de tickets
cket inspector le contrôleur/la
contrôleuse
cket office le guichet
de la marée
low tide la marée basse
high tide la marée haute
dy bien rangé(e)
tidy up tout ranger
e la cravate
ght (fitting) serré(e)
ghts le collant
le (on roof) la tuile
(on wall, floor) le carreau
ll (cash desk) la caisse
ll (until) jusqu'à
till 2 o'clock jusqu'à deux heures
me le temps
(of day) l'heure (f)
this time cette fois
what time is it? quelle heure est-il?
mer le minuteur
metable l'horaire (m)
n (can) la boîte
nfoil le papier alu(minium)
n-opener l'ouvre-boîtes (m)
p (to waiter, etc) le pourboire

to tip (waiter, etc) donner un pourboire à
tipped (cigarette) à bout filtre
tired fatigué(e)
tissue (Kleenex®) le kleenex®
to à
(with name of country) en/au
to London à Londres
to the airport à l'aéroport
to France en France
to Canada au Canada
toadstool le champignon vénéneux
toast (to eat) le pain grillé ; le toast
tobacco le tabac
tobacconist's le bureau de tabac
today aujourd'hui
toddler le bambin
toe le doigt de pied
together ensemble
toilet les toilettes
toilet for disabled les toilettes pour
handicapés
toilet brush la balayette pour les WC
toilet paper le papier hygiénique
toiletries les articles de toilette
token le jeton
toll (motorway) le péage
tomato la tomate
tomato soup la soupe de tomates
tinned tomatoes les tomates en boîte
tomorrow demain
tomorrow morning demain matin
tomorrow afternoon demain après-
midi
tomorrow evening demain soir
tongue la langue
tonic water le tonic
tonight ce soir
tonsillitis l'angine (f)
too (also) aussi
it's too big c'est trop grand
it's too hot il fait trop chaud
it's too noisy il y a trop de bruit
toolkit la trousse à outils
tools les outils
tooth la dent
toothache le mal de dents
I have toothache j'ai mal aux dents
toothbrush la brosse à dents
toothpaste le dentifrice
toothpick le cure-dent
top: the top floor le dernier étage
top (of bottle) le bouchon
(of pen) le capuchon
(of pyjamas, bikini, etc) le haut
(of hill, mountain) le sommet
on top of sur

topless: *to go topless* enlever le haut
torch la lampe de poche
torn déchiré(e)
total *(amount)* le total
to touch toucher
tough *(meat)* dur(e)
tour l'excursion *(f)*
  guided tour la visite guidée
tour guide le/la guide
tour operator le tour-opérateur ;
  le voyagiste
tourist le/la touriste
tourist (information) office le syndicat
  d'initiative
tourist route l'itinéraire touristique *(m)*
tourist ticket le billet touristique
to tow remorquer
towbar *(on car)* le crochet d'attelage
tow rope le câble de remorquage
towel la serviette
tower la tour
town la ville
town centre le centre-ville
town hall la mairie
town plan le plan de la ville
toxic toxique
toy le jouet
toyshop le magasin de jouets
tracksuit le survêtement
traditional traditionnel(-elle)
traffic la circulation
traffic jam l'embouteillage *(m)*
traffic lights les feux
traffic warden le/la contractuel(le)
trailer la remorque
train le train
  by train par le train
  the next train le prochain train
  the first train le premier train
  the last train le dernier train
trainers les baskets
tram le tramway
tranquillizer le tranquillisant
to translate traduire
translation la traduction
to travel voyager
travel agent's l'agence de voyages *(f)*
travel guide le guide
travel insurance l'assurance voyage *(f)*
travel pass la carte de transport
travel sickness le mal des transports
traveller's cheques les chèques
  de voyage
tray le plateau

tree l'arbre *(m)*
trip l'excursion *(f)*
trolley le chariot
trouble les ennuis
  to be in trouble avoir des ennuis
trousers le pantalon
truck le camion
true vrai(e)
trunk *(luggage)* la malle
trunks *(swimming)* le maillot (de bain)
to try essayer
to try on *(clothes, shoes)* essayer
t-shirt le tee-shirt
Tuesday mardi
tumble dryer le sèche-linge
tunnel le tunnel
to turn tourner
  to turn round faire demi-tour
to turn off *(light, etc)* éteindre
  (to turn off engine) couper le moteur
to turn on *(light, etc)* allumer
  (engine) mettre en marche
turquoise *(colour)* turquoise
tweezers la pince à épiler
twice deux fois
twin-bedded room la chambre
  à deux lits
twins *(male)* les jumeaux
  (female) les jumelles
to type taper à la machine
typical typique
tyre le pneu
tyre pressure la pression des pneus

U

ugly laid(e)
ulcer l'ulcère *(m)*
  mouth ulcer l'aphte *(m)*
umbrella le parapluie
  (sunshade) le parasol
uncle l'oncle *(m)*
uncomfortable inconfortable
unconscious sans connaissance
under sous
undercooked pas assez cuit(e)
underground le métro
underpants *(man's)* le caleçon
underpass le passage souterrain
to understand comprendre
  I don't understand je ne comprends pas
  do you understand? vous comprenez?
underwear les sous-vêtements
to undress se déshabiller
unemployed au chômage

to unfasten *(clothes, etc)* défaire *(door)* ouvrir
United Kingdom le Royaume-Uni
United States les États-Unis
university l'université *(f)*
unkind pas gentil(-ille)
unleaded petrol l'essence sans plomb *(f)*
unlikely peu probable
to unlock ouvrir
to unpack *(suitcase)* défaire
unpleasant désagréable
to unplug débrancher
to unscrew dévisser
up: *to get up (out of bed)* se lever
upside down à l'envers
upstairs en haut
urgent urgent(e)
urine l'urine *(f)*
us nous
to use utiliser
useful utile
username le nom d'utilisateur
usual habituel(-elle)
usually d'habitude
U-turn le demi-tour

V

vacancy *(in hotel)* la chambre
vacant libre
vacation les vacances
vaccination le vaccin
vacuum cleaner l'aspirateur *(m)*
vagina le vagin
valid *(ticket, driving licence, etc)* valable
valley la vallée
valuable d'une grande valeur
valuables les objets de valeur
value la valeur
valve la soupape
van la camionnette
vase le vase
VAT la TVA
vegan végétalien(ne)
  I'm a vegan je suis végétalien(ne)
vegetables les légumes
vegetarian végétarien(ne)
  I'm vegetarian je suis végétarien(ne)
vehicle le véhicule
vein la veine
velvet le velours
vending machine le distributeur automatique
venereal disease la maladie vénérienne
ventilator le ventilateur

very très
vest le maillot de corps
vet le/la vétérinaire
via par
to video *(from TV)* enregistrer
video *(machine)* le magnétoscope *(cassette)* la (cassette) vidéo
video camera la caméra vidéo
video cassette la cassette vidéo
video game le jeu vidéo
video recorder le magnétoscope
video tape la cassette vidéo
view la vue
  a room with a sea view une chambre avec vue sur la mer
villa la maison de campagne
village le village
vinegar le vinaigre
vineyard le vignoble
viper la vipère
virus le virus
visa le visa
visit le séjour
to visit visiter
visiting hours les heures de visite
visitor le/la visiteur(-euse)
vitamin la vitamine
voice la voix
voicemail la messagerie vocale
volcano le volcan
volleyball le volley-ball
voltage le voltage
to vomit vomir
voucher le bon

W

wage le salaire
waist la taille
waistcoat le gilet
to wait for attendre
waiter le/la serveur(-euse)
waiting room la salle d'attente
waitress la serveuse
to wake up se réveiller
Wales le pays de Galles
walk la promenade
  to go for a walk faire une promenade
to walk aller à pied ; marcher
walking boots les chaussures de marche
walking stick la canne
Walkman® le walkman®
wall le mur
wallet le portefeuille

to want vouloir
I want... je veux...
we want... nous voulons...
war la guerre
ward (hospital) la salle
wardrobe l'armoire (f)
warehouse l'entrepôt (m)
warm chaud(e)
it's warm (weather) il fait bon
it's too warm il fait trop chaud
to warm up (milk, etc) faire chauffer
warning triangle le triangle de présignalisation
to wash laver
to wash oneself se laver
washbasin le lavabo
washing machine la machine à laver
washing powder la lessive
washing-up bowl la cuvette
washing-up liquid le produit pour la vaisselle
wasp la guêpe
wasp sting la piqûre de guêpe
waste bin la poubelle
watch la montre
to watch (look at) regarder
watchstrap le bracelet de montre
water l'eau (f)
bottled water l'eau en bouteille
cold water l'eau froide
drinking water (fit to drink) l'eau potable
hot water l'eau chaude
sparkling mineral water l'eau minérale gazeuse
still mineral water l'eau minérale plate
waterfall la cascade
water heater le chauffe-eau
watermelon la pastèque
waterproof imperméable
water-skiing le ski nautique
water sports les sports nautiques
waterwings les bracelets gonflables
waves (on sea) les vagues
waxing (hair removal) l'épilation à la cire (f)
way (manner) la manière
(route) le chemin
way in (entrance) l'entrée (f)
way out (exit) la sortie
we nous
weak faible
(coffee, etc) léger(-ère)
to wear porter
weather le temps
weather forecast la météo
web (internet) le Web

website le site web   .
wedding le mariage
wedding anniversary l'anniversaire de mariage (m)
wedding present le cadeau de mariage
Wednesday mercredi
week la semaine
last week la semaine dernière
next week la semaine prochaine
per week par semaine
this week cette semaine
weekday le jour de semaine
weekend le week-end
next weekend le week-end prochain
this weekend ce week-end
weekly par semaine ; hebdomadaire
(pass, ticket) valable pendant une semaine
to weigh peser
weight le poids
welcome! bienvenu(e)!
well (for water) le puits
well (healthy) en bonne santé
he's not well il est souffrant
I'm very well je vais très bien
well done (steak) bien cuit(e)
wellingtons les bottes en caoutchouc
Welsh gallois(e)
west l'ouest (m)
wet mouillé(e)
wetsuit la combinaison de plongée
what que ; quel/quelle ; quoi
what is it? qu'est-ce que c'est?
wheel la roue
wheelchair le fauteuil roulant
wheel clamp le sabot
when quand
(at what time?) à quelle heure?
when is it? c'est quand? ; à quelle heure?
where où
where is it? c'est où?
where is the hotel? où est l'hôtel?
which quel/quelle
which (one)? lequel/laquelle?
which (ones)? lesquels/lesquelles?
while pendant que
in a while bientôt ; tout à l'heure
white blanc (blanche)
who qui
who is it? qui c'est?
whole entier(-ière)
wholemeal bread le pain complet
whose: *whose is it?* c'est à qui?
why pourquoi
wide large

widow la veuve
widower le veuf
width la largeur
wife la femme
wig la perruque
to win gagner
wind le vent
windbreak *(camping, etc)* le pare-vent
windmill le moulin à vent
window la fenêtre
   (shop) la vitrine
windscreen le pare-brise
windscreen wipers les essuie-glaces
windsurfing la planche à voile
   to go windsurfing faire de la planche
   à voile
windy: *it's windy* il y a du vent
wine le vin
   dry wine le vin sec
   house wine le vin en pichet
   red wine le vin rouge
   rosé wine le rosé
   sparkling wine le vin mousseux
   sweet wine le vin doux
   white wine le vin blanc
wine list la carte des vins
wing *(bird, aircraft)* l'aile *(f)*
wing mirror le rétroviseur latéral
winter l'hiver *(m)*
wire le fil
wireless internet l'internet sans fil
with avec
   with ice avec des glaçons
   with milk/sugar avec du lait/sucre
without sans
   without ice sans glaçons
   without milk/sugar sans lait/sucre
witness le témoin
woman la femme
wonderful merveilleux(-euse)
wood le bois
wooden en bois
wool la laine
word le mot
work le travail
to work *(person)* travailler
   (machine, car) fonctionner ; marcher
   it doesn't work ça ne marche pas
work permit le permis de travail
world le monde
worried inquiet(-iète)

worse pire
worth: *it's worth...* ça vaut...
to wrap (up) emballer
wrapping paper le papier d'emballage
wrinkles les rides
wrist le poignet
to write écrire
   please write it down vous me
   l'écrivez, s'il vous plaît?
writing paper le papier à lettres
wrong faux (fausse)
wrought iron le fer forgé

X

X-ray la radiographie
to x-ray radiographier

Y

yacht le yacht
year l'an *(m)* ; l'année *(f)*
   this year cette année
   next year l'année prochaine
   last year l'année dernière
yearly annuel(le)
yellow jaune
Yellow Pages les pages jaunes
yes oui
   yes please oui, merci
yesterday hier
yet: *not yet* pas encore
yoghurt le yaourt
   plain yoghurt le yaourt nature
yolk le jaune d'œuf
you *(familiar)* tu
   (polite) vous
young jeune
your *(familiar sing)* ton/ta
   (familiar plural) tes
   (polite singular) votre
   (polite plural) vos
youth hostel l'auberge de jeunesse *(f)*

Z

zebra crossing le passage pour
   piétons
zero le zéro
zip la fermeture éclair
zone la zone
zoo le zoo
zoom lens le zoom

A

à to ; at
abbaye f abbey
abcès m abscess
abeille f bee
abîmer to damage
abonné(e) m/f subscriber ; season ticket holder
abonnement m subscription ; season ticket
abri m shelter
abrité(e) sheltered
accélérateur m accelerator
accepter to accept
accès m access
  accès aux trains to the trains
  accès aux quais to the trains
  accès interdit no entry
  accès internet internet access
  accès réservé authorized entry only
  avez-vous l'accès internet? do you have internet access?
accident m accident
accompagner to accompany
accord m agreement
accotement m verge
accueil m reception ; information
accueillir to greet ; to welcome
ACF m Automobile Club de France
achat m purchase
acheter to buy
acier m steel
acte de naissance m birth certificate
activité f activity
adaptateur m adaptor (electrical)
addition f bill
adhérent(e) m/f member
adolescent(e) m/f teenager
adresse f address
adresse électronique e-mail address
adresser to address
  adressez-vous à enquire at (office)
adroit(e) skilful
adulte m/f adult
aérogare f terminal
aéroglisseur m hovercraft
aéroport m airport
affaires fpl business ; belongings
  bonne affaire bargain
affiche f poster ; notice
affluence f crowd
affreux(-euse) awful
âge m age
  d'un certain âge middle-aged
  du troisième âge senior citizen

âgé(e) elderly
  âgé de ... ans aged ... years
agence f agency ; branch
  agence de voyages travel agency
  agence immobilière estate agent's
agenda m diary
  agenda électronique m personal organizer (electronic)
agent m agent
  agent de police police officer
agiter to shake
  agiter avant emploi shake before use
agneau m lamb
agrandissement m enlargement
agréable pleasant ; nice
agréé(e) registered ; authorized
agression f attack (mugging)
aider to help
aigre sour
aiguille f needle
ail m garlic
aimer to enjoy ; to love (person)
air: *en plein air* in the open air
aire: *aire de jeux* play area
  aire de repos rest area
  aire de service service area
  aire de stationnement layby
airelles fpl bilberries ; cranberries
alarme f alarm
alcool m alcohol ; fruit brandy
alcoolisé(e) alcoholic
alentours mpl surroundings
algues fpl seaweed
alimentation f food
allée f driveway ; path
allégé(e) low-fat
Allemagne f Germany
allemand(e) German
aller to go
aller (simple) m single ticket
aller-retour m return ticket
allergie f allergy
allô? hello? (on telephone)
allumage m ignition
allumé(e) on (light)
allume-feu m fire lighter
allumer to turn on ; to light
  allumez vos phares switch on headlights
allumette f match
alpinisme m mountaineering
alsacien(ne) Alsatian
ambassade f embassy
ambulance f ambulance
améliorer to improve

amende f fine
amer(-ère) bitter
américain(e) American
Amérique f America
ameublement m furniture
ami(e) m/f friend
  petit(e) ami(e) boyfriend/girlfriend
amortisseur m shock absorber
amour m love
  faire l'amour to make love
ampoule f blister ; light bulb
amusant(e) funny (amusing)
amuser to entertain
  (bien) s'amuser to enjoy oneself
an m year
  Nouvel An m New Year
analgésique m painkiller
ananas m pineapple
ancien(ne) old ; former
ancre f anchor
anesthésique m anaesthetic
ange m angel
angine f tonsillitis
  angine de poitrine angina
Anglais m Englishman
anglais m English (language)
anglais(e) English
Angleterre f England
animal m animal
  animal domestique pet
animations fpl entertainment ; activities
anis m aniseed
anisette f aniseed liqueur
année f year ; vintage
  bonne année! happy New Year!
anniversaire m anniversary ; birthday
annonce f advertisement
annuaire m directory
annulation f cancellation
annuler to cancel
antenne f aerial
  antenne parabolique f satellite dish
anti-insecte m insect repellent
antibiotique m antibiotic
antigel m antifreeze
antihistaminique m antihistamine
antimoustique m mosquito repellent
antiquaire m/f antique dealer
antiquités fpl antiques
antiseptique m antiseptic
antivol m bike lock ; immobilizer (on car)
août August
apéritif m apéritif
aphte m mouth ulcer

appareil m appliance ; camera
  appareil acoustique hearing aid
  appareil photo camera
appartement m apartment ; flat
appât m bait (for fishing)
appel m phone call
appeler to call (speak, phone)
  appeler en PCV to reverse the charges
appendicite f appendicitis
apporter to bring
apprendre to learn
  il a des difficultés d'apprentissage
  he/she has a learning disability
appuyer to press
après after
après-midi m afternoon
après-rasage m after-shave
après-shampooing m conditioner
aquarium m fish tank
arachide f groundnut
araignée f spider
arbre m tree
arête f fishbone
argent m money ; silver (metal)
  argent de poche pocket money
  argent liquide cash
argot m slang
armoire f wardrobe
arranger to arrange
arrêt m stop
  arrêt d'autobus bus stop
  arrêt facultatif request stop
arrêter to arrest ; to stop
  arrêter le moteur to turn off the engine
arrêtez! stop!
arrhes fpl deposit (part payment)
arrière m rear ; back
arrivées fpl arrivals
arriver to arrive ; to happen
arrobase @
arrondissement m district (in large city)
art m art
arthrite f arthritis
article m item ; article
  articles de toilette toiletries
articulation f joint (body)
artisan(e) m/f craftsman/woman
artisanat m arts and crafts
artiste m/f artist
ascenseur m lift
aspirateur m vacuum cleaner
aspirine f aspirin
assaisonnement m seasoning ; dressing
asseoir to sit (someone) down
  s'asseoir to sit down

assez enough ; quite *(rather)*
assiette f plate
associé(e) m/f partner *(business)*
assorti(e) assorted ; matching
assurance f insurance
assuré(e) insured
assurer to assure ; to insure
asthme m asthma
atelier m workshop ; artist's studio
attacher to fasten *(seatbelt)*
attaque f fit *(medical)*
  attaque (d'apoplexie) stroke
attendre to wait *(for)*
attention! look out!
  attention au feu danger of fire
  faire attention to be careful
atterrissage m landing *(aircraft)*
attestation f certificate
  l'attestation d'assurance green card
attrayant(e) attractive
au-delà de beyond
au-dessus de above ; on top of
au lieu de instead of
au revoir goodbye
au secours! help!
aube f dawn
auberge f inn
  auberge de jeunesse youth hostel
aubergine f aubergine
aucun(e) none ; no ; not any
audiophone m hearing aid
augmenter to increase
aujourd'hui today
aussi also
aussitôt immediately
  aussitôt que possible as soon
  as possible
Australie f Australia
australien(ne) Australian
autel m altar
auteur m author
auto-école f driving school
auto-stop m hitch-hiking
autobus m bus
autocar m coach
automatique automatic
automne m autumn
automobiliste m/f motorist
autoradio m car radio
autorisé(e) permitted ; authorized
autoroute f motorway
autre other
  autres directions other routes
auvent m awning *(for caravan etc)* ; car port

avalanche f avalanche
avaler to swallow
  ne pas avaler not to be taken internally
avance f advance
  à l'avance in advance
avant before ; front
  à l'avant at the front
  en avant forward
avec with
avenir m future
avenue f avenue
avertir to inform ; to warn
avion m aeroplane
aviron m oar ; rowing *(sport)*
avis m notice ; warning
aviser to advise
avocat m avocado ; lawyer
avoine f oats
avoir to have
avortement m abortion
avril April

B

bacon m bacon
bagages mpl luggage
  bagages à main hand luggage
  faire les bagages to pack
bague f ring *(on finger)*
baguette f stick of French bread
baie f bay *(along coast)*
baignade f bathing
  baignade interdite no bathing
baignoire f bath *(tub)*
bain m bath
  bain de bouche mouthwash
  bain moussant bubble bath
baiser kiss
baisser to lower
bal m ball ; dance
balade f walk ; drive ; trek
balai m broom *(brush)*
  balai à franges mop *(for floor)*
balance f scales *(for weighing)*
balançoire f swing *(for children)*
balcon m circle *(theatre)* ; balcony
ball-trap m clay pigeon shooting
balle f ball *(small: golf, tennis, etc)*
ballet m ballet
ballon m balloon ; ball *(large)* ;
  brandy glass
bambin m toddler
banane f banana ; bumbag
banc m seat ; bench
banlieue f suburbs
banque f bank

bar *m* bar
barbe *f* beard
  barbe à papa candy floss
barque *f* rowing boat
barrage *m* dam
  barrage routier road block
barré: route barrée road closed
barrer to cross out
barrière *f* barrier
bas *m* bottom *(of page, etc)* ; stocking
  en bas below ; downstairs
bas(se) low
baskets *fpl* trainers
bassin *m* pond ; washing-up bowl
bateau *m* boat ; ship
  bateau à rames rowing boat
  bateau-mouche river boat
bâtiment *m* building
bâton (de ski) *m* ski pole
batte *f* bat *(baseball, cricket)*
batterie *f* battery *(for car)*
  batterie à plat flat battery
baume pour les lèvres *m* lip salve
bavoir *m* bib *(baby's)*
beau (belle) lovely ; handsome ;
  beautiful ; nice *(enjoyable)*
beau-frère *m* brother-in-law
beau-père *m* father-in-law ; stepfather
beaucoup (de) much/many ; a lot of
bébé *m* baby
beignet *m* fritter ; doughnut
belge Belgian
Belgique *f* Belgium
belle-fille *f* daughter-in-law
belle-mère *f* mother-in-law ; step-mother
béquilles *fpl* crutches
berger *m* shepherd
berlingots *mpl* boiled sweets
besoin: avoir besoin de to need
beurre *m* butter
  beurre doux unsalted butter
biberon *m* baby's bottle
bibliothèque *f* library
bicyclette *f* bicycle
bien well ; right ; good
  bien cuit(e) well done *(steak)*
bientôt soon ; shortly
bienvenu(e) welcome!
bière *f* beer
  bière (à la) pression draught beer
  bière blonde lager
  bière bouteille bottled lager
  bière brune bitter
bifteck *m* steak
bijouterie *f* jeweller's ; jewellery

bijoux *mpl* jewellery
bikini *m* bikini
billet *m* note ; ticket
  billet aller-retour return ticket
  billet d'avion plane ticket
  billet de banque banknote
  billet simple one-way ticket
biologique organic
biscotte *f* breakfast biscuit ; rusk
biscuit *m* biscuit
bisque *f* thick seafood soup
blanc (blanche) white ; blank
  en blanc blank *(on form)*
blanc d'œuf *m* egg white
blanchisserie *f* laundry
blé *m* wheat
blessé(e) injured
blesser to injure
bleu *m* bruise
bleu(e) blue ; very rare *(steak)*
  bleu marine navy blue
bloc-notes *m* note pad
blond(e) fair *(hair)*
bloqué(e) stuck
body *m* body *(clothing)*
bœuf *m* beef
boire to drink
bois *m* wood
boisson *f* drink
  boisson non alcoolisée soft drink
boîte *f* can ; box
  boîte à fusibles fuse box
  boîte à lettres post box
  boîte de conserve tin *(of food)*
  boîte de nuit night club
  boîte de vitesses gearbox
bol *m* bowl *(for soup, etc)*
bombe *f* aerosol ; bomb
bon *m* token ; voucher
bon (bonne) good ; right ; nice
  bon anniversaire happy birthday
  bon marché inexpensive
bonbon *m* sweet
bondé(e) crowded
bonhomme *m* chap
  bonhomme de neige snowman
bonjour hello ; good morning/afternoon
bonnet *m* hat
  bonnet de bain bathing cap
bonneterie *f* hosiery
bonsoir good evening
bord *m* border ; edge ; verge
  à bord on board
  au bord de la mer at the seaside
bosse *f* lump *(swelling)*
botte *f* boot ; bunch

bottillons mpl ankle boots
bouche f mouth
  bouche d'incendie fire hydrant
bouché(e) blocked
bouchée f mouthful ; chocolate
  bouchée à la reine vol-au-vent
boucherie f butcher's shop
bouchon m cork ; plug (for sink) ;
top (of bottle)
boucle d'oreille f earring
bouée de sauvetage f life belt
bougie f candle ; spark plug
bouillabaisse f rich fish soup/stew
bouilli(e) boiled
bouillir to boil
bouilloire f kettle
bouillon m stock
bouillotte f hot-water bottle
boulangerie f bakery
boule f ball
boules fpl game similar to bowls
bouquet m bunch (of flowers)
Bourgogne Burgundy
boussole f compass
bout m end
  à bout filtre filter-tipped
bouteille f bottle
boutique f shop
bouton m button ; switch ; spot
  bouton de fièvre cold sore
  boutons de manchette cufflinks
boxe f boxing
bracelet m bracelet
  bracelet de montre watchstrap
braisé(e) braised
bras m arm
brasserie f café ; brewery
Bretagne f Brittany
breton(ne) from Brittany
bricolage m do-it-yourself
briquet m cigarette lighter
briser to break ; to smash
britannique British
brocante f second-hand goods ;
flea market
broche f brooch ; spit
brochette f skewer ; kebab
brocoli m broccoli
brodé main hand-embroidered
bronzage m suntan
bronze m bronze
brosse f brush
  brosse à cheveux hairbrush
  brosse à dents toothbrush

  brosse à dents électrique electric
toothbrush
brouillard m fog
bru f daughter-in-law
bruit m noise
brûlé(e) burnt
brûler to burn
brûlures d'estomac fpl heartburn
brun(e) brown ; dark
brushing m blow-dry
brut(e) gross ; raw
Bruxelles Brussels
bûche f log (for fire)
buisson m bush
bulletin de consigne m left-luggage
ticket
bureau m desk ; office
  bureau de change foreign exchange
office
  bureau de location booking office
  bureau de poste post office
  bureau de renseignements
information office
  bureau des objets trouvés lost
property office
bus m bus
butane m camping gas

C

ça va it's OK ; I'm OK
  ça va? are you OK?
cabaret m cabaret
cabine f beach hut ; cubicle ; cabin
  cabine d'essayage changing room
cabinet m office
câble de frein brake cable
câble d'embrayage gear cable
câble de remorquage m tow rope
cacahuète f peanut
cacao m cocoa
cacher to hide
cadeau m gift
cadenas m padlock
cadre m picture frame
cafard m cockroach
café m coffee ; café
  café au lait white coffee
  café crème white coffee
  café décaféiné decaff coffee
  café instantané instant coffee
  café noir black coffee
cafetière f coffee pot
cahier m exercise book
caisse f cash desk ; case
  caisse d'épargne savings bank
caissier(-ière) m/f cashier ; teller

calculatrice f calculator
caleçon m boxer shorts
calendrier m calendar ; timetable
calmant m sedative
cambriolage m break-in
cambrioleur(-euse) m/f burglar
caméra vidéo f video camera
caméscope m camcorder
camion m lorry ; truck
camionnette f van
camomille f camomile
campagne f countryside ; campaign
camper to camp
camping m camping ; camp-site
  camping-gaz® camping stove
  camping sauvage camping on
  unofficial sites
Canada m Canada
canadien(ne) Canadian
canal m canal
canapé m sofa ; open sandwich
  canapé-lit sofa bed
canard m duck
canif m penknife
canne f walking stick
  canne à pêche fishing rod
cannelle f cinnamon
canoë m canoe
canot m boat
  canot de sauvetage lifeboat
canotage m boating
caoutchouc m rubber (material)
capable efficient
capitale f capital (city)
capot m bonnet ; hood (of car)
câpres fpl capers
capuchon m hood ; top (of pen)
car m coach
carabine de chasse f hunting rifle
carafe f carafe ; decanter
caravane f caravan
carburateur m carburettor
Carême m Lent
carnet m notebook ; book
  carnet de billets book of tickets
  carnet de chèques cheque book
carotte f carrot
carré m square
carreau m tile (on wall, floor)
carrefour m crossroads
carte f map ; card ; menu ; pass (bus, train)
  carte bleue credit card
  carte d'abonnement season ticket
  carte d'embarquement boarding
  card/pass

carte d'identité identity card
carte de crédit credit card
carte de paiement charge card ;
debit card
carte des vins wine list
carte grise log book (car)
carte magnétique swipecard
carte orange monthly or yearly
season ticket (for Paris transport system)
carte postale postcard
carte routière road map
carte SIM SIM card
carte vermeille senior citizen's rail pass
carte-clé électronique keycard
(electronic key)
cartes (à jouer) fpl playing cards
carton m cardboard
cartouche f carton (of cigarettes)
cas m case
cascade f waterfall
caserne f barracks
casier m rack ; locker
casino m casino
casque m helmet
  casque (à écouteurs) headphones
casquette f cap (hat)
cassé(e) broken
casse-croûte m snacks
casser to break
  casser la croûte to have a snack
casserole f saucepan
cassette f cassette
catch m wrestling
cathédrale f cathedral
catholique Catholic
cause f cause
  pour cause de on account of
caution f security (for loan) ; deposit
  caution à verser deposit required
cave f cellar
caveau m cellar
caviar m caviar(e)
CD m CD
CD-Rom CD ROM
ceci this
cédez le passage give way
CE f EC (European Community)
ceinture f belt
  ceinture de sécurité seatbelt
  ceinture porte-monnaie moneybelt
cela that
célèbre famous
célibataire single (unmarried)
cendrier m ashtray
cent m hundred
centimètre m centimetre

central(e) central
centre m centre
  centre commercial shopping centre
  centre de loisirs leisure centre
  centre des affaires business centre
  centre équestre riding school
  centre-ville city centre
céramique f ceramics
cercle m circle ; ring
céréales fpl cereal (for breakfast)
cerise f cherry
certain(e) certain (sure)
certificat m certificate
cerveau m brain
cervelle f brains (as food)
cesser to stop
cette this ; that
ceux-ci/celles-ci these ones
ceux-là/celles-là those ones
CFF mpl Swiss Railways
chacun/chacune each
chaîne f chain ; channel ;
  (mountain) range
  chaîne (stéréo) stereo
  chaînes obligatoires snow chains
  compulsory
chair f flesh
chaise f chair
  chaise de bébé high chair
  chaise longue deckchair
châle m shawl
chalet m chalet
chambre f bedroom ; room
  chambre à air inner tube
  chambre à coucher bedroom
  chambre à deux lits twin-bedded room
  chambre d'hôte bed and breakfast
  chambre individuelle single room
  chambre pour deux personnes
  double room
  chambres rooms to let
champ m field
  champ de courses racecourse
champagne m champagne
champignon m mushroom
  champignon vénéneux toadstool
chance f luck
change m exchange
changement m change
changer to change
  changer de l'argent to change money
  changer de train to change train
  se changer to change clothes
chanson f song
chanter to sing
chanterelle f chanterelle

chantier m building site ; roadworks
chapeau m hat
chapelle f chapel
chaque each ; every
charbon m coal
  charbon de bois charcoal
charcuterie f pork butcher's ;
  delicatessen ; cooked meat
chariot m trolley
charter m charter flight
chasse f hunting ; shooting
  chasse gardée private hunting
chasse-neige m snowplough
chasser to hunt
chasseur m hunter
chat m cat
châtaigne f chestnut
château m castle ; mansion
chaud(e) hot
chauffage m heating
chauffer to heat up (milk, water)
chauffeur m driver
chaussée f carriageway
  chaussée déformée uneven road surface
  chaussée rétrécie road narrows
  chaussée verglacée icy road
chaussette f sock
chaussure f shoe ; boot
chauve bald (person)
chauve-souris f bat (creature)
chef m chef ; chief ; head ; leader
  chef de train guard (on train)
chef-d'œuvre m masterpiece
chef-lieu m county town
chemin m path ; lane ; track ; way
  chemin de fer railway
cheminée f chimney ; fireplace
chemise f shirt
  chemise de nuit nightdress
chemisier m blouse
chèque m cheque
  chèque de voyage traveller's cheque
cher (chère) dear ; expensive
chercher to look for
  aller chercher to fetch ; to collect
cheval m horse
  faire du cheval to ride (horse)
cheveux mpl hair
cheville f ankle
chèvre f goat
chevreau m kid (goat, leather)
chevreuil m venison
chez at the house of
  chez moi at my home
chien m dog

hiffon m duster ; rag
hili con carne chilli (dish)
hips fpl crisps
hirurgien m surgeon
hocolat m chocolate
  chocolat à croquer plain chocolate
  chocolat au lait milk chocolate
hoisir to choose
noix m range ; choice ; selection
hômage: au chômage unemployed
hope f tankard
horale f choir
hose f thing
hou m cabbage
hou-fleur m cauliflower
hute f fall
idre m cider
iel m sky
igare m cigar
igarette f cigarette
l m eyelash
imetière m cemetery ; graveyard
inéma m cinema
intre m coat hanger
irage m shoe polish
ircuit m round trip ; circuit
irculation f traffic
irculer to operate (train, bus, etc)
ire f wax ; polish
irque m circus
iseaux mpl scissors
ité f city ; housing estate
itron m lemon
  citron vert lime
itronnade f still lemonade
itronnelle lemongrass
lair(e) clear ; light
lasse f grade ; class
lavicule f collar bone
lavier m keyboard
lé f key ; spanner
  clé de contact ignition key
  clé minute keys cut while you wait
lef f key
lient(e) m/f client ; customer
lignotant m indicator (on car)
limatisation f air-conditioning
limatisé(e) air-conditioned
limatisateur f air-conditioning unit
linique f clinic (private)
loche f bell (church, school)
locher m steeple
lou m nail (metal)
  clou de girofle clove

cocher to tick (on form)
cochon m pig
cocktail m cocktail
  cocktail-bar cocktail bar
cocotte f casserole dish
cocotte-minute f pressure cooker
code m code
  code barres barcode
  code postal postcode
  code secret pin number
cœur m heart
coffre-fort m strongbox ; safe
cognac m brandy
coiffeur m hairdresser ; barber
coiffeuse f hairdresser
coin m corner
coincé(e) jammed ; stuck
col m collar ; pass (in mountains)
colis m parcel
collant m pair of tights
colle f glue
collège m secondary school
collègue m/f colleague
coller to stick ; to glue
collier m necklace ; dog collar
colline f hill
collision f crash (car)
colonne f column
  colonne vertébrale spine
combien how much/many
combinaison de plongée f wetsuit
combinaison de ski f ski suit
combustible m fuel
comédie f comedy
  comédie musicale musical (show)
commande f order (in restaurant)
commander to order
comme like
  comme ça like this ; like that
commencer to begin
comment? pardon? ; how?
commerçant(e) m/f trader
commerce m commerce ; business ;
  trade
commissariat (de police) m police station
commode f chest of drawers
commotion f shock
  commotion (cérébrale) concussion
communication f communication ;
  call (on telephone)
communion f communion
compagne f girlfriend
compagnie f firm ; company
compagnon m boyfriend
compartiment m compartment (train)

complet(-ète) full (up)
complètement completely
comporter to consist of
  se comporter to behave
composer to dial (a number)
composter to date-stamp/punch (ticket)
  composter votre billet validate your
  ticket
comprenant including
comprendre to understand
comprimé m tablet
compris(e) included
  non compris not included
comptant m cash
compte m number ; account
  compte en banque bank account
compter to count (add up)
compteur m speedometer ; meter
comptoir m counter (in shop, bar, etc)
comte m count ; earl
concert m concert
concierge m/f caretaker ; janitor
concours m contest ; aid
concurrent(e) m/f competitor
conducteur(-trice) m/f driver
conduire to drive
conduite f driving ; behaviour
confection f ready-to-wear clothes
conférence f conference
confession f confession
confirmer to confirm
confiserie f sweetshop
confiture f jam ; preserve
congélateur m freezer
congelé(e) frozen
connaître to know
conseil m advice ; council
conseiller to advise
conserver to keep ; to retain (ticket, etc)
consigne f deposit ; left luggage
consommation f drink
consommé m clear soup
constat m report
constipé(e) constipated
construire to build
consulat m consulate
contacter to contact
contenir to contain
content(e) pleased
contenu m contents
continuer to continue
contraceptif m contraceptive
contrat m contract
  contrat de location lease

contravention f fine (penalty)
contre against ; versus
contre-filet m sirloin
contrôle m check
  contrôle des passeports passport contro
  contrôle radar speed trap
contrôler to check
contrôles de sécurité mpl security chec
contrôleur(-euse) m/f ticket inspector
convenu(e) agreed
convoi exceptionnel m large load
copie f copy (duplicate)
copier to copy
coque f shell ; cockle
coquelicot m poppy
coquet(te) pretty (place, etc)
coquillages mpl shellfish
coquille f shell
  coquille Saint-Jacques scallop
corail m coral ; type of train
corde f rope
  corde à linge clothes line
cordonnerie f shoe repair shop
cornet m cone
corniche f coast road
cornichon m gherkin
corps m body
correspondance f connection (transport)
correspondant(e) m/f penfriend
corrida f bull-fight
Corse f Corsica
costume m suit (man's)
côte f coast ; hill ; rib
  Côte d'Azur French Riviera
côté m side
  à côté de beside ; next to
côtelette f cutlet
coton m cotton
  coton hydrophile cotton wool
  coton-tige® cotton bud
cou m neck
couche (de bébé) f nappy
coucher de soleil m sunset
couchette f bunk ; berth
coude m elbow
coudre to sew
couette f continental quilt ; duvet
couler to run (water)
couleur f colour
coulis m purée
couloir m corridor ; aisle
coup m stroke ; shot ; blow
  coup de pied kick
  coup de soleil sunburn
  coup de téléphone phone call

coupe f goblet (ice cream)
  coupe (de cheveux) haircut
coupe-ongles m nail clippers
couper to cut
couple m couple (two people)
coupure f cut
  coupure de courant power cut
cour f court ; courtyard
courant m power ; current
courant(e) common ; current
courir to run
couronne f crown
courrier m mail ; post
  courrier électronique e-mail
courroie de ventilateur f fan belt
cours m lesson ; course ; rate
course f race (sport) ; errand
  course hippique horse race
  faire des courses to go shopping
court de tennis m tennis court
court(e) short
cousin(e) m/f cousin
coussin m cushion
coût m cost
couteau m knife
coûter to cost
coûteux(-euse) expensive
couture f sewing ; seam
couvent m convent ; monastery
couvercle m lid
couvert m cover charge ; place setting
  couverts cutlery
couvert(e) covered
couverture f blanket ; cover
crabe m crab
cranberry (jus de) cranberry juice
crapaud m toad
cravate f tie
crayon m pencil
crème f cream (food, lotion)
  crème à raser shaving cream
  crème anglaise custard
  crème Chantilly whipped cream
  crème fermentée soured cream
  crème hydratante moisturizer
  crème pâtissière confectioner's
  custard
  crème solaire suncream
crémerie f dairy
crêpe f pancake
crêperie f pancake shop/restaurant
cresson m watercress
crevaison f puncture
crevette f shrimp ; prawn
cric m jack (for car)

crier to shout
crime m crime ; offence ; murder
crise f crisis ; attack (medical)
  crise cardiaque heart attack
cristal m crystal
crochet d'attelage m towbar
croire to believe
croisement m junction (road)
croisière f cruise
croix f cross
croquant(e) crisp ; crunchy
croque-madame m toasted cheese
  sandwich with ham and fried egg
croque-monsieur m toasted ham and
  cheese sandwich
croustade f pastry shell with filling
croûte f crust
cru(e) raw
crudités fpl raw vegetables
crue subite f flash flood
crustacés mpl shellfish
cube de bouillon m stock cube
cuiller f spoon
  cuiller à café teaspoon
cuir m leather
cuisiné(e) cooked
cuisine f cooking ; cuisine ; kitchen
  cuisine familiale home cooking
  faire la cuisine to cook
cuisiner to cook
cuisinier m cook
cuisinière f cook ; cooker
cuisse f thigh
  cuisses de grenouille frogs' legs
cuit(e) cooked
  bien cuit well done (steak)
cuivre m copper
  cuivre jaune brass
culotte f panties
curieux(-euse) strange
curseur m cursor (computer)
cuvée f vintage
cuvette f washing up bowl
cyclisme m cycling
cystite f cystitis

D

daltonien(ne) colour-blind
dame f lady
  dames ladies
danger m danger
dangereux(-euse) dangerous
dans into ; in ; on
danser to dance

date f date (day)
  date de naissance date of birth
  date limite de vente sell-by date
daube f stew
de from ; of ; some
dé m dice
début m beginning
débutant(e) m/f beginner
décaféiné(e) decaffeinated
décembre December
décès m death
décharge f electric shock
  décharge publique rubbish dump
déchargement m unloading
déchirer to rip
déclaration f statement ; report
  déclaration de douane customs declaration
décollage m takeoff
décoller to take off (plane)
décolleté m low neck
décongeler to defrost
découvrir to discover
décrire to describe
décrocher to lift the receiver
dedans inside
défaire to unfasten ; to unpack
défaut m fault ; defect
défectueux(-euse) faulty
**défense de... ** no.../... forbidden
  défense de fumer no smoking
  défense de stationner no parking
dégâts mpl damage
dégeler to thaw
dégivrer to de-ice (windscreen)
dégustation f tasting
  dégustation de vins wine tasting
dehors outside ; outdoors
déjeuner m lunch
délicieux(-euse) delicious
délit m offence
deltaplane m hang-glider
demain tomorrow
demande f application ; request
  demandes d'emploi situations wanted
demander to ask (for)
demandeur d'emploi m job seeker
démaquillant m make-up remover
démarqué(e) reduced (goods)
démarreur m starter (in car)
demi(e) half
demi-pension f half board
demi-sec medium-dry
demi-tarif m half fare

demi-tour m U-turn
dent f tooth
dentelle f lace
dentier m dentures
dentifrice m toothpaste
dentiste m/f dentist
déodorant m deodorant
dépannage m breakdown service
dépanneuse f breakdown van
départ m departure
département m county
dépasser to exceed ; to overtake
dépenses fpl expenditure
dépliant m brochure
dépôt m deposit ; depot
  dépôt d'ordures rubbish dump
dépression f depression ; nervous breakdown
depuis since
déranger to disturb
dérapage skid
  déraper to skid
dernier(-ère) last ; latest
derrière at the back ; behind
derrière m bottom (buttocks)
dès from ; since
  dès votre arrivée as soon as you arrive
désagréable unpleasant
descendre to go down ; to get off
description f description
déshabiller to undress
  se déshabiller to get undressed
désirer to want
désodorisant m air freshener
désolé(e) sorry
dessein m design ; plan
desserré(e) loose (not fastened)
dessert m pudding
dessous (de) underneath (of)
dessus (de) on top (of)
destinataire m/f addressee
destination f destination
  à destination de bound for
détail m detail
  au détail retail
détergent m detergent
détourner to divert
deux two
  deux fois twice
  les deux both
deuxième second
devant in front (of)
développer to develop
devenir to become

déviation f diversion
devis m quotation (price)
devises fpl currency
dévisser to unscrew
devoir to have to; to owe
diabète m diabetes
diabétique diabetic
diamant m diamond
diaphragme m cap (contraceptive)
diapositive f slide (photograph)
diarrhée f diarrhoea
dictionnaire m dictionary
diététique f dietary ; health foods
différent(e) different
difficile difficult
digue f dyke ; jetty
dimanche m Sunday
dinde f turkey
dîner to have dinner
dîner m dinner
  dîner spectacle cabaret dinner
dire to say ; to tell
direct: train direct through train
directeur m manager ; headmaster
direction f management ; direction
directrice f manageress ; headmistress
discothèque f disco ; nightclub
discussion f argument
disjoncteur m circuit breaker
disloquer to dislocate
disparaître to disappear
disparu(e) missing (disappeared)
disponible available
disque m record ; disk (computer)
  disque de stationnement parking disk
  disque dur hard disk
disquette f floppy disk
dissolvant m nail polish remover
distractions fpl entertainment
distributeur m dispenser
  distributeur automatique vending
  machine ; cash machine
divers(e) various
divertissements mpl entertainment
divorcé(e) divorced
docteur m doctor
doigt m finger
  doigt de pied toe
domestique m/f servant ; maid
domicile m home ; address
donner to give ; to give away
doré(e) golden
dormir to sleep
dos m back (of body)

dossier m file
  dossier attaché attachment
douane f customs
double double
doubler to overtake
douche f shower
douleur f pain
douloureux(-euse) painful
doux (douce) mild ; gentle ; soft ; sweet
douzaine f dozen
dragée f sugared almond
drap m sheet
drapeau m flag
drogue f drug
droguerie f hardware shop
droit m right (entitlement)
droit(e) right (not left) ; straight
droite f right-hand side
  à droite on/to the right
  tenez votre droite keep to right
dur(e) hard ; hard-boiled ; tough
durée f duration
DVD DVD
  lecteur de DVD DVD player

E

eau f water
  eau de Javel bleach
  eau douce fresh water (not salt)
  eau du robinet tap-water
  eau minérale mineral water
  eau potable drinking water
  eau salée salt water
  eau-de-vie brandy
ébène f ebony
échanger to exchange
échantillon m sample
échapper to escape
écharpe f scarf (woollen)
échelle f ladder
  échelle de secours fire escape
éclairage m lighting
éclairs mpl lightning
éclatement m blowout (of tyre)
écluse f lock (in canal)
école f school
  école maternelle nursery school
écologique ecological
écossais(e) Scottish
Écosse f Scotland
écotourisme m eco-tourism
écouter to listen to
écran m screen
  écran solaire sunscreen (lotion)
  écran total sunblock

écrire to write
écrivain m author
écrou m nut *(for bolt)*
écurie f stable
édulcorant m sweetener
église f church
élastique m elastic band
électricien m electrician
électricité f electricity
électrique electric
électronique electronic
élément m unit ; element
élevé(e) en plein air free-range
emballer to wrap (up)
embarcadère m jetty *(landing pier)*
embarquement m boarding
embouteillage m traffic jam
embrayage m clutch *(in car)*
émission f programme ; broadcast
emplacement m parking space ; pitch
    (place for tent/caravan)
emploi m use ; job
emporter to take away
    à emporter take-away
emprunter to borrow
en some ; any ; in ; to ; made of
    en cas de in case of
    en face de opposite
    en gros in bulk ; wholesale
    en panne out of order
    en retard late
    en train/voiture by train/car
encaisser to cash *(cheque)*
enceinte pregnant
enchanté(e)! pleased to meet you!
encore still ; yet ; again
encre f ink
endommager to damage
endroit m place ; spot
enfant m/f child
enfler to swell *(bump, eye, etc)*
enlever to take away ; to take off *(clothes)*
    enlever le haut to go topless
enneigé(e) snowed up
ennui m boredom ; nuisance ; trouble
ennuyeux boring
enregistrement m check-in desk
enregistrer to record ; to check in ;
    to video
enseignement m education
enseigner to teach
ensemble together
ensuite next ; after that
entendre to hear

entier(-ière) whole
entorse f sprain
entracte m interval
entre between
entrecôte f rib steak
entrée f entrance ; admission ; starter
    (food)
    entrée gratuite admission free
    entrée interdite no entry
entreprise f firm ; company
entrer to come in ; to go in
entretien m maintenance ; interview
entrez! come in!
enveloppe f envelope
    enveloppe matelassée padded
    envelope
envers: l'envers wrong side
    à l'envers upside down ; back to front
environ around ; about
environs mpl surroundings
envoyer to send
    envoyer un SMS à to text
    je t'enverrai un SMS I'll text you
épais(se) thick
épargner to save *(money)*
épaule f shoulder
épi m ear (of corn)
    épi de maïs corn-on-the-cob
épice f spice
épicerie f grocer's shop
    épicerie fine delicatessen
épilation f hair removal
    épilation à la cire f waxing
épileptique epileptic
épinards mpl spinach
épine f thorn
épingle f pin
    épingle de sûreté safety pin
éponge f sponge
époque f age
    d'époque period *(furniture)*
épuisé(e) sold out ; used up
épuiser to use up ; to run out of
équipage m crew
équipe f team ; shift
équipement m equipment
équitation f horse-riding
erreur f mistake
escalade f climbing
escalator m escalator
escalier m stairs
    escalier de secours fire escape
    escalier mécanique escalator
escargot m snail
escarpement m cliff *(in mountains)*

Espagne f Spain
espagnol(e) Spanish
espèce f sort
espérer to hope
esquimau m ice lolly
essai m trial ; test
essayer to try ; to try on
essence f petrol
  essence sans plomb unleaded petrol
essorer to spin(-dry) ; to wring
essoreuse f spin dryer
essuie-glace m windscreen wipers
essuie-tout m kitchen paper
esthéticienne f beautician
estivants mpl summer holiday-makers
estomac m stomach
estragon m tarragon
et and
étage m storey
  le dernier étage the top floor
étain m tin ; pewter
étang m pond
étape f stage
état m state
  États-Unis United States
été m summer
éteindre to turn off
éteint(e) out (light)
étiquette f label
  étiquette à bagages luggage tag
étoile f star
étranger(-ère) m/f foreigner
  à l'étranger overseas ; abroad
être to be
étroit(e) narrow ; tight
étudiant(e) m/f student
étudier to study
étui m case (camera, glasses)
étuvée: à l'étuvée braised
eurocheque m eurocheque
Europe f Europe
européen(ne) European
eux them
évanoui(e) fainted
événement m occasion ; event
éventail m fan (handheld)
éventé(e) flat (beer)
évêque m bishop
évier m sink (washbasin)
éviter to avoid
exact(e) right (correct)
examen m examination
excédent de bagages m excess baggage
excellent(e) excellent

excès de vitesse m speeding
exclu(e) excluded
exclure to expel
exclusif(-ive) exclusive
excursion f trip ; outing ; excursion
excuses fpl apologies
excusez-moi! excuse me!
exemplaire m copy
exercice m exercise
expéditeur m sender
expert(e) m/f expert
expirer to expire (ticket, passport)
expliquer to explain
exporter to export
exposition f exhibition
exprès on purpose ; deliberately
  en exprès express (parcel, etc)
extérieur(e) outside
extincteur m fire extinguisher
extra top-quality ; first-rate

F

fabrication f manufacturing
fabriquer to manufacture
  fabriqué en... made in...
face: en face (de) opposite
fâché(e) angry
facile easy
façon f way ; manner
facteur(-trice) m/f postman
facture f invoice
  facture détaillée itemized bill
faible weak
faïence f earthenware
faim f hunger
  avoir faim to be hungry
faire to make ; to do
  faire du stop to hitchhike
faisan m pheasant
fait main handmade
falaise f cliff
famille f family
farci(e) stuffed
fard à paupières m eye shadow
farine f flour
fatigue f tiredness
fatigué(e) tired
fausse couche f miscarriage
faute f mistake ; foul (football)
fauteuil m armchair ; seat
  fauteuil roulant wheelchair
faux (fausse) fake ; false ; wrong
fax m fax
faxer to fax

félicitations *fpl* congratulations
femme *f* woman ; wife
  femme au foyer housewife
  femme d'affaires businesswoman
  femme de chambre chambermaid
  femme de ménage cleaner
  femme policier policewoman
fenêtre *f* window
fenouil *m* fennel
fente *f* crack ; slot
fer *m* iron *(material, golf club)*
  fer à repasser iron *(for clothes)*
férié(e): *jour férié* public holiday
ferme *f* farmhouse ; farm
fermé(e) closed
fermer to close/shut ; to turn off
  fermer à clé to lock
fermeture *f* closing
  fermeture Éclair® zip
ferroviaire railway ; rail
ferry *m* car ferry
fête *f* holiday ; fête ; party
  fête des rois Epiphany
  fête foraine funfair
feu *m* fire ; traffic lights
  feu (de joie) bonfire *(celebration)*
  feu d'artifice fireworks
  feu de position sidelight
  feu rouge red light
feuille *f* leaf ; sheet *(of paper)*
feuilleton *m* soap opera
feutre *m* felt ; felt-tip pen
février February
fiancé(e) engaged *(to be married)*
ficelle *f* string ; thin French stick
fiche *f* token ; form ; slip *(of paper)*
fichier *m* file *(computer)*
fièvre *f* fever
  avoir de la fièvre to have a temperature
figue *f* fig
fil *m* thread ; lead *(electrical)*
  fil dentaire dental floss
file *f* lane ; row
filet *m* net ; fillet *(of meat, fish)*
  filet à bagages luggage rack
fille *f* daughter ; girl
film *m* film
Filofax Filofax®
fils *m* son
filtre *m* filter *(on cigarette)*
  filtre à huile oil filter
fin *f* end
fin(e) thin *(material)* ; fine *(delicate)*
fini(e) finished
finir to end ; to finish
fixer to fix

flacon *m* bottle *(small)*
flamand(e) Flemish
flan *m* custard tart
flash *m* flash *(for camera)*
fleur *f* flower
fleuriste *m/f* florist
fleuve *m* river
flipper *m* pinball
flûte *f* long, thin loaf
foie *m* liver
  foie gras goose liver
foire *f* fair
  foire à/aux... special offer on...
fois *f* time
  cette fois this time
  une fois once
folle mad
foncé(e) dark *(colour)*
fonctionner to work *(machine)*
fond *m* back *(of hall, room)* ; bottom
fondre to melt
force *f* strength
forêt *f* forest
forfait *m* fixed price ; ski pass
forme *f* shape ; style
formidable great *(wonderful)*
formulaire *m* form *(document)*
fort(e) loud; strong
forteresse *f* fort
forum chatroom *(internet)*
fosse *f* pit ; grave
  fosse septique septic tank
fou (folle) mad
fouetté(e) whipped *(cream, eggs)*
foulard *m* scarf *(headscarf)*
foule *f* crowd
four *m* oven
  four à micro-ondes microwave
fourchette *f* fork
fournir to supply
fourré(e) filled ; fur-lined
fourrure *f* fur
fraîche fresh ; cool ; wet *(paint)*
frais fresh ; cool
frais *mpl* costs ; expenses
fraise *f* strawberry
framboise *f* raspberry
français(e) French
Français(e) Frenchman/woman
frapper to hit ; to knock *(on door)*
frein *m* brake
freiner to brake
fréquent(e) frequent
frère *m* brother

fret m freight (goods)
frigo m fridge
frit(e) fried
friterie f chip shop
frites fpl french fries ; chips
friture f small fried fish
froid(e) cold
fromage m cheese
froment m wheat
front m forehead
frontière f border ; boundary
frotter to rub
fruit m fruit
 fruit de la passion passionfruit
 fruits de mer seafood
 fruits secs dried fruit
fuite f leak
fumé(e) smoked
fumée f smoke
fumer to smoke
fumeurs smokers
fumier m manure
funiculaire m funicular railway
fuseau m ski pants
fusible m fuse
fusil m gun

G

gagner to earn ; to win
galerie f art gallery ; arcade ; roof-rack
gallois(e) Welsh
gambas fpl large prawns
gant m glove
 gant de toilette face cloth
 gants de ménage rubber gloves
garage m garage
garantie f guarantee
garçon m boy ; waiter
garde f custody ; guard
 garde-côte coastguard
garder to keep ; to look after
gardien(ne) m/f caretaker ; warden
gare f railway station
 gare routière bus terminal
garer to park
garni(e) served with vegetables or chips
gas-oil m diesel fuel
gâteau m cake ; gateau
gauche left
 à gauche to/on the left
gâteau m cake
gaufre f waffle
gaz m gas
 gaz d'échappement exhaust fumes

gaz-oil m diesel fuel
gazeux(-euse) fizzy
gel m frost
 gel pour cheveux hair gel
gelé(e) frozen
gelée f jelly ; aspic
gênant inconvenient
gendarme m policeman (in rural areas)
gendarmerie f police station
gendre m son-in-law
généreux(-euse) generous
genou m knee
gentil(-ille) kind (person)
gérant(e) m/f manager/manageress
gérer to manage (be in charge of)
gibier m game (hunting)
gilet m waistcoat
 gilet de sauvetage life jacket
gingembre m ginger
gîte m self-catering house/flat
glace f ice ; ice cream ; mirror
glacé(e) chilled ; iced
glacier m glacier ; ice-cream maker
glacière f cool-box (for picnic)
glaçon m ice cube
glissant(e) slippery
glisser to slip
gluten gluten
gomme f rubber (eraser)
gorge f throat ; gorge
gosse m/f kid (child)
gothique Gothic
goût m flavour ; taste
goûter to taste
goyave guava
graine f seed
gramme m gram
grand(e) great ; high (speed, number) ;
 big ; tall
grand-mère f grandmother
grand-père m grandfather
Grande-Bretagne f Great Britain
grands-parents mpl grandparents
grange f barn
granité m flavoured crushed ice
grappe f bunch (of grapes)
gras(se) fat ; greasy
gratis for free
gratuit(e) free of charge
grave serious
gravure f print (picture)
grêle f hail
grenier m attic
grenouille f frog

grève f strike
grillé(e) grilled
grille-pain m toaster
Grèce f Greece
grippe f flu
gris(e) grey
gros(se) big ; large ; fat
gros lot m jackpot
grotte f cave
groupe m group ; party ; band
   groupe sanguin blood group
guêpe f wasp
guerre f war
gueule de bois f hangover
guichet m ticket office ; counter
guide m guide ; guidebook
   guide de conversation phrase book
guidon m handlebars
guitare f guitar
gynécologue gynaecologist

H

habillé(e) dressed
habiller to dress
   s'habiller to get dressed
habitant(e) m/f inhabitant
habiter to live (in)
habituel(le) usual ; regular
haché(e) minced
   steak haché m hamburger
hachis m minced meat
halles fpl central food market
hamburger m burger
hameçon m hook (fishing)
hanche f hip
handicapé(e) disabled (person)
haricot m bean
haut m top (of ladder, bikini, etc)
   en haut upstairs
haut débit broadband
haut(e) high ; tall
hauteur f height
haut-parleur loudspeaker
hebdomadaire weekly
hébergement m lodging
hélicoptère médical m air ambulance
hépatite f hepatitis
herbe f grass
   fines herbes herbs
hernie f hernia
heure f hour ; time of day
   à l'heure on time
   heure de pointe rush hour
heureux(-euse) happy

hibou m owl
hier yesterday
hippisme m horse riding
hippodrome m racecourse
historique historic
hiver m winter
hollandais(e) Dutch
homard m lobster
homéopathie f homeopathy
homéopathique homeopathic
   (remedy etc)
homme m man
   homme au foyer house-husband
   homme d'affaires businessman
   hommes gents
homo m gay (person)
honnête honest
honoraires mpl fee
hôpital m hospital
horaire m timetable ; schedule
horloge f clock
hors: *hors de* out of
   hors-saison off-season
   hors service out of order
   hors-taxe duty-free
hôte m host ; guest
hôtel m hotel
   hôtel de ville town hall
hôtesse f stewardess
huile f oil
   huile d'arachide peanut oil
   huile d'olive olive oil
   huile de tournesol sunflower oil
huître f oyster
hypermarché m hypermarket
hypermétrope long-sighted
hypertension f high blood pressure

I

ici here
idée f idea
il y a... there is/are...
   il y a un défaut there's a fault
   il y a une semaine a week ago
île f island
illimité(e) unlimited
immédiatement immediately
immeuble m building (offices, flats)
immunisation f immunisation
impair(e) odd (number)
impasse f dead end
imperméable waterproof
important(e) important
importer to import
impossible impossible

impôt m tax
imprimer to print
incendie m fire
inclus(e) included ; inclusive
inconfortable uncomfortable
incorrect(e) wrong
indicateur m guide ; timetable
indicatif m dialling code
indications fpl instructions ; directions
indice UVA m factor (sunblock)
  indice 25 factor 25
indigestion f indigestion
indispensable essential
infectieux(-euse) infectious
infection f infection
inférieur(e) inferior ; lower
infirmerie f infirmary
infirmier(-ière) m/f nurse
informations fpl news ; information
infusion f herbal tea
ingénieur m/f engineer
ingrédient m ingredient
inhalateur m inhaler
inondation f flood
inquiet(-iète) worried
inscrire to write (down) ; to enrol
insecte m insect
insolation f sunstroke
installations fpl facilities
instant m moment
  un instant! just a minute!
institut m institute
  institut de beauté beauty salon
insuline f insulin
intelligent(e) intelligent
interdit forbidden
intéressant(e) interesting
intérieur: à l'intérieur indoors
international(e) international
internet sans fil wireless internet
interprète m/f interpreter
intervention f operation (surgical)
intoxication alimentaire f food poisoning
introduire to introduce ; to insert
inutile useless ; unnecessary
invalide m/f disabled person
invité(e) m/f guest (house guest)
inviter to invite
iPod (m) iPod®
irlandais(e) Irish
Irlande f Ireland
Irlande du Nord f Northern Ireland
issue de secours f emergency exit
Italie f Italy

italien(ne) Italian
itinéraire m route
  itinéraire touristique scenic route
ivoire m ivory
ivre drunk

J

jaloux(-ouse) jealous
jamais never
jambe f leg
jambon m ham
janvier January
Japon m Japan
jardin m garden
jauge (de niveau d'huile) f dipstick
jaune yellow
jaune d'œuf m egg yolk
jaunisse f jaundice
jetable disposable
jetée f pier
jeter to throw
jeton m token
jeu m game ; set (of tools, etc) ;
  gambling
  jeu électronique computer game
  jeu vidéo video game
  jeu-concours quiz
jeudi m Thursday
jeune young
jeunesse f youth
joindre to join ; to enclose
joli(e) pretty
jonquille f daffodil
joue f cheek
jouer to play (games)
jouet m toy
jour m day
  jour férié public holiday
journal m newspaper
journaliste m/f journalist
journée f day (length of time)
juge m/f judge
juif (juive) Jewish
juillet July
juin June
jumeaux mpl twins
jumelles fpl twins ; binoculars
jupe f skirt
jus m juice
  jus de fruit fruit juice
  jus d'orange orange juice
  jus de viande gravy
jusqu'à (au) until ; till
juste fair ; reasonable

K

kart m go-cart
kas(c)her kosher
kayak m canoe
kilo m kilo
kilométrage m mileage
  kilométrage illimité unlimited mileage
kilomètre m kilometre
kiosque m kiosk ; newsstand
kit mains-libres hands-free kit *(for phone)*
kiwi kiwi fruit
klaxonner to sound one's horn
kyste m cyst

L

là there
lac m lake
lacets mpl shoelaces
laid(e) ugly
laine f wool
  laine polaire fleece *(top/jacket)*
laisse f leash
laisser to leave
  laissez en blanc leave blank
lait m milk
  lait cru unpasteurised milk
  lait démaquillant cleansing milk
  lait demi-écrémé semi-skimmed milk
  lait écrémé skim(med) milk
  lait entier full-cream milk
  lait longue conservation long-life milk
  lait maternisé baby milk *(formula)*
  lait solaire suntan lotion
laiterie f dairy
laitue f lettuce
lame f blade
  lames de rasoir razor blades
lampe f light ; lamp
  lampe de poche torch
landau m pram ; baby carriage
langue f tongue ; language
lapin m rabbit
laque f hair spray
lard m fat ; *(streaky)* bacon
lardons mpl diced bacon
large wide ; broad
largeur f width
laurier m sweet bay ; bay leaves
lavable washable
lavabo m washbasin
  lavabos toilets
lavage m washing
lavande f lavender
lave-auto m car wash
lave-glace m screen wash

lave-linge m washing machine
laver to wash
  se laver to wash oneself
laverie automatique f launderette
lave-vaisselle m dishwasher
laxatif m laxative
layette f baby clothes
leçon f lesson
  leçons particulières private lessons
lecture f reading
légal(e) legal
léger(-ère) light ; weak *(tea, etc)*
légume m vegetable
lendemain m next day
lent(e) slow
lentement slowly
lentille f lentil ; lens *(of glasses)*
  lentille de contact contact lens
lesbienne f lesbian
lessive f soap powder ; washing
lettre f letter
  lettre recommandée registered letter
leur(s) their
levée f collection *(of mail)*
lever to lift
  se lever to get up *(out of bed)*
lever de soleil m sunrise
lèvre f lip
levure f yeast
libellule f dragonfly
librairie f bookshop
libre free ; vacant
libre-service self-service
lieu m place *(location)*
lièvre m hare
ligne f line ; service ; route
lime à ongles f nail file
limitation de vitesse f speed limit
limonade f lemonade
lin m linen *(cloth)*
linge m linen *(bed, table)* ; laundry
lingerie f lingerie
lingettes fpl baby wipes
lion m lion
liquide f liquid
  liquide de freins brake fluid
lire to read
liste f list
lit m bed
  grand lit double bed
  lit d'enfant cot
  lit simple single bed
  lits jumeaux twin beds
litre m litre

livraison f delivery (of goods)
 livraison des bagages baggage reclaim
livre f pound
livre m book
local(e) local
locataire m/f tenant ; lodger
location f hiring (out) ; letting
logement m accommodation
loger to stay (reside for while)
logiciel m computer software
loi f law
loin far
lointain(e) distant
loisir m leisure
Londres London
long(ue) long
 le long de along
longe f loin (of meat)
longtemps for a long time
longueur f length
lot m prize ; lot (at auction)
loterie f lottery
lotion f lotion
loto m numerical lottery
lotte f monkfish ; angler fish
louer to let ; to hire ; to rent
 à louer for hire/to rent
loup m wolf ; sea perch
loupe f magnifying glass
lourd(e) heavy
loyer m rent
luge f sledge ; toboggan
lumière f light
lundi m Monday
lune f moon
 lune de miel honeymoon
lunettes fpl glasses
 lunettes de soleil sunglasses
 lunettes protectrices goggles
luxe m luxury
lycée m secondary school

M

M sign for the Paris metro
machine f machine
 machine à laver washing machine
mâchoire f jaw
Madame f Mrs ; Ms ; Madam
madeleine f small sponge cake
Mademoiselle f Miss
madère m Madeira (wine)
magasin m shop
 grand magasin department store
magnétophone m tape recorder

magnétoscope m video-cassette
 recorder
magret de canard m breast fillet of duck
mai May
maigre lean (meat)
maigrir to slim
maillet m mallet
maillot m vest
 maillot de bain swimsuit
main f hand
maintenant now
maire m mayor
mairie f town hall
mais but
maison f house ; home
 maison de campagne villa
maître d'hôtel m head waiter
majuscule f capital letter
mal badly
mal m harm ; pain
 mal de dents toothache
 mal de mer seasickness
 mal de tête headache
 faire du mal à quelqu'un to harm
 someone
malade sick (ill)
malade m/f sick person ; patient
maladie f disease
malentendu m misunderstanding
malle f trunk (luggage)
maman f mummy
manche m sleeve
mangue mango
Manche f the Channel
mandat m money order
manger to eat
manicure manicure
manière f way (manner)
manifestation f demonstration
manque m shortage ; lack
manteau m coat
maquereau m mackerel
maquillage m make-up
marais m marsh
marbre m marble (material)
marc m white grape spirit
marchand m dealer ; merchant
 marchand de poisson fishmonger
 marchand de vin wine merchant
marche f step ; march; walking
 marche arrière reverse gear
marché m market
 marché aux puces flea market
 marché d'artisanat craft fair
 marché fermier farmers' market

marcher to walk ; to work *(machine, car)*
  en marche on *(machine)*
mardi *m* Tuesday
  mardi gras Shrove Tuesday
marée *f* tide
  marée basse low tide
  marée haute high tide
margarine *f* margarine
mari *m* husband
mariage *m* wedding
marié *m* bridegroom
marié(e) married
mariée *f* bride
marier to marry
  se marier to get married
mariné(e) marinated
marionnette *f* puppet
marque *f* make ; brand *(name)*
marquer to score *(goal, point)*
marron brown
marron *m* chestnut
mars March
marteau *m* hammer
masculin male *(person, on forms)*
massage massage
mât *m* mast
match de football *m* football match
match en nocturne *m* floodlit fixture
matelas *m* mattress
  matelas pneumatique lilo®
matériel *m* equipment ; kit
matin *m* morning
mauvais(e) bad ; wrong ; off *(food)*
maximum *m* maximum
mazout *m* oil *(for heating)*
mécanicien *m* mechanic
méchant(e) naughty ; wicked
médecin *m* doctor
médicament *m* medicine ; drug ; medication
médiéval(e) medieval
Méditerranée *f* Mediterranean Sea
méduse *f* jellyfish
mégaoctet megabyte
  128 mégaoctets 128 megabytes
meilleur(e) best ; better
  meilleurs vœux best wishes
mél *m* e-mail address
membre *m* member *(of club, etc)*
même same
mémoire *f* memory
ménage *m* housework
méningite *f* meningitis
mensuel(le) monthly

menthe *f* mint ; mint tea
menu *m* menu *(set)*
  menu à prix fixe set price menu
  menu du jour today's menu
mer *f* sea
  mer du Nord North Sea
mercerie *f* haberdasher's
merci thank you
mercredi *m* Wednesday
mère *f* mother
merlan *m* whiting
merlu *m* hake
mérou *m* grouper
merveilleux(-euse) wonderful
message *m* message
  message SMS SMS message
messagerie vocale voicemail
messe *f* mass *(church)*
messieurs *mpl* men
  Messieurs gentlemen
messieurs gents
mesure *f* measurement
mesurer to measure
métal *m* metal
météo *f* weather forecast
métier *m* trade ; occupation ; craft
mètre *m* metre
  mètre à ruban tape measure
métro *m* underground railway
mettre to put ; to put on
  mettre au point focus *(camera)*
  mettre en marche to turn on
meublé(e) furnished
meubles *mpl* furniture
  meubles de style period furniture
mi-bas *mpl* pop-socks ; knee-highs
micro(phone) microphone
midi *m* midday ; noon
Midi *m* the south of France
miel *m* honey
mieux better ; best
migraine *f* headache ; migraine
milieu *m* middle
mille *m* thousand
millimètre *m* millimetre
million *m* million
mince slim ; thin
mine *f* expression ; mine *(coal, etc)*
mineur *m* miner
mineur(e) under age ; minor
mini-brasserie micro-brewery
minidisque minidisk
minimum *m* minimum
minuit *m* midnight

minuscule tiny
minute f minute
minuteur m timer
mirabelle f plum ; plum brandy
miroir m mirror
mise en plis f set (for hair)
mistral m strong cold dry wind
mite f moth (clothes)
mixte mixed
Mo Mb (megabyte)
mobile (portable) mobile (phone)
mobilier m furniture
mode f fashion
  à la mode fashionable
  mode d'emploi instructions for use
modem m modem
moderne modern
moelle f marrow (beef, etc)
moi me
moineau m sparrow
moins less ; minus
  moins (de) less (than)
  moins cher cheaper
moins m the least
mois m month
moississure f mould (fungus)
moitié f half
  à moitié prix half-price
moka m coffee cream cake ; mocha
  coffee
molle soft
moment m moment
  en ce moment at the moment
mon/ma/mes my
monastère m monastery
monde m world
  il y a du monde there's a lot of people
moniteur m instructor ; coach
monitrice f instructress ; coach
monnaie f currency ; change
monnayeur m automatic change
  machine
monsieur m gentleman
Monsieur m Mr ; Sir
montagne f mountain
montant m amount (total)
monter to take up ; to go up ; to rise ;
  to get in (car)
  monter à cheval to horse-ride
montre f watch
montrer to show
monument m monument
moquette f fitted carpet
morceau m piece ; bit ; cut (of meat)
mordu(e) bitten

morsure f bite
  morsure de serpent snake bite
mort(e) dead
mosquée f mosque
mot m word ; note (letter)
  mot de passe password
  mots croisés crossword puzzle
motel m motel
moteur m engine ; motor
motif m pattern
moto f motorbike
mou (molle) soft
mouche f fly
moucheron m midge
mouchoir m handkerchief
mouette f seagull
mouillé(e) wet
moule f mussel
moulin m mill
  moulin à vent windmill
moulinet m reel (fishing)
mourir to die
mousse f foam ; mousse
  mousse à raser shaving foam
  mousse coiffante hair mousse
mousseux(-euse) sparkling (wine)
moustache f moustache
moustique m mosquito
moutarde f mustard
mouton m sheep ; lamb ; mutton
moyen(ne) average
moyenne f average
MP3 (lecteur de) MP3 player
muguet m lily of the valley ; thrush
  (candida)
muni(e) de supplied with ;
  in possession of
mur m wall
mûr(e) mature ; ripe
mûre f blackberry
muscade f nutmeg
musée m museum
  musée d'art art gallery
musique f music
Musulman(e) Muslim
myope short-sighted

N

nager to swim
naissance f birth
nappe f tablecloth
nappé(e) coated (with chocolate, etc)
natation f swimming
national(e) national

nationalité f nationality
natte f plait
nature f wildlife
naturel(le) natural
nautique nautical ; water
navette f shuttle *(bus service)*
navigation f sailing
navire m ship
né(e) born
négatif m negative *(photography)*
neige f snow
neiger to snow
nettoyage m cleaning
  nettoyage à sec dry-cleaning
nettoyer to clean
neuf (neuve) new
neveu m nephew
névralgie f headache
nez m nose
niche f kennel
nid m nest
  nid de poule pothole
nièce f niece
niveau m level ; standard
noce f wedding
nocturne m late opening
Noël m Christmas
  joyeux Noël! merry Christmas!
noir(e) black
noisette f hazelnut
noix f nut ; walnut
nom m name ; noun
  nom de famille family name
  nom de jeune fille maiden name
  nom d'utilisateur username
nombre m number
nombreux(-euse) numerous
non no ; not
non alcoolisé(e) non-alcoholic
non-fumeur non-smoking
nord m north
normal(e) normal ; standard *(size)*
nos our
notaire m solicitor
note f note ; bill ; memo
notre our
nœud m knot
nourrir to feed
nourriture f food
nouveau (nouvelle) new
  de nouveau again
nouvelles fpl news
novembre November
nu(e) naked ; bare

nuage m cloud
nuageux(-euse) cloudy
nucléaire nuclear
nuit f night
  bonne nuit good night
numéro m number ; act ; issue
  numéro de mobile/de portable mobile number

O

objectif m objective ; lens *(of camera)*
objet m object
  objets de valeur valuable items
  objets trouvés lost property
obligatoire compulsory
oblitérer to stamp *(ticket, stamp)*
obsèques fpl funeral
obtenir to get ; to obtain
occasion f occasion ; bargain
occupé(e) busy ; hired *(taxi)*
occupé(e) engaged
océan m ocean
octobre October
odeur f smell
œuf m egg
  œuf de Pâques Easter egg
office m service *(church)* ; office
  office du tourisme tourist office
offre f offer
oie f goose
oignon m onion
œil m eye
œillet m carnation
oiseau m bird
olive f olive
ombre f shade/shadow
  à l'ombre in the shade
oncle m uncle
onde f wave
ongle m nail *(finger)*
opéra m opera
or m gold
orage m storm
orange orange ; amber *(traffic light)*
orange f orange
orangeade f orange squash
orchestre m orchestra ; stalls *(in theatre)*
ordinaire ordinary
ordinateur m computer
  l'ordinateur de poche palmtop computer
ordonnance f prescription
ordre m order
  à l'ordre de payable to
ordures fpl litter *(rubbish)*

oreille f ear
oreiller m pillow
oreillons mpl mumps
organiser to organize
organiseur PDA m PDA
orge f barley
origan m oregano
os m bone
oseille f sorrel
osier m wicker
ou or
où where
oublier to forget
ouest m west
oui yes
ours(e) m/f bear (animal)
oursin m sea urchin
outils mpl tools
ouvert(e) open ; on (tap, gas, etc)
ouvert(e) open
ouverture f overture ; opening
ouvrable working (day)
ouvre-boîtes m tin-opener
ouvre-bouteilles m bottle-opener
ouvrir to open

P

page f page
   pages jaunes Yellow Pages
paiement m payment
paille f straw
pain m bread ; loaf of bread
   pain bis brown bread
   pain complet wholemeal bread
   pain grillé toast
pair(e) even
paire f pair
paix f peace
palais m palace
pâle pale
palmes fpl flippers
palourde f clam
pamplemousse m grapefruit
panaché m shandy
pané(e) in breadcrumbs
panier m basket
   panier repas packed lunch
panne f breakdown
panneau m sign
pansement m bandage
pantalon m trousers
pantoufles fpl slippers
pape m pope
papeterie f stationer's shop

papier m paper
   papier à lettres writing paper
   papier alu(minium) foil
   papier cadeau gift-wrap
   papier hygiénique toilet paper
   papiers identity papers ; driving
   licence
papillon m butterfly
pâquerette f daisy
Pâques m or fpl Easter
paquet m package ; pack ; packet
par by ; through ; per
   par example for example
   par jour per day
   par téléphone by phone
   par voie orale take by mouth
   (medicine)
paradis m heaven
paralysé(e) paralysed
parapluie m umbrella
parasol m sunshade
parc m park
   parc d'attractions funfair
parce que because
parcmètre m parking meter
parcours m route
pardon! sorry! ; excuse me!
parer to ward off
pare-brise m windscreen
pare-chocs m bumper
parent(e) m/f relative
parents mpl parents
paresseux(-euse) lazy
parfait(e) perfect
parfum m perfume ; flavour
parfumerie f perfume shop
pari m bet
parier sur to bet on
parking m car park
   parking assuré parking facilities
   parking souterrain underground
   car park
   parking surveillé attended car park
parler (à) to speak (to) ; to talk (to)
paroisse f parish
partager to share
parterre m flowerbed
parti m political party
partie f part ; match (game)
partir to leave ; to go
   à partir de from
partout everywhere
pas not
   pas encore not yet
pas m step ; pace

passage m passage
  passage à niveau level crossing
  passage clouté pedestrian crossing
  passage interdit no through way
  passage souterrain underpass
passager(-ère) m/f passenger
passé(e) past
passe-temps m hobby
passeport m passport
passer to pass ; to spend (time)
  se passer to happen
passerelle f gangway (bridge)
passionnant(e) exciting
passoire f sieve ; colander
pastèque f watermelon
pasteur m minister (of religion)
pastille f lozenge
pastis m aniseed-flavoured apéritif
pataugeoire f paddling pool
pâte f pastry ; dough ; paste
pâté m pâté
pâtes fpl pasta
patient(e) m/f patient (in hospital)
patin m skate
  patins à glace ice skates
  patins à roulettes roller skates
patinoire f skating rink
pâtisserie f cake shop ; little cake
patron m boss ; pattern (knitting,
  dress, etc)
patronne f boss
pauvre poor
payer to pay (for)
  payé(e) paid
  payé(e) d'avance prepaid
pays m land ; country
  du pays local
Pays-Bas mpl Netherlands
paysage countryside ; scenery
péage m toll (motorway, etc)
peau f hide (leather) ; skin
pêche f peach ; fishing
pêcher to fish
pêcheur m angler
pédale f pedal
pédalo m pedal boat/pedalo
pédicure m/f chiropodist
peigne m comb
peignoir m dressing gown ; bath-robe
peindre to paint ; to decorate
peinture f painting ; paintwork
peler to peel (fruit)
pèlerinage m pilgrimage
pelle f spade
  pelle à poussière dustpan

pellicule f film (for camera)
  pellicule couleur colour film
  pellicule noir et blanc black and
  white film
pelote f ball (of string, wool)
  pelote basque pelota (ball game
  for 2 players)
pelouse f lawn
pencher to lean
pendant during
pendant que while
pénicilline f penicillin
péninsule f peninsula
pénis m penis
penser to think
pension f guesthouse
  pension complète full board
pente f slope
Pentecôte f Whitsun
pépin m pip
perceuse électrique f electric drill
perdre to lose
perdu(e) lost (object)
père m father
périmé(e) out of date
périphérique m ring road
perle f bead ; pearl
permanente f perm
permettre to permit
permis m permit ; licence
  permis de chasse hunting permit
  permis de conduire driving licence
  permis de pêche fishing permit
perruque f wig
persil m parsley
personne f person
peser to weigh
pétanque f type of bowls
pétillant(e) fizzy
petit(e) small ; slight
  petit déjeuner breakfast
  petit pain roll
petit-fils m grandson
petite-fille f granddaughter
pétrole m oil (petroleum) ; paraffin
peu little ; few
  à peu près approximately
  un peu (de) a bit (of)
peur f fear
  avoir peur (de) to be afraid (of)
peut-être perhaps
phare m headlight ; lighthouse
pharmacie f chemist's ; pharmacy
pharmacien(ne) pharmacist
phoque m seal (animal)
photo f photograph

photocopie f photocopy
photocopier to photocopy
photocopieuse photocopier
piano m piano
pichet m jug ; carafe
pie f magpie
pièce f room (in house) ; play (theatre) ; coin
  pièce d'identité means of identification
  pièce de rechange spare part
pied m foot
  à pied on foot
pierre f stone
piéton m pedestrian
pignon m pine kernel
pile f pile ; battery (for radio, etc)
pilon m drumstick (of chicken)
pilote m/f pilot
pilule f pill
piment chilli (fruit)
pin m pine
pince f pliers
  pince à cheveux hairgrip
  pince à épiler tweezers
  pince à linge clothes peg
pipe f pipe (smoking)
piquant(e) spicy ; hot
pique-nique m picnic
piquer to sting
piquet m peg (for tent)
piqûre f insect bite ; injection ; sting
pire worse
piscine f swimming pool
pissenlit m dandelion
pistache f pistachio (nut)
piste f ski-run ; runway (airport)
  piste cyclable cycle track
  piste de luge toboggan run
  piste pour débutants nursery slope
  pistes tous niveaux slopes for all
  levels of skiers
pistolet m pistol
placard m cupboard
place f square (in town) ; seat ; space (room)
  places debout standing room
plafond m ceiling
plage f beach
  plage seins nus topless beach
plainte f complaint
plaisanterie f joke
plaisir m enjoyment ; pleasure
plaît: s'il vous/te plaît please
plan m map (of town)
  plan de la ville street map
planche f plank
  planche à découper chopping board
  planche à repasser ironing board

planche à voile sailboard ; wind-surfing
  planche de surf surfboard
plancher m floor (of room)
plante f plant ; sole (of foot, shoe)
plaque f sheet ; plate
  plaque d'immatriculation f numberplate
plat m dish ; course (of meal)
  plat à emporter take-away meal
  plat de résistance main course
  plat principal main course
plat(e) level (surface) ; flat
  à plat flat (battery)
platane m plane tree
plateau m tray
plâtre m plaster
plein(e) (de) full (of)
  le plein! fill it up! (car)
  plein sud facing south
  plein tarif peak rate
pleurer to cry (weep)
pleuvoir to rain
  il pleut it's raining
plier to fold
plomb m lead ; fuse
plombage m filling (in tooth)
plombier m plumber
plonger to dive
pluie f rain
plume f feather
plus more ; most
  plus grand(e) (que) bigger (than)
  plus tard later
plusieurs several
pneu m tyre
  pneu dégonflé flat tyre
  pneu de rechange spare tyre
  pneus cloutés snow tyres
poche f pocket
poché(e) poached
poêle f frying-pan
poème m poem
poids m weight
  poids lourd heavy goods vehicle
poignée f handle
poignet m wrist
poil m hair ; coat (of animal)
poinçonner to punch (ticket, etc)
point m place ; point ; stitch ; dot
  à point medium rare (meat)
pointure f size (of shoes)
poire f pear ; pear brandy
poireau m leek
pois m pea ; spot (dot)
  petits pois peas
poison m poison
poisson m fish

poissonnerie f fishmonger's shop
poitrine f breast ; chest
poivre m pepper
poivron m pepper *(capsicum)*
police f policy *(insurance)* ; police
policier m policeman ; detective film/novel
pollué(e) polluted
pommade f ointment
pomme f apple ; potato
pomme de terre f potato
pompe f pump
  pompe à vélo bicycle pump
pompes funèbres fpl undertaker's
pompier m fireman
  pompiers fire brigade
poney m pony
pont m bridge ; deck *(of ship)*
  faire le pont to have a long weekend
populaire popular
porc m pork ; pig
port m harbour ; port
portable m mobile phone ; laptop
portatif portable
porte f door ; gate
portefeuille m wallet
porter to wear; to carry
porte-bagages m luggage rack
porte-clefs m keyring
porte-monnaie m purse
porteur m porter
portier m doorman
portion f helping ; portion
porto m port *(wine)*
poser to put ; to lay down
posologie f dosage
posséder to own
poste f post ; post office
  poste de contrôle checkpoint
  poste de secours first-aid post
poste m radio/television set ; extension *(phone)*
poster m poster *(decorative)*
poster to post
pot m pot ; carton *(yoghurt, etc)*
  pot d'échappement exhaust pipe
potable ok to drink
potage m soup
poteau m post *(pole)*
  poteau indicateur signpost
poterie f pottery
poubelle f dustbin
pouce m thumb
poudre f powder
poule f hen
poulet m chicken

poumon m lung
poupée f doll
pour for
pourboire m tip
pourquoi why
pourri(e) rotten *(fruit, etc)*
pousser to push
poussette f push chair
pousser to push
poussière f dust
pouvoir to be able to
pré m meadow
préfecture de police f police headquarters
préféré(e) favourite
préférer to prefer
premier(-ière) first
  premier cru first-class wine
  premiers secours first aid
prendre to take ; to get ; to catch
prénom m first name
préparer to prepare ; to cook
près de near (to)
présenter to present ; to introduce
préservatif m condom
pressé(e) squeezed ; pressed
pressing m dry cleaner's
pression f pressure
  pression des pneus tyre pressure
prêt(e) ready
  prêt à cuire ready to cook
prêt-à-porter m ready-to-wear
prêter to lend
prêtre m priest
prévision f forecast
prier to pray
prière de... please...
prince m prince
princesse f princess
principal(e) main
printemps m spring
priorité f right of way
  priorité à droite give way to traffic from right
prise f plug ; socket
privé(e) private
prix m price ; prize
  à prix réduit cut-price
  prix d'entrée admission fee
  prix de détail retail price
probablement probably
problème m problem
prochain(e) next
proche close *(near)*
produits mpl produce ; product

professeur m teacher
profiter de to take advantage of
profond(e) deep
programme m schedule ; programme
(list of performers, etc)
  programme informatique computer
  program
promenade f walk ; promenade ; ride
(in vehicle)
  faire une promenade to go for a walk
promettre to promise
promotionnel(le) special low-price
prononcer to pronounce
propre clean ; own
propriétaire m/f owner
propriété f property
protège-slip m panty-liner
protestant(e) Protestant
provenance f origin ; source
provisions fpl groceries
province f province
provisoire temporary
provisoirement for the time being
proximité: à proximité nearby
prune f plum ; plum brandy
pruneau m prune
public m audience
public(-ique) public
publicité f advertisement (on TV)
puce f flea
puissance f power
puits m well (for water)
pull m sweater
pullover m sweater
purée f purée ; mashed
PV m parking ticket
pyjama m pyjamas

Q

quai m platform
qualifié(e) skilled
qualité f quality
quand when
quantité f quantity
quarantaine f quarantine
quart m quarter
quartier m neighbourhood ; district
que that ; than ; whom ; what
  qu'est-ce que c'est? what is it?
quel(le) which ; what
quelqu'un someone
quelque some
quelque chose something
quelquefois sometimes
question f question

queue f queue ; tail
  faire la queue to queue (up)
qui who ; which
quincaillerie f hardware ; hardware shop
quinzaine f fortnight
quitter to leave a place
quoi what
quotidien(ne) daily

R

rabais m reduction
raccourci m short cut
raccrocher to hang up (phone)
race f race (people)
racine f root
radiateur m radiator
radio f radio
radiographie f X-ray
radis m radish
rafraîchissements mpl refreshments
rage f rabies
ragoût m stew ; casserole
raide steep
raie f skate (fish)
raifort m horseradish
raisin m grapes
  raisin blanc green grapes
  raisin noir black grapes
  raisins secs sultanas ; raisins ; currants
raison f reason
ralentir to slow down
ralentissement m tailback
rallonge f extension (electrical)
randonnée f hike
  randonnée à cheval pony-trekking
râpe f grater
râpé(e) grated
rappel m reminder (on signs)
rappeler to remind
  se rappeler to remember
rapide quick ; fast
rapide m express train
raquette f racket ; bat ; snowshoe
rare rare ; unusual
raser to shave off
  se raser to shave
rasoir m razor
  rasoir électrique shaver
rater to miss (train, flight etc)
RATP f Paris transport authority
rayé(e) striped
rayon m shelf ; department (in store) ;
spoke (of wheel)
  rayon hommes menswear
RC ground floor

reboucher to recork
récemment recently
récepteur m receiver (of phone)
réception f reception ; check-in
réceptionniste m/f receptionist
recette f recipe
recharge f refill
rechargeable refillable (lighter, pen)
recharger to recharge (battery, etc)
réchaud de camping m camping stove
réclamation f complaint
réclame f advertisement
recommandé(e) registered (mail)
recommander to recommend
récompense f reward
reconnaître to recognize
reçu m receipt
réduction f reduction ; discount; concession
réduire to reduce
refuge m mountain hut
refuser to reject ; to refuse
regarder to look at
régime m diet (slimming)
région f region
règle f rule ; ruler (for measuring)
règles fpl period (menstruation)
  règles douloureuses cramps
règlement m regulation ; payment
régler to pay ; to settle
réglisse f liquorice
reine f queen
relais routier m roadside restaurant
rembourser to refund
remède m remedy
remercier to thank
remettre to put back
  remettre à plus tard to postpone
  se remettre to recover (from illness)
remonte-pente m ski tow
remorque f trailer
remorquer to tow
remplir to fill ; to fill in/out/up
renard m fox
rencontrer to meet
rendez-vous m date ; appointment
rendre to give back
renouveler to renew
renseignements mpl information
rentrée f return to work after break
  rentrée (des classes) start of the new school year
renverser to knock down (in car)
réparations fpl repairs
réparer to fix (repair)

repas m meal
repasser to iron
répondeur automatique m answer-phone
répondre (à) to reply ; to answer
réponse f answer ; reply
repos m rest
  se reposer to rest
représentation f performance
requis(e) required
RER m Paris high-speed commuter train
réseau m network
réservation f reservation ; booking
réserve naturelle f nature reserve
réservé(e) reserved
réserver to book (reserve)
réservoir m tank
  réservoir d'essence fuel tank
respirer to breathe
ressort m spring (metal)
restaurant m restaurant
reste m rest (remainder)
rester to remain ; to stay
restoroute m roadside or motorway restaurant
retard m delay
retirer to withdraw ; to collect (tickets)
retour m return
retourner to go back
retrait m withdrawal ; collection
  retrait d'espèces cash withdrawal
retraité(e) retired
retraité(e) m/f old-age pensioner
rétrécir to shrink (clothes)
rétroviseur m rearview mirror
  rétroviseur latéral wing mirror
réunion f meeting
réussir (à) to succeed
réussite f success ; patience (game)
réveil m alarm clock
réveiller to wake (someone)
  se réveiller to wake up
réveillon m Christmas/New Year's Eve
revenir to come back
réverbère m lamppost
revue f review ; magazine
rez-de-chaussée m ground floor
rhum m rum
rhumatisme m rheumatism
rhume m cold (illness)
  rhume des foins hay fever
riche rich
rideau m curtain
rides fpl wrinkles
rien nothing ; anything
  rien à déclarer nothing to declare

re to laugh
vage m shore
ve f river bank
vière f river
z m rice
N trunk road
be f gown ; dress
binet m tap
cade f ringroad
cher m rock (boulder)
gnon m kidney (to eat)
oi m king
oman m novel
oman(e) Romanesque
omantique romantic
omarin m rosemary
ond(e) round
ond-point m roundabout
ose pink
ose f rose
ossignol m nightingale
ôti(e) roast
ôtisserie f steakhouse ; roast meat counter
oue f wheel
  roue de secours spare wheel
ouge red
ouge à lèvres m lipstick
ouge-gorge m robin
ougeole f measles
ougeur f rash (skin)
ouillé(e) rusty
ouleau à pâtisserie m rolling pin
ouler to roll ; to go (by car)
oute f road ; route
  route barrée road closed
  route nationale trunk road
  route principale major road
  route secondaire minor road
outier m lorry driver
Royaume-Uni m United Kingdom
ruban m ribbon ; tape
rubéole f rubella
rue f street
  rue sans issue no through road
ruelle f lane ; alley
ruisseau m stream
russe Russian

S

SA Ltd ; plc
sable m sand
  sables mouvants quicksand
sabot m wheel clamp
sac m sack ; bag
  sac à dos backpack

sac à main handbag
sac de couchage sleeping bag
sac poubelle bin liner
sachet de thé m tea bag
sacoche f panniers (for bike)
sacoche d'ordinateur portable laptop
  bag
safran m saffron
sage good (well-behaved) ; wise
saignant(e) rare (steak)
saigner to bleed
saint(e) m/f saint
Saint-Sylvestre f New Year's Eve
saisir to seize
saison f season
  basse saison low season
  de saison in season
  haute saison high season
saisonnier seasonal
salade f lettuce ; salad
  salade de fruits fruit salad
salaire m salary ; wage
sale dirty
salé(e) salty ; savoury
salle f lounge (airport) ; hall ; ward (hospital)
  salle à manger dining room
  salle d'attente waiting room
  salle de bains bathroom
salon m sitting room ; lounge
  salon de beauté beauty salon
salut! hi!
samedi m Saturday
SAMU m emergency services
sandales fpl sandals
sandwich m sandwich
sang m blood
sanglier m wild boar
sans without
  sans alcool alcohol-free
  sans connaissance unconscious
  sans issue no through road
  sans OGM GM-free
santé f health
  santé! cheers!
  en bonne santé well (healthy)
sapeurs-pompiers mpl fire brigade
SARL f Ltd ; plc
sauce f sauce
sauf except (for)
saumon m salmon
sauter to jump
sauvegarder to back up (computer)
sauver to rescue
savoir to know (be aware of)
  savoir faire quelque chose to know
  how to do sth

savon m soap
Scellofrais® m Clingfilm®
scène f stage
scie f saw
score m score (of match)
scotch m whisky
séance f meeting ; performance
seau m bucket
sec (sèche) dried (fruit, beans)
sèche-cheveux m hairdryer
sèche-linge m tumble dryer
sécher to dry
seconde f second (in time)
  en seconde second class
secouer to shake
secours m help
secrétaire m/f secretary
secrétariat m office
secteur m sector ; mains
sécurité f security ; safety
séjour m stay ; visit
sel m salt
self m self-service restaurant
selle f saddle
semaine f week
sens m meaning ; direction
  sens interdit no entry
  sens unique one-way street
sentier m footpath
  sentier écologique nature trail
sentir to feel
septembre September
séparément separately
série f series ; set
seringue f syringe
serré(e) tight (fitting)
serrer to grip ; to squeeze
  serrez à droite keep to the right
serrure f lock
serrurerie f locksmith's
serveur m waiter
serveuse f waitress
servez-vous help yourself
service m service ; service charge ; favour
  service compris service included
  service d'urgences A & E
serviette f towel ; briefcase
  serviette hygiénique sanitary towel
servir to dish up ; to serve
seul(e) alone ; lonely
seulement only
sexe m sex
shampooing m shampoo
  shampooing antipelliculaire anti-dandruff shampoo

short m shorts
si if ; yes (to negative question)
SIDA m AIDS
siècle m century
siège m seat ; head office
  siège pour bébés/enfants car seat (for children)
signaler to report
signer to sign
simple simple ; single ; plain
site m site
  site internet site (website)
  site web web site
situé(e) located
ski m ski ; skiing
  ski de piste downhill skiing
  ski de randonnée/fond cross-country skiing
  ski nautique water-skiing
slip m underpants ; panties
  slip (de bain) trunks (swimming)
snack m snack bar
SNCB f Belgian Railways
SNCF f French Railways
société f company ; society
sœur f sister
soie f silk
soif f thirst
  avoir soif to be thirsty
soin m care
  soins du visage facial
soir m evening
soirée f evening ; party
soja m soya ; soya bean
sol m ground ; soil
soldat m soldier
solde m balance (remainder owed)
soldes mpl sales
  soldes permanents sale prices all year round
sole f sole (fish)
soleil m sun ; sunshine
somme f sum
sommelier m wine waiter
sommet m top (of hill, mountain)
somnifère m sleeping pill
sonner to ring ; to strike
sonnette f doorbell
sonner to ring bell
sorbet m water ice
sorte f kind (sort, type)
sortie f exit
  sortie de secours emergency exit
  sortie interdite no exit
sortir to go out (leave)
soucoupe f saucer

oudain suddenly
ouhaiter to wish
oûl(e) drunk
oulever to lift
oupape f valve
oupe f soup
ouper m supper
ourcils mpl eyebrows
ourd(e) deaf
ourire to smile
ouris f mouse (also for computer)
ous underneath ; under
ous-sol m basement
ous-titres mpl subtitles
ous-vêtements mpl underwear
outerrain(e) underground
outien-gorge m bra
ouvenir m memory ; souvenir
ouvent often
spam spam (email)
sparadrap m sticking plaster
spécial(e) special
spécialité f speciality
spectacle m show (in theatre) ;
 entertainment
spectateurs mpl audience
spiritueux mpl spirits
sport m sport
 sports nautiques water sports
sportif(-ive) sports ; athletic
stade m stadium
stage m course (period of training)
standard m switchboard
station f station (metro) ; resort
 station balnéaire seaside resort
 station de taxis taxi rank
 station thermale spa
 station-service service station
stationnement m parking
stérilet m coil (IUD)
stick mémoire memory stick (for camera
 etc)
stimulateur (cardiaque) m pacemaker
store m blind ; awning
stylo m pen
sucette f lollipop ; dummy
sucre m sugar
sucré(e) sweet
sud m south
suisse Swiss
Suisse f Switzerland
suite f series ; continuation ; sequel
suivant(e) following
suivre to follow
 faire suivre please forward

super m four-star petrol
supermarché m supermarket
supplément m extra charge
supplémentaire extra
sur on ; onto ; on top of ; upon
 sur place on the spot
sûr safe ; sure
surcharger to overload
surchauffer to overheat
surf m surfing
 faire du surf to surf
 surf des neiges snowboard
 surf sur neige snowboarding
surgelés mpl frozen foods
surveillé(e) supervised
survêtement m tracksuit
sympa(thique) nice ; pleasant
synagogue f synagogue
syndicat d'initiative m tourist office
système de navigation GPS GPS
 (global positioning system)
système de navigation satellite satnav
 (satellite navigation system, for car)

T

tabac m tobacco ; tobacconist's
table f table
tableau m painting ; picture ; board
 tableau de bord dashboard
tablier m apron
tache f stain
taie d'oreiller f pillowcase
taille f size (of clothes) ; waist
 taille unique one size
 grande taille outsize (clothes)
tailleur m tailor ; suit (women's)
talc m talc
talon m heel ; stub (counterfoil)
 talon minute shoes reheeled while
 you wait
tampon m tampon
 tampon Jex® scouring pad
tante f aunt
taper to strike ; to type
tapis m carpet
 tapis de sol groundsheet
tard late
 au plus tard at the latest
tarif m price-list ; rate ; tarif
tarte f flan ; tart
tartine f slice of bread and butter (or jam)
tartiner: à tartiner for spreading
tasse f cup ; mug
taureau m bull
tauromachie f bull-fighting

taux m rate
  taux de change exchange rate
  taux fixe flat rate
taxe f duty ; tax (on goods)
taxi m cab (taxi)
TCF m Touring Club de France (AA)
teinture f dye
teinturerie f dry cleaner's
télé f TV
télébenne f gondola lift
télécabine f gondola lift
télécarte f phonecard
télécommande f remote control
téléphérique m cable-car
téléphone m telephone
  téléphone portable mobile phone
  téléphone portable appareil-photo camera phone
  téléphone sans fil cordless phone
téléphoner (à) to phone
téléphoniste m/f operator
télésiège m chair-lift
téléviseur m television (set)
télévision f television
température f temperature
tempête f storm
temple m temple ; synagogue ; protestant church
temps m weather ; time
tendon m tendon
tenir to hold ; to keep
tennis m tennis
tension f voltage ; blood pressure
tente f tent
tenue f clothes ; dress
  tenue de soirée evening dress
terrain m ground ; land ; pitch ; course
terrasse f terrace
terre f land ; earth ; ground
  terre cuite terracotta
tête f head
tétine f dummy (for baby) ; teat (for bottle)
TGV m high-speed train
thé m tea
  thé au lait tea with milk
  thé nature tea without milk
théâtre m theatre
théière f teapot
thermomètre m thermometer
ticket m ticket (bus, cinema, museum)
  ticket de caisse receipt
tiède lukewarm
tiers m third ; third party
timbre m stamp
tirage m printing ; print (photo)

  tirage le mercredi lottery draw on Wednesdays
tire-bouchon m corkscrew
tire-fesses m ski tow
tirer to pull
  tirez pull
tiroir m drawer
tisane f herbal tea
tissu m material ; fabric
titre m title
  à titre indicatif for info only
  à titre provisoire provisionally
titulaire m/f holder of (card, etc)
toile f canvas ; web (spider)
  Toile World Wide Web
toilettes fpl toilet ; powder room
toit m roof
  toit ouvrant sunroof
tomate f tomato
tomber to fall
tonalité f dialling tone
tongs fpl flip flops
tonneau m barrel (wine/beer)
tonnerre m thunder
torchon m tea towel
tordre to twist
tôt early
total m total (amount)
toucher to touch
toujours always ; still ; forever
tour f tower
tour m trip ; walk ; ride
tourisme m sightseeing
touriste m/f tourist
touristique tourist (route, resort, etc)
tourner to turn
tournesol m sunflower
tournevis m screwdriver
  tournevis cruciforme phillips screwdriver
tourte f pie
tous all (plural)
  tous les jours daily (each day)
Toussaint f All Saints' Day
tousser to cough
tout(e) all ; everything
  tout à l'heure in a while
  tout compris all inclusive
  tout de suite straight away
  tout droit straight ahead
tout le monde everyone
toutes all (plural)
  toutes directions all routes
toux f cough
tradition f custom (tradition)
traditionnel(-elle) traditional
traduction f translation

traduire to translate
train m train
trajet m journey
tramway m tram
tranchant sharp (razor, knife)
tranche f slice
tranquille quiet (place)
transférer to transfer
transpirer to sweat
travail m work
travailler to work (person)
  travailler à son compte to be self employed
travaux mpl road works ; alterations
travers: à travers through
traversée f crossing (voyage)
traverser to cross (road, sea, etc)
tremplin m diving-board
  tremplin de ski ski jump
très very ; much
triangle de présignalisation m warning triangle
tricot m knitting ; sweater
tricoter to knit
trimestre m term
trisomie Down's syndrome
  il/elle est trisomique he/she has Down's syndrome
triste sad
trop too ; too much
trottoir m pavement ; sidewalk
trou m hole
trousse f pencil case
  trousse de premiers secours first aid kit
trouver to find
  se trouver to be (situated)
tuer kill
tunnel m tunnel
tuyau m pipe (for water, gas)
  tuyau d'arrosage hosepipe
TVA f VAT
typique typical

U

UE f EU
ulcère m ulcer
ultérieur(e) later (date, etc)
un(e) one ; a ; an
  l'un ou l'autre either one
uni(e) plain (not patterned)
Union européenne f European Union
unité fpl credit (on mobile phone)
université f university
urgence f urgency ; emergency
  Urgences A & E

urgentiste m/f paramedic
urine f urine
usage m use
usine f factory
utile useful
utiliser to use

V

vacances fpl holiday(s)
  en vacances on holiday
  grandes vacances summer holiday
vaccin m vaccination
vache f cow
vagin m vagina
vague f wave (on sea)
vaisselle f crockery
valable valid (ticket, licence, etc)
valeur f value
valider to validate
valise f suitcase
vallée f valley
valoir to be worth
  ça vaut... it's worth...
vanille f vanilla
vapeur f steam
varicelle f chickenpox
varié(e) varied ; various
vase m vase
veau m calf ; veal
vedette f speedboat ; star (film)
végétal(e) vegetable
végétarien(ne) vegetarian
véhicule m vehicle
  véhicules lents slow-moving vehicles
veille f the day before ; eve
  veille de Noël Christmas Eve
veine f vein
vélo m bike
  vélo tout terrain (VTT) mountain bike
velours m velvet
venaison f venison
vendange(s) fpl harvest (of grapes)
vendeur(-euse) m/f sales assistant
vendre to sell
  à vendre for sale
vendredi m Friday
  vendredi saint Good Friday
vénéneux poisonous
venir to come
vent m wind
vente f sale
  vente aux enchères auction
ventilateur m ventilator ; fan
verglas m black ice
vérifier to check ; to audit

vernis m varnish
  vernis à ongles nail varnish
verre m glass
  verres de contact contact lenses
verrouillage central m central locking
vers toward(s) ; about
versement m payment ; instalment
verser to pour ; to pay
vert(e) green
veste f jacket
vestiaire m cloakroom
vêtements mpl clothes
vétérinaire m/f vet
veuf m widower
veuillez... please...
veuve f widow
via by (via)
viande f meat
  viande hachée mince (meat)
vidange f oil change (car)
vide empty
videoclub m video shop
vie f life
vieux (vieille) old
vierge blank (disk, tape)
vigile m security guard
vigne f vine ; vineyard
vignoble m vineyard
VIH m HIV
village m village
ville f town ; city
vin m wine
  vin en pichet house wine
  vin pétillant sparkling wine
vinaigre m vinegar
violer to rape
violet(-ette) purple
vipère f adder ; viper
virage m bend ; curve ; corner
vis f screw
  vis platinées points (in car)
visage m face
visite f visit ; consultation (of doctor)
  visite guidée guided tour
visiter to visit (a place)
visiteur(-euse) m/f visitor
visser to screw on
vite quickly ; fast
vitesse f gear (of car) ; speed
  vitesse limitée à... speed limit...
vitrail m stained-glass window
vitrine f shop window
vivre to live
VO: en VO with subtitles (film)
vœu m wish

voici here is/are
voie f lane (of road) ; line ; track
voilà there is/are
voile f sail ; sailing
voilier m sailing boat
voir to see
voisin(e) m/f neighbour
voiture f car ; coach (of train)
vol m flight ; theft
  vol intérieur domestic flight
volaille f poultry
volant m steering wheel
voler to fly (bird) ; to steal
volet m shutter (on window)
voleur(-euse) m/f thief
volonté f will
  à volonté as much as you like
vomir to vomit
v.o.s.t. original version with subtitles (film)
vouloir to want
voyage m journey
  voyage d'affaires business trip
  voyage organisé package holiday
voyager to travel
voyageur(-euse) m/f traveller
vrai(e) real ; true
VTT m mountain bike
vue f view ; sight

W

w-c mpl toilet
wagon m carriage ; waggon
wagon-couchettes m sleeping car
wagon-restaurant m dining car
web m internet

X

xérès m sherry

Y

yacht m yacht
yaourt m yoghurt
  yaourt nature plain yoghurt
yeux mpl eyes
youyou m dinghy

Z

zéro m zero
zona m shingles (illness)
zone f zone
  zone piétonne pedestrian area
zoo m zoo

How French Works

Nouns

> A **noun** is a word such as **car**, **horse** or **Mary** which is used to refer to a person or thing.

Unlike English, French nouns have a gender: they are either *masculine* (**le**) or *feminine* (**la**). Therefore words for *the* and *a(n)* must agree with the noun they accompany – whether *masculine*, *feminine* or *plural*:

	masc.	*fem.*	*plural*
the	**le chat**	**la rue**	**les chats, les rues**
a, an	**un chat**	**une rue**	**des chats, des rues**

If the noun begins with a vowel (**a**, **e**, **i**, **o** or **u**) or an unsounded **h**, **le** and **la** shorten to **l'**, i.e. **l'avion** *(m)*, **l'école** *(f)*, **l'hôtel** *(m)*.

NOTE: **le** and **les** used after the prepositions **à** (to, at) and **de** (any, some, of) contract as follows:

> **à** + **le** = **au** (**au cinéma** but **à** <u>la</u> **gare**)
> **à** + **les** = **aux** (**aux magasins** - applies to both *(m)* and *(f)*)
> **de** + **le** = **du** (**du pain** but **de** <u>la</u> **confiture**)
> **de** + **les** = **des** (<u>des</u> **pommes** - applies to both *(m)* and *(f)*)

There are some broad rules as to noun endings which indicate whether they are *masculine* or *feminine*:

Generally *masculine* endings:
-er, -ier, -eau, -t, -c, -age, -ail, -oir, -é, -on, -acle, -ège, -ème, -o, -ou.

Generally *feminine* endings:
-euse, -trice, -ère, -ière, -elle, -te, -tte, -de, -che, -age, -aille, -oire, -ée, -té, -tié, -onne, -aison, -ion, -esse, -ie, -ine, -une, -ure, -ance, -anse, -ence, -ense.

Plural

The general rule is to add an **s** to the singular:

> **le chat** → **les chats**

Exceptions occur with the following noun endings: **-eau, -eu, -al**

> **le bat<u>eau</u>** → **les bat<u>eaux</u>**
> **le nev<u>eu</u>** → **les nev<u>eux</u>**
> **le chev<u>al</u>** → **les chev<u>aux</u>**

Nouns ending in **-s**, **-x**, or **-z** do not change in the plural.

> **le dos** → **les dos**
> **le prix** → **les prix**
> **le nez** → **les nez**

Adjectives

> An **adjective** is a word such as **small**, **pretty** or **practical** that
> describes a person or thing, or gives extra information about them.

Adjectives normally follow the noun they describe in French,

e.g.   **la pomme verte** (the green apple)

Some common exceptions which go before the noun are: **beau** beautiful, **bon**
good, **grand** big, **haut** high, **jeune** young, **long** long, **joli** pretty, **mauvais** bad,
nouveau new, **petit** small, **vieux** old.

e.g.   **un bon livre** (a good book)

French adjectives have to reflect the gender of the noun they describe. To make
an adjective *feminine*, an **e** is added to the *masculine* form (where this does
not already end in an **e**, e.g. **jeune**).

NOTE: The addition of an **e** to the final consonant (which is usually silent in the
masculine) means that you should pronounce the ending in the *feminine*.

masc.	**le livre vert**	*fem.*	**la pomme verte**
	luh leevr vehr		*la pom vehrt*
	(the green book)		(the green apple)

To make an adjective plural, an **s** is added to the singular form: *masculine
plural* – **verts** (remember – the ending is still silent: *vehr*) or *feminine plural* –
vertes (because of the **e**, the **t** ending is sounded: *vehrt*).

My, your, his, her, our, their

These words also reflect the gender and number of the noun (whether *masculine,
feminine* or *plural*) they accompany and not on the sex of the 'owner'.

	with masc. sing. noun	with fem. sing. noun	with plural nouns
my	**mon**	**ma**	**mes**
your *(familiar, singular)*	**ton**	**ta**	**tes**
his/her	**son**	**sa**	**ses**
our	**notre**	**notre**	**nos**
your *(polite and plural)*	**votre**	**votre**	**vos**
their	**leur**	**leur**	**leurs**

Pronouns

> A **pronoun** is a word that you use to refer to someone or something
> when you do not need to use a noun, often because the person or thing
> has been mentioned earlier. Examples are **it**, **she**, **something** and **myself**.

subject		*object*	
I	**je, j'**	me	**me, m'**
you *(familiar)*	**tu**	you	**te, t'**
you *(polite and plural)*	**vous**	you	**vous**
he/it	**il**	him/it	**le, l'**
she/it	**elle**	her/it	**la, l'**
we	**nous**	us	**nous**
they *(masculine)*	**ils**	them	**les**
they *(feminine)*	**elles**	them	**les**

In French there are two forms for *you* – **tu** and **vous**. **Tu** is the familiar form which is used with children and people you know as friends. **Vous**, as well as being the plural form for *you*, is also the polite form of addressing someone. You should probably use this form until the other person invites you to use the more familiar **tu** ('**on se dit 'tu'?**').

Object pronouns are placed before the verb:

e.g.   il <u>vous</u> aime (he loves <u>you</u>)

              nous <u>la</u> connaissons (we know <u>her</u>)

However, in commands or requests, object pronouns follow the verb,

e.g.   écoutez-<u>le</u> (listen to <u>him</u>)

              aidez-<u>moi</u> (help <u>me</u>)

NOTE: this does not apply to negative commands or requests,

e.g.   ne <u>le</u> faites pas (don't do <u>it</u>)

The object pronouns shown above are also used to mean **to me**, **to us**, etc. except,

              le and **la** which become **lui** (to him, to her)

              les which becomes **leur** (to them)

e.g.   il le <u>lui</u> donne (he gives it <u>to him</u>)

Verbs

> A **verb** is a word such as *sing*, *walk* or *cry* which is used with a subject to say what someone or something does or what happens to them. **Regular verbs** follow the same pattern of endings. **Irregular verbs** do not follow a regular pattern so you need to learn the different endings.

There are three main patterns of endings for verbs in French – those ending -**er**, -**ir** and -**re** in the dictionary.

DONNER	TO GIVE
je donne	I give
tu donnes	you give
il/elle donne	he/she gives
nous donnons	we give
vous donnez	you give
ils/elles donnent	they give

past participle: **donné** (with **avoir**)

FINIR	TO FINISH
je finis	I finish
tu finis	you finish
il/elle finit	he/she finishes
nous finissons	we finish
vous finissez	you finish
ils/elles finissent	they finish

past participle: **fini** (with **avoir**)

RÉPOND<u>RE</u>	TO REPLY
je réponds	I reply
tu réponds	you reply
il/elle répond	he/she replies
nous répondons	we reply
vous répondez	you reply
ils/elles répondent	they reply

past participle: **répondu** (with **avoir**)

Irregular Verbs

Among the most important irregular verbs are the following:

ÊTRE	TO BE
je suis	I am
tu es	you are
il/elle est	he/she is
nous sommes	we are
vous êtes	you are
ils/elles sont	they are

past participle: **été** (with **avoir**)

AVOIR	TO HAVE
j'ai	I have
tu as	you have
il/elle a	he/she has
nous avons	we have
vous avez	you have
ils/elles ont	they have

past participle: **eu** (with **avoir**)

ALLER	TO GO
je vais	I go
tu vas	you go
il/elle va	he/she goes
nous allons	we go
vous allez	you go
ils/elles vont	they go

past participle: **allé** (with **être**)

VENIR	TO COME
je viens	I come
tu viens	you come
il/elle vient	he/she comes
nous venons	we come
vous venez	you come
ils/elles viennent	they come

past participle: **venu** (with **être**)

FAIRE	TO DO
je fais	I do
tu fais	you do
il/elle fait	he/she does
nous faisons	we do
vous faites	you do
ils/elles font	they do

past participle: **fait** (with **avoir**)

VOULOIR	TO WANT
je veux	I want
tu veux	you want
il/elle veut	he/she wants
nous voulons	we want
vous voulez	you want
ils/elles veulent	they want

past participle: **voulu** (with **avoir**)

POUVOIR	TO BE ABLE TO
je peux	I can
tu peux	you can
il/elle peut	he/she can
nous pouvons	we can
vous pouvez	you can
ils/elles peuvent	they can

past participle: **pu** (with **avoir**)

DEVOIR	TO HAVE TO
je dois	I have to
tu dois	you have to
il/elle doit	he/she has to
nous devons	we have to
vous devez	you have to
ils/elles doivent	they have to

past participle: **dû** (with **avoir**)

Past Tense

> To make a simple past tense, you need an **auxiliary verb** with the past participle of the main verb, e.g. **I have** (auxiliary) **been** (past participle), **I have** (auxiliary) **eaten** (past participle). In French the basic auxiliary verbs are **avoir** (to have) and **être** (to be). A **reflexive verb** is one where the subject and object are the same e.g. **to enjoy yourself**, **to dress yourself**. These verbs take **être** as their auxiliary verb.

To form the simple past tense, I gave/I have given, I finished/I have finished, combine the present tense of the verb **avoir** – to have with the past participle of the verb (**donné, fini, répondu**),

e.g.	**j'ai donné**	I gave/I have given
	j'ai fini	I finished/I have finished
	j'ai répondu	I replied/I have replied

Not all verbs take **avoir** (**j'ai..., il a...**) as their auxiliary verb. The reflexive verb (**s'amuser, se promener**, etc) take **être** (**je me suis..., il s'est...**), and so do a dozen or so other verbs which generally express the idea of motion or staying such as **aller** (to go) and **rester** (to stay),

e.g.	**je me suis amusé**	I had fun
	je suis allé	I went
	je suis resté	I stayed

When the auxiliary verb **être** is used, the past participle (**amusé, allé, resté**, etc) becomes like an adjective and agrees with the subject of the verb in number and gender:

e.g.	**je me suis amusée**	I had fun (female)
	nous nous sommes amusés	we had fun (plural)
	je suis allée	I went (female)
	nous sommes allés	we went (plural)
	je suis restée	I stayed (female)
	nous sommes restés	we stayed (plural)

To make a sentence negative e.g. I am not eating, you use **ne ... pas** around the verb or auxilliary verb.

e.g.	**je ne mange pas**	I am not eating
	je ne suis pas amusé	I did not have fun